WRITERS AND THEIR WORK

ISOBEL ARMSTRONG
General Editor

VIRGINIA WOOLF

VIRGINIA WOOLF

From a photograph of 1939 by Gisèle Freund
in the collection of the National Portrait Gallery, London

VIRGINIA WOOLF

Laura Marcus

Second Edition

For Daniel,
youngest of bibliophiles

© Copyright 1997 and 2004 by Laura Marcus
Second edition 2004

First published in 1997 by Northcote House Publishers Ltd, Horndon House,
Horndon, Tavistock, Devon, PL19 9NQ, United Kingdom.
Tel: +44 (0) 1822 810066 Fax: +44 (0) 1822 810034.

All rights reserved. No part of this work may be reproduced or stored in an
information retrieval system (other than short extracts for the purposes of review)
without the express permission of the Publishers given in writing.

British Library Cataloguing-in-Publication Data
A catalogue record for this book is available from the British Library

ISBN 0 7463 0966 X

Typeset by PDQ Typesetting, Newcastle-under-Lyme
Printed and bound in the United Kingdom by Athenaeum Press Ltd., Gateshead

Contents

Acknowledgements

I am very grateful to Isobel Armstrong for inviting me to write about Virginia Woolf: I have found it an enriching experience. My thanks to Jan Montefiore and Alison Mark for their helpful comments on the manuscript and to William Outhwaite for advice, support, childcare, and much else. I would also like to offer (belated) thanks to Hilary Walford for her meticulous copy-editing of the first edition; to Bryony Randall, for her expert help in updating the bibliography for the new edition; and to Brian Hulme, for his patience and encouragement throughout. Finally, my publishers and I gratefully acknowledge the Trustees of the Literary Estate of Virginia Woolf and the Hogarth Press, Random House for permission to quote from the works of Virginia Woolf.

Biographical Outline

1882   Born Adeline Virginia Stephen on 25 January in London, daughter of Julia Prinsep Stephen and Leslie Stephen, philosopher and biographer. Younger sister of Vanessa (b. 30 May 1879) and Julian Thoby (b. 8 September 1880).

1883   Birth of brother, Adrian Leslie Stephen, 27 October.

1895   Death of Julia Stephen on 5 May. Virginia's first breakdown in summer. Lease of Talland House, St Ives, is sold.

1897   Virginia begins to keep a regular diary. Marriage of Stella Duckworth, Virginia's half-sister, to Jack Hills on 10 April. Stella dies of peritonitis on 19 July. Virginia begins studies of Greek and History at King's College, London, in November.

1899   Thoby Stephen, Virginia's brother, enters Trinity College, Cambridge, in October.

1902   Virginia begins private lessons in Greek with Janet Case.

1904   Death of Sir Leslie Stephen on 22 February. Beginning of Virginia's second serious breakdown in May. Stephen children move from 22 Hyde Park Gate to 46 Gordon Square, Bloomsbury. In October, Virginia goes to stay with aunt Caroline Emelia Stephen in Cambridge. She helps F. W. Maitland with his *Life of Leslie Stephen*. Virginia returns to London in December. Her first publication, an unsigned review, is printed in the *Guardian*.

1905   Thoby Stephen starts 'Thursday Evenings' at 46 Gordon Square: birth of 'The Bloomsbury Group'.

1906   Virginia, Vanessa, and Violet Dickinson leave London

	for Greece on 8 September, joining Thoby and Adrian. Thoby dies of typhoid fever in London on 20 November. Vanessa agrees to marry Clive Bell 22 November.
1907	Vanessa marries Clive Bell 7 February. Virginia and Adrian move to 29 Fitzroy Square, London in April. Virginia works on her novel (*Melymbrosia*).
1908	Vanessa gives birth to a son, Julian Heward Bell, 8 February.
1910	In January Virginia begins work for Women's Suffrage. Birth of Vanessa's second son, Claudian [Quentin] Bell, 19 August. First Post-Impressionist exhibition, organized by Roger Fry, shown at Grafton Galleries, London, November–January 1911.
1911	In November, Virginia moves to 38 Brunswick Square, Bloomsbury, sharing house with Adrian, Maynard Keynes, Duncan Grant, and Leonard Woolf. Virginia also takes lease of Asham House, Beddingham, Sussex.
1912	Marriage of Virginia and Leonard Woolf in London, 10 August. In second part of year, Virginia ill, depressed, and suicidal. Second Post-Impressionist exhibition, October–January 1913.
1915	In January, Virginia starts to keep a diary again and Virginia and Leonard decide to take Hogarth House, Richmond and to buy a printing press. Publication of first novel, *The Voyage Out*, in March. Virginia suffers severe breakdown and is ill for much of the year.
1917	In spring the Woolfs buy a printing press. Publication No. 1 of The Hogarth Press – Virginia Woolf's 'The Mark on the Wall' and Leonard Woolf's 'Three Jews' – published in July.
1918	Birth of Vanessa's daughter Angelica on 25 December.
1919	Hogarth Press publishes Virginia's *Kew Gardens* in May. Woolfs buy Monk's House, Rodmell, Sussex, in July. *Night and Day* published by Duckworth in October.
1920	First meeting of the Memoir Club takes place in March.
1921	Publication of *Monday or Tuesday* in March.
1922	*Jacob's Room* published in October by Hogarth Press.
1923	Death of Katherine Mansfield on 9 January. Leonard accepts literary editorship of *The Nation*.

1924   Woolfs move from Richmond to 52 Tavistock Square, Bloomsbury. *Mr Bennett and Mrs Brown* published in October.

1925   Death of Jacques Raverat on 7 March. *The Common Reader* is published in April. *Mrs Dalloway* is published in May. Virginia's growing friendship with Vita Sackville-West.

1926   Virginia works on *To the Lighthouse*. Writes the 'Time Passes' section of the novel during the General Strike.

1927   *To the Lighthouse* published in May. Virginia starts to write *Orlando* in October.

1928   Virginia awarded the *Femina Vie Heureuse* prize for *To the Lighthouse*. *Orlando* published in October. Woolf gives Cambridge lectures which become *A Room of One's Own*. *The Well of Loneliness* case is heard in November.

1929   Publication of *A Room of One's Own* in October.

1930   Virginia works on *The Waves*.

1931   Publication of *The Waves* in October.

1932   Death of Lytton Strachey on January 21. Publication of *The Common Reader: A Second Series* in October.

1933   Virginia works on *The Years*. *Flush* published in October.

1934   Virginia continues work on *The Years*. Death of Roger Fry on 9 September.

1935   Virginia's play *Freshwater* is performed before friends in London.

1936   Woolf is ill for much of year. Works on *The Years*.

1937   *The Years* is published in March. Julian Bell dies in Spain on 18 July.

1938   *Three Guineas* published in June.

1939   Woolfs move from Tavistock Square to 37 Mecklenburgh Square, but with advance of war are primarily resident in Sussex.

1940   Publication of *Roger Fry: A Biography* in July. Mecklenburgh Square is bombed and The Hogarth Press is moved to Letchworth, Hertfordshire.

1941   Virginia finishes *Pointz Hall* (*Between the Acts*) in February. Virginia commits suicide by drowning on 28 March.

Abbreviations

BA   *Between the Acts* (Harmondsworth: Penguin, 1992)

CDB   *The Captain's Death Bed* (London: Hogarth Press)

CDML   *The Crowded Dance of Modern Life*, ed. Rachel Bowlby (Harmondsworth: Penguin, 1993)

CSF   *The Complete Shorter Fiction of Virginia Woolf*, ed. Susan Dick (London: Grafton, 1991)

D.   *The Diary of Virginia Woolf*, Anne Olivier Bell with Andrew McNeillie (5 vols.; London: Hogarth Press, 1977–84)

E.   *The Essays of Virginia Woolf*, ed. Andrew McNeillie (6 vols.; London: Hogarth Press, 1986–)

JR   *Jacob's Room* (Harmondsworth: Penguin, 1992)

L.   *The Letters of Virginia Woolf*, eds. Nigel Nicolson and Joanne Trautmann (6 vols.; London: Chatto & Windus, 1975–80)

M&M   R. Majumdar and A. McLaurin (eds.), *Virginia Woolf: The Critical Heritage* (London: Routledge and Kegan Paul, 1975)

MB   *Moments of Being: Unpublished Autobiographical Writings*, ed. Jeanne Schulkind (rev. edn., London: Hogarth Press, 1985)

MD   *Mrs Dalloway* (Harmondsworth: Penguin, 1976)

ND   *Night and Day* (Harmondsworth: Penguin, 1969)

O.   *Orlando* (Harmondsworth: Penguin, 1993)

P.   *The Pargiters: The Novel-Essay Portion of* The Years, ed. and intro. Mitchell A. Leaska (London: Hogarth Press, 1978)

PA   *A Passionate Apprentice: The Early Journals 1897–1909*, ed. Mitchell A. Leaska (London: Hogarth Press, 1990)

QB   Quentin Bell, *Virginia Woolf: A Biography* (2 vols.) (London: Hogarth Press, 1972)

ROO   *A Room of One's Own* (Harmondsworth: Penguin, 1993)

TG	*Three Guineas* (Harmondsworth: Penguin, 1993)
TL	*To the Lighthouse* (Harmondsworth: Penguin, 1992)
TW	*The Waves: The Two Holograph Drafts*, ed. J. W. Graham (London: Hogarth Press, 1976)
VO	*The Voyage Out* (Harmondsworth: Penguin, 1970)
W.	*The Waves* (Harmondsworth: Penguin, 1992)
WE	*A Woman's Essays*, ed. Rachel Bowlby (Harmondsworth: Penguin, 1992)
WW	*Women and Writing*, ed. Michèle Barrett (London: The Women's Press, 1979)
Y.	*The Years* (Harmondsworth: Penguin, 1968)

Note on the Text

Virginia Woolf used ellipses, parentheses, and square brackets frequently. In order to distinguish between these and ellipses which indicate that something has been omitted, in quotations from her texts my ellipses are in angled brackets: i.e. <...>. In quotations from other sources, the ellipses are mine.

Prologue

In 1962 Bernard Blackstone added a postscript to his monograph on Virginia Woolf in which he wrote: 'It must be admitted that Virginia Woolf's stock has fallen in the post-war years.'[1] Blackstone was writing before a number of events and turns in the history of literary studies caused an extraordinary *rise* in Woolf's 'stock'. Her *œuvre* has expanded substantially: in addition to the novels, we now have in print her short stories, letters, diaries, autobiographical sketches, and a vast body of reviews and essays which command as much critical interest as her fiction. The publication of her autobiographical writings – diaries, letters, memoirs – has not only fuelled a large and ever-growing body of biographical studies, but her recording of her culture and her times has revealed a writer radically at odds with the image of the detached 'Bloomsbury aesthete'.[2] She has become a different writer from the one read at mid-twentieth century.

The massive change in the reception of her work has also come about as a result of feminist criticism and theory. Woolf is undoubtedly the central figure in the English-speaking countries for feminist literary criticism, and *A Room of One's Own* remains a key text for an understanding of women's place in literary tradition and history. Her feminism no longer seems anachronistic or irrelevant in the face of Fascism and war, as it did to many of her male (and some of her female) contemporaries; her writings of the 1930s make a crucial link between the oppression of women and the authoritarian structures of Fascist societies. Many elements of her work have been central to feminist theory and politics of the later twentieth century: her explorations of the gendered relationship between the private and the public sphere; her model of the mother–daughter relationship as a paradigm for a female literary tradition; her accounts of men's and women's different relationships to their culture.

1

Each epoch creates writers in its own image. Literary criticism also has a tendency to reinvent the wheel; the contemporary critic who excitedly discovers Virginia Woolf as a writer of the modern city, for example, may well overlook the fact that this facet of her work was obvious to her earlier commentators.[3] In this brief study of her work, I hope to open up something of the 'Virginia Woolf' of her time as well as ours. Recent critical, theoretical, and cultural concerns have, however, inevitably coloured the ways in which I have read her work. I, too, find myself excited by the Virginia Woolf who wrote about the city and the cinema, the Woolf of 'modernity'. I am taken up with her radical explorations of gender and identity, of subjectivity and selfhood, of patriarchy and militarism, of history and of the present moment or 'now-time'.[4]

Woolf's representations of 'subjectivity' and 'consciousness' have determined critical responses from the outset. Yet these are not static concepts. Early critics tended to read Woolf's work through Henri Bergson's theories of the temporal fluidity of consciousness and emphasized her explorations of the 'inner' self. In the 1970s, when there was a revival of interest in Woolf's writing, a number of critics focused on 'the world without a self' in her texts: the evacuation of subjectivity and the representation of an 'impersonal' universe. Contemporary postmodern and feminist criticism has focused on Woolf's representations of the subject by pointing up the multiple selves she postulates and the absence of an 'essential' selfhood in her work.

In this study I point to a further aspect of Woolf's writing: her models of 'intersubjectivity' and of the interrelationship between ostensibly separate selves. 'Intersubjectivity' is revealed in Woolf's narrative techniques, through which she moves in and out of 'consciousnesses' and emphasizes the connections between them: in her emphases on the relationship between 'I' and 'we' and on the permeable boundaries between selves; and, perhaps most strikingly, in her novel *The Waves*, in which she articulates the voices of six characters who are also one. In exploring this aspect of her work, we see not only how far removed she was from the writer limited 'to one's own sensations', as she phrased it (*L.* ii. 597–8), but also the extent to which she was a critic of a 'philosophy of consciousness'. Her concern was with the interrelationship between self, language, and world.

2

In 1939, two years before her death, Virginia Woolf began to write the memoir subsequently published as 'A Sketch of the Past'. Here she explores what it means to recover the past from the standpoint of the present and points to the limitations of autobiographical writing:

> Here I come to one of the memoir-writer's difficulties – one of the reasons why, though I read so many, so many are failures. They leave out the person to whom things happened. The reason is that it is so difficult to describe any human being. So they say: 'This is what happened': but they do not say what the person was like to whom it happened. And the events mean very little unless we know first to whom they happened. Who was I then? (MB 75)

We can begin to answer this question with a simple biographical sketch. Adeline Virginia Stephen was born on 25 January 1882 into an upper-middle-class, intellectual family. Her father, Leslie Stephen, was a Victorian 'man of letters', a disappointed philosopher whose lasting literary legacy was the monumental *Dictionary of National Biography*. His study and his library gave the young Virginia an exceptional access to literature of all kinds – one in which she immersed herself from a very early age. Her mother, Julia Stephen, Leslie's second wife (his first wife, Minnie Thackeray, had died in 1875, leaving him with one daughter, Laura), was, Woolf writes, 'central': she provided the 'atmosphere' in which Virginia as a child lived. Julia's first husband, Herbert Duckworth, had died only four years into their marriage, leaving her with three children. She then had a further four children with Leslie Stephen: Thoby, Vanessa (who became the artist Vanessa Bell), Virginia, and Adrian. She died in 1895, at the age of 49, when Virginia was 13, exhausted, her children believed, by the demands of family, her exacting husband, and the strains of her philanthropic work. Her death shattered the family; it was followed two years later by the death of Stella Duckworth, Julia's daughter by her first marriage. 'Death', as Gillian Beer writes, was Woolf's 'special knowledge', as it was the knowledge of her generation, whose lives encompassed two world wars.[5]

After Leslie Stephen's death in 1904 the Stephen children moved from the family house in Kensington and set up home in Bloomsbury, considered by their older relatives to be a disturbingly Bohemian area. Freed from their 'Victorian' past, and from their half-brothers' attempts to turn them into society ladies, Virginia and Vanessa dedicated themselves to writing and painting respectively. Thoby Stephen, the brother to whom Virginia was most attached, introduced his sisters to his Cambridge University friends. Thoby died of typhoid in 1906, at the age of 26, after travelling with his brother and sisters in Greece. In 1907 Vanessa married Clive Bell, the art historian, and in 1912 Virginia married Leonard Woolf, who had spent some years in Ceylon after Cambridge and returned to make a career of writing, editing, publishing, and political work on the Left. Their marriage was an intellectual partnership which lasted until Virginia Woolf's death in 1941. Much has been written about the 'madness' (defined by Leonard Woolf as 'manic depression') that erupted at intervals throughout Woolf's life and that culminated in her suicide. As readers of Woolf, we need to know not only that it was an aspect of her life and of her writing, but that the writing was in part her way of living through, and with, a sometimes terrifying intensity of response.

Woolf, of course, was not just a creator of poetic masterpieces. She was also a writer of comic genius, a professional journalist, reviewer, and publisher, and a political and feminist pamphleteer. We now have at last a much fuller picture of Woolf as one of the most important literary and cultural figures of the twentieth century. We can never fully grasp, perhaps, the Woolf 'to whom things happened'; 'A Sketch of the Past' set out to explore rather than answer this question. Her concern in the memoir is primarily with those intense experiences that she feels made her a writer: the vividness of her first memories; her powerful early responses to the rhythms of language; her capacity for receiving 'shocks' and for transmuting them into the stuff of art. It might be fruitful to think of Woolf's life and writing not in 'pathological' frameworks (as in those studies that have sought to understand her life as a product of sexual abuse[6]) but as a negotiation of what she herself called 'shock' – a response to modernity as well as to her personal circumstances and her psychic world[7]. 'The shock-receiving capacity' she speculated, 'is what makes me a writer.' Ordinary life buffers the shocks of experience; for Woolf, this buffering is necessary for living, but for her writing, she believed, the shocks had to penetrate the 'cotton-wool' and reveal 'a token of something real behind appearances'. Moreover, and despite this neat Platonic formulation, the terms in which Woolf thought were continually negotiated, questioned, and subverted. This is her endless fascination for critics and for readers.

In the first two chapters of this study, I look briefly at Woolf's first novels, *The Voyage Out* and *Night and Day*, and at the short stories and essays she wrote in her search for a new form for the novel, culminating in her third novel, *Jacob's Room*. Chapter 3 is a discussion of Woolf's feminism, focusing on *A Room of One's Own*; Chapter 4 focuses on the representation of the city in the essay 'Street-Haunting' and in *Mrs Dalloway*. In the remaining chapters of the book I look at the directions in which Woolf took the novel as a genre. Her dissatisfactions with the forms of the conventional novel and her acute sense of her responsibilities (political as well as aesthetic) as a writer led her to ceaseless exploration of the novel's limits and possibilities and to experimentation with 'hybrid' genres: the novel-elegy, the novel as biography, the novel-essay, the play-poem, the novel-play. I will be pointing to themes and forms that run throughout her work, but I have wanted to take the space to begin – and it can only be a beginning – to unpack a number of her novels in their extraordinary complexity and richness.

For this new edition, I have not changed the emphases of the original study, other than to point up more emphatically the importance of war-consciousness in *Mrs Dalloway*. I have, however, given a fuller discussion of *The Waves* and have added a new section on Woolf's mock-biography *Flush*, a text which, while popular from the moment of its publication, has not, until recently, received a great deal of critical attention. In bringing *Flush* to the fore in this study, I have sought to lay greater emphasis on the centrality of biography as a genre to Woolf's work and thought. The extended bibliography also gives some indication of the very substantial amount of new work in Virginia Woolf studies, and of the continuing, and indeed growing, interest in Woolf's life and work. I am very grateful for the further opportunity to contribute to this critical field.

1

Women's Future, Women's Fiction

Virginia Woolf's career as a published writer (she had been keeping journals and diaries since childhood) began in the first years of the century with reviews and articles, primarily for the *Guardian*, the *Times Literary Supplement*, and the *Cornhill Magazine*. After her father's death in 1904, Woolf, then Virginia Stephen, went to stay with her father's sister, Caroline Stephen, who, on her death in 1909, left her, in John Mepham's words, 'sufficient capital to give her an income something approaching the famous £500 pounds a year, enough for her financial independence, a vital condition for the autonomy of the woman writer'.[1] Woolf also travelled Europe with her brothers and sister during these years (it was soon after a trip to Greece that Thoby Stephen died from typhoid fever), and for two years taught history and writing at Morley College, an adult education institute in south London.

Her early writings also included short stories, some of them unpublished in her lifetime.[2] Her first pieces are nearly all explorations of women's lives at various historical periods, and of the difficulties of representing them adequately. In 'Memoirs of a Novelist' (1909) she invents a two-volume 'life and letters' of a fictional Victorian woman writer, Miss Willatt, written by her friend, a Miss Linsett. Woolf satirizes the typical eulogistic Victorian biography and shows up the extent to which conventional biography (and, by extension, literary naturalism) kills 'life' rather than creating and expressing it: this theme pervades her writing. 'The Journal of Mistress Joan Martyn' (1906) is an exploration of women's history, cast in the form of a 'found' manuscript, as Woolf's present-day historian, Rosalind

Merridew, researching the land-tenure system of medieval England, uncovers a journal, written in 1480, by Joan Martyn, a young woman keeping house during the civil wars. Again, Woolf explores the ways in which one woman writes the life of another. 'Joan Martyn' anticipates Woolf's many explorations of hidden histories and obscure lives – in her essay 'Lives of the Obscure' she describes herself as 'a deliverer advancing < ... > to the rescue of some stranded ghost' (E. iv. 119) – and her inventions of lives and stories that must be created because they would otherwise have no representation.

Woolf began her first novel, *The Voyage Out*, in 1908; it was finally published in 1915, by which time it had been through some ten drafts.[3] Both this novel and the one that followed it, *Night and Day* (1919), have often been underrated by critics, for whom they represent a plot-driven realism which Woolf was later to transcend: Woolf herself was to express her ambivalence towards these apprentice novels. Yet in many ways they laid down the tracks which she was to follow throughout her writing career.

Both novels are versions of the *Bildungsroman*, the 'novel of formation'.[4] There has been substantial discussion about whether this is intrinsically a male genre; the classics of the form recount the formative experiences of their heroes, often culminating with their entry into the public world as fully social subjects. Honoré de Balzac, for example, closes *Père Goriot* (1834) with the triumphal image of his young hero standing on a hilltop with Paris laid out before him, awaiting his entry. Such a trajectory was rarely ascribed or available to women, and Woolf indeed seems to follow more conservative traditions by closing her first novels with death and marriage respectively. Yet both novels actively struggle with the conventional narratives of 'a woman's life' and begin to open up one of the most important questions for modernist writing: that of the relationship between the future of women and the future of fiction.[5]

The heroine of *The Voyage Out*, Rachel Vinrace, is a young woman travelling to South America with her father (who owns the ship on which they sail), her uncle and aunt, Ridley and Helen Ambrose, whose characters anticipate those of Mr and Mrs Ramsay in *To the Lighthouse*, and assorted travellers, including Richard and Clarissa Dalloway, who pass abruptly from this novel but reappear in *Mrs Dalloway*, though in rather altered forms. Rachel's aunt, Helen, takes on the task of 'bringing out' her niece, whose sheltered upbringing by spinster aunts has left her ignorant of sexual and emotional relationships between men and women; Rachel's father asks Helen to help in 'making a woman of her', by which he means teaching her to be a successful Tory hostess. On their arrival in Santa Marina, Helen persuades him that Rachel should stay with Ridley and herself in a resort popular with the British community. Rachel meets a young man, Terence Hewet, a Cambridge graduate and aspiring novelist, and they become engaged on a river trip into the interior of the country. They plan a future together, but Rachel is stricken with fever shortly afterwards, from which she does not recover. The last section of the novel charts the decline of Rachel, passive from the outset, into semi-consciousness and death.

Night and Day, by contrast, offers a self-consciously comic resolution, in the tradition of a Shakespeare play or a Mozart opera, in which the curtains of drawing rooms part and close on scenes and in which courtship is played out in London's ludic spaces – Regent's Park Zoo (where human relationships are satirically contrasted with those of animals), Hampton Court, Kew Gardens. At the opening of the novel, Katherine Hilbery is engaged to the literary, and somewhat pompous, William Rodney; she meets Ralph Denham, an intense, complex young lawyer from a far less prosperous and 'well-connected' family than her own, and, after a prolonged dance of attraction and repulsion, falls in love with him. William Rodney is not left bereft; he has found himself drawn to Katherine's cousin, Cassandra, and the novel's denouement comes in the form of a double engagement.

Katherine and Ralph have a mutual acquaintance in Mary Datchet, a suffrage worker in love with Ralph. Woolf clearly struggled with the depiction of Mary as an alternative heroine to the apolitical Katherine and, at the close of a novel deeply ambivalent about marriage, places Mary at a far remove from the marriage plot. She becomes one of Woolf's 'outsiders', a woman alone, 'working out her plans far into the night' (*ND* 469), functioning as both Katherine and Ralph's image of an autonomy and 'impersonality' they have not claimed for themselves.

Rachel's strongest passion is for music, not literature; Katherine yearns for escape from the world of letters into her passion, mathematics. Music and mathematics are both figured as abstract, non-representational, 'impersonal' forms, ways of escaping from the social world of lives and their stories. In *The Voyage Out* Rachel leaves the company of her aunt and Clarissa Dalloway, who, in talking about their children, 'made her feel outside their world and motherless', neither mothered nor mothering, and retreats to her room:

> In three minutes she was deep in a very difficult, very impersonal expression of complete absorption and anxious satisfaction. Now she stumbled; now she faltered and had to play the same bar twice over; but an invisible line seemed to string the notes together, from which rose a shape, a building. (*VO* 54)

Katherine Hilbery's intellectual and imaginative passion cannot be publicly aired. She escapes from work on the interminable biography her mother is composing of her own father, the eminent poet Richard Alardyce, into science. Whereas Jane Austen is reputed to have slipped the pages of the novel she was writing under her blotter whenever someone entered the drawing room (an image Woolf uses in *A Room of One's Own*), Katherine, whenever steps are heard on the staircase, conceals her notations 'between the leaves of a great Greek dictionary which she had purloined from her father's room for this purpose':

> Perhaps the unwomanly nature of the science made her instinctively wish to conceal her love of it. But the more profound reason was that in her mind mathematics were directly opposed to literature. She would not have cared to confess how infinitely she preferred the exactitude, the star-like impersonality, of figures to the confusion, agitation, and vagueness of the finest prose. (*ND* 41)

In later novels, and in her descriptions of her writing practice, Woolf appropriates geometry and architecture, 'shape' and 'building', for fiction itself, 'making the squares shape up' and inserting white spaces on the pages of the work, breaking up the busy detail of novelistic form. But such shapes are not simply abstract forms; Woolf also saw in them the lineaments of women's desires, so that her first imaginings of the novel that was to become *Orlando* are embodied in 'dreams of golden domes', the shapes of cities (*D.* iii. 131). While Rachel and Katherine must project themselves out of the biographical limits of both literature and life into the abstract systems of music and mathematics, later novels appropriate the 'shapes' of artistic form and human desire for fiction itself.

In *Night and Day* the 'confusion, agitation and shapelessness' of prose are directly linked to the life of the city: 'The incessant and tumultuous hum of the distant traffic seemed, as she stood there, to represent the thick texture of her life, for her life was so hemmed in with the progress of other lives that the sound of its own advance was inaudible' (*ND* 97). This 'thick texture' is more suffocating than sustaining. In *The Voyage Out* Rachel, trying to describe to Terence her circumscribed daily existence in the London suburb of Richmond, realized that it was 'her aunts who built up the fine, closely woven substance of their life at home <...> making an atmosphere and building up a solid mass, a background' (*VO* 216). The lines echo the early short story 'Memoirs of a Novelist', in which Woolf both creates a space for women's culture and history and hints at its limitations:

> George Eliot and Charlotte Brontë between them must share the parentage of many novels at this period, for they disclosed the secret that the precious stuff of which books are made lies all about one, in drawing-rooms and kitchens where women live, and accumulates with every tick of the clock. (*CSF* 75)

Both Rachel and Katherine recognize the comforts afforded by this busy domesticity and yet yearn for an escape from it, for space of their own and even for loneliness. This conflict runs throughout Woolf's writing and the work of many of her women contemporaries. The novelist Dorothy Richardson, author of the multi-volumed autobiographical novel *Pilgrimage*, wrote in a note on her early writing career that she had 'planned a book on the inviolability of feminine solitude, or alternatively, loneliness'.[6] Woolf at times also suggests that women are most themselves when they are most alone: 'It was in her loneliness that Katherine was unreserved', she writes in *Night and Day* (*ND* 312). Lily Briscoe, the artist figure in *To the Lighthouse*, refuses to marry: 'she need not undergo that degradation. She was saved from that dilution' (*TL* 111). In each of Woolf's novels we see glimpses of a story she never wrote in full, a story of a woman's life: 'I sketched the possibilities which an unattractive woman, penniless, alone, might yet bring into being', she wrote in her diary in March 1927, when her first imaginings of the novel that became *Orlando* (whose eponymous hero/heroine is a very different figure) came to her (*D*. iii. 131).

It is through the image of such a woman – unattractive,

penniless, alone – that Woolf, in *The Voyage Out*, dramatizes the relationship and division between art and politics that was to absorb her throughout her life. Richard Dalloway, a Tory politician, tells Rachel that he is prouder of ameliorating the working conditions of Lancashire mill girls than he should be of writing the works of Keats and Shelley. Rachel tentatively counters this with 'her shivering private visions' of 'an old widow in her room', whose 'affections' are left untouched by the small material gains and losses brought about by politicians. Richard points out that the widow's material situation will affect her 'spiritual outlook'. Woolf was indeed to insist upon the relationship between material circumstances and the creative life in *A Room of One's Own*, but in *The Voyage Out* she seems to resist the link by associating it with the conservative and unimaginative Richard, whose politics are those of the social engineer, both organicist and mechanistic: 'It was impossible to combine the image of a lean black widow, gazing out of her window, and longing for someone to talk to, with the image of a vast machine, such as one sees at South Kensington, thumping, thumping, thumping. The attempt at communication had been a failure' (*VO* 63).

In a number of her essays on the novel, Woolf made 'the widow' one of the figures of fiction itself, as she shifts between the representation of fiction as a young and flighty female, a phantom or will-o'-the-wisp, and an elderly and vulnerable woman, all of whom elude the novelist who attempts to pin them down. The most significant of Woolf's embodiments of this last figure is the Mrs Brown of her essay 'Mr Bennett and Mrs Brown', in which, as we shall see, she argues that the Edwardian novelists, rather like Richard Dalloway, have failed to 'capture' character, represented here in the figure of Mrs Brown the widow, either using her as a means to an end – the conveying of a political message – or burying her beneath the naturalist detail of her material surroundings. Rachel's 'lean black widow' is as surprising an image of fiction as Mrs Brown, to whom she is surely linked: in her narrative of a young woman's formation, Woolf none the less gives 'fiction' its embodiment in a different kind of woman's life.

Terence Hewit, in *The Voyage Out*, tells Rachel that he wants 'to write a book about Silence <...> the things people don't say' (*VO* 218). This is ambiguous: it could mean the re-enactment of the 'Silence' or its breaking, and this ambiguity, and the

12

paradoxes to which it leads, are omnipresent in Woolf's work. This silence is also linked to women's lives, as Terence suggests:

> 'I've often walked about the streets where people live all in a row, and one house is exactly like another house, and wondered what on earth the women were doing inside,' he said. 'Just consider: it's the beginning of the twentieth century, and until a few years ago no woman had ever come out by herself and said things at all. There it was going on in the background, for all these thousands of years, this curious silent unrepresented life. Of course we're always writing about women – abusing them, or jeering at them, or worshipping them; but it's never come from women themselves. I believe we still don't know in the least how they live, or what they feel, or what they do precisely.' (*VO* 215)

In one sense Terence, Woolf's novelist within the novel, shares her lifelong fascination with the unwritten lives of women and with 'the lives of the obscure'; in another, Woolf hints that there is something aggressive and voyeuristic about 'his determination to know'. The books Helen gives Rachel to read include George Meredith's novel *Diana of the Crossways* and Henrik Ibsen's play *The Doll's House*, both extremely influential late-nineteenth-century works of 'New Woman' literature written by men.[7] These alone are able to distract her from her music; her identification with their heroines is total, creating in her 'some sort of change' (*VO* 122), yet Rachel later finds that the experiences of love they delineate have little connection with her own. The explicit reference to 'New Woman' writing calls attention to Woolf's own ambivalent relationship to this genre, and to the novel's refusal to allow to Rachel the fruits of her transformation. Sex and death seem inextricably linked; the shock of Richard Dalloway's sexual advances leads to the same nightmare of entrapment and deformity that accompanies her fatal illness. Male sexual desire, as Rachel comes to understand it, is responsible for the London prostitutes, who in turn are the reason for her lack of freedom: 'So that's why I can't walk alone!'

> By this new light she saw her life for the first time a creeping hedged-in thing, driven cautiously between high walls, here turned aside, there plunged in darkness, made dull and crippled for ever – her life that was the only chance she had – a thousand words and actions became plain to her. (*VO* 79)

Her 'life', like that of Katherine Hilbery's, is both personified and objectified, becoming here a pitiable, abject 'thing'. The very term 'life', repeated again and again in the novel, often in the context of 'women and life' (*VO* 122), is one Woolf interrogated throughout her writing: 'What is this "Life" that keeps on cropping up so mysteriously and so complacently in books about fiction' ('The Art of Fiction', *WE* 123). The passage quoted above also anticipates Woolf's exploration, in *The Years*, and, most overtly, in the earlier version of this novel, *The Pargiters*, of the crippling restrictions placed on women. The existence of 'street or common love', as Woolf terms it, confines the Pargiter girls to the home or to a chaperoned existence, turning the streets of London's West End into areas as impassable 'as any swamp alive with crocodiles', or 'a fever-stricken den'.

These issues are also at the heart of *The Voyage Out*: the paradox of attempting to speak or write about that which cannot be spoken or written is even more acute in the earlier novel. 'You've no conception what it's like – to be a young woman', Rachel tells Terence: the 'terrors and agonies' are again linked to 'women one sees in the streets' and 'men kissing one'. Rachel's faltering attempts to talk to Terence about sexuality are halted by the entry of 'the great space of life into which no one had ever penetrated' (*VO* 217). In one sense this 'space' is freedom, a subterranean depth below the busy surface of life; in another, it is the 'space' of repression, the silence of women.

Writing to her friend Lytton Strachey (essayist, biographer, and historian) in 1909 while she was at work on the novel, Woolf described herself as 'a painstaking woman who wishes to treat of life as she finds it, and to give voice to some of the perplexities of her sex' (*L.* i. 381). These 'perplexities' are reflected in the uneven tone of the novel, which veers between visionary consciousness and social satire. Shifting perspectives are also an aspect of the novel's concern with relativity, with the varying relations of time and space, and with the ways in which what Woolf called the 'difference of view' (referring in *A Room of One's Own* and in her essay 'Women and Fiction' to the different ways in which men and women see the world) commands a difference of values. As in *Jacob's Room*, *To the Lighthouse*, and *Between the Acts*, Woolf alternates between the view from the shore and the view from the sea, representing the perspectival and spatial changes brought about by these alternating views: 'From a distance the *Euphrosyne* looked very small' (*VO* 85).

Value, meaning, significance are contingent and subject to alteration, a fact uncomfortably realized by Rachel and Terence:

> They stood together in front of the looking-glass, and with a brush tried to make themselves look as though they had been feeling nothing all the morning, neither pain nor happiness. But it chilled them to see themselves in the glass, for instead of being vast and indivisible they were really very small and separate, the size of the glass leaving a large space for the reflection of other things. (*VO* 308)

For Rachel, consciousness entails a perpetual shift between, in cinematic terms, close-up and long-shot. The coherence and singularity of the self or personality are not radically questioned, as they are in Woolf's later writings, but the self is subject to continual alteration in stature and significance, at times occupying the whole 'glass', screen, or foreground, at others retreating and diminishing as time and history, which have preceded and will succeed the self, place it in 'perspective'.

The vertiginous effects of such alterations are linked both to sexual passion and to dying in the novel. Rachel and Terence's declarations of their feelings for each other are accompanied for Rachel by a return to a state prior to consciousness:

> A hand dropped abrupt as iron on Rachel's shoulder; it might have been a bolt from heaven. She fell beneath it, and the grass whipped across her eyes and filled her mouth and ears. Through the waving stems she saw a figure, large and shapeless against the sky. Helen was upon her. Rolled this way and that, now seeing only forests of green, and now the high blue heaven; she was speechless and almost without sense. At last she lay still, all the grasses shaken round her and before her by her panting. Over her loomed two great heads, the heads of a man and woman, of Terence and Helen.
>
> Both were flushed, both laughing, and the lips were moving; they came together and kissed in the air above her. Broken fragments of speech came down to her on the ground. She thought she heard them speak of love and then of marriage. Raising herself and sitting up, she too realized Helen's soft body, the strong and hospitable arms, and happiness swelling and breaking in one vast wave. When this fell away, and the grasses once more lay low, and the sky became horizontal, and the earth rolled out flat on each side, and the trees stood upright, she was the first to perceive a little row of human figures standing patiently in the distance. For the moment she could not remember who they were. (*VO* 287–8)

The confused and disordered perspectives in this passage suggest a disordering of sexual and familial relationships which the reader, like Rachel, must recompose in order to understand that it is Helen who has come upon Rachel and Terence and that Helen and Terence are speaking not of their love and marriage but of that of Rachel and Terence. Seen from Rachel's perspective, Rachel, 'speechless and almost without sense', becomes the infant looking up at the Titanic figures of Father and Mother, Terence and Helen. The lover's body is not Terence's but the maternal body, all-powerful, infinitely desired but also terrifying: 'Helen was upon her.' Talk of love and 'then of marriage' inscribes the conventional narrative of a woman's life. At the same time the text itself returns Rachel to (and buries her beneath) the imaginary space of maternal plenitude, a time before separation and loss, closely linked to the novel's representations of the matriarchal, 'primitive' society to which Rachel has journeyed. It is perhaps unsurprising that Rachel's *Bildung*, her formation, is cut short by death, the return journey to non-being.

In a later exchange of letters with Lytton Strachey about *The Voyage Out*, Woolf agreed with his assessment that the whole 'was really only the beginning of an enormous novel, which had been – almost accidentally – cut short by the death of Rachel': 'What I wanted to do', she writes, 'was to give the feeling of a vast tumult of life, as various and disorderly as possible, which should be cut short for a moment by the death, and go on again – and the whole was to have a sort of pattern, and be somehow controlled. <...> I really wanted three volumes' (*L*. iii. 82). It is ironic that Woolf, having written what Strachey applauds as a 'very, very unvictorian' novel, should seem to lament the passing of the expansive Victorian 'three-decker novel'. In an 'unvictorian' way, however, she envisaged that the heroine's death would not end the novel, so that 'the life' and the life of the narrative would not be coterminous. In later texts, Woolf was to find new ways of contracting and condensing time and of making biographical and narrative time asynchronous. Both *Mrs Dalloway* and *Between the Acts* are 'one-day novels' which contain much of the past, both near and remote, while in *To the Lighthouse* the death of the central figure, Mrs Ramsay, half-way through the novel allowed for a radical experiment in 'writing beyond the ending'.[8]

2

A Shape that Fits

> I think a great deal of my future, and settle what book I am
> to write, how I shall re-form the novel and capture
> multitudes of things at present fugitive, enclose the whole,
> and shape infinite strange shapes.
>
> (Letter to Clive Bell, 19 Aug. 1908 (*L.* i. 356))

> These little pieces in Monday or (and) Tuesday were written
> by way of diversion; they were the treats I allowed myself
> when I had done my exercise in the conventional style
> [*Night and Day*]. I shall never forget the day I wrote The
> Mark on the Wall – all in a flash, as if flying, after being kept
> stone breaking for months. The Unwritten Novel was the
> great discovery, however. That – again in one second –
> showed me how I could embody all my deposit of
> experience in a shape that fitted it – not that I have ever
> reached that end; but anyhow I saw, branching out of the
> tunnel I made, when I discovered that method of approach,
> Jacobs Room [1922], Mrs Dalloway [1925] etc – How I
> trembled with excitement <...>
>
> (Letter to Ethel Smyth, Thursday, 16 Oct. 1930 (*L.* iv. 231))

In 1921 the Hogarth Press published a collection of Woolf's short
stories under the title *Monday or Tuesday*. Two of the stories, 'The
Mark on the Wall' and 'Kew Gardens', had already appeared in
pamphlet form as Hogarth Press publications, hand-set and
printed by Leonard and Virginia Woolf for the Press they had
founded in 1917.[1] Virginia Woolf wrote to David Garnett, after
he had admired 'The Mark on the Wall':

> I'm very glad you liked the story. In a way its easier to do a short
> thing, all in one flight than a novel. Novels are frightfully clumsy and
> overpowering of course; still if one could only get hold of them it
> would be superb. I daresay one ought to invent a completely new

form. Anyhow, it's very amusing to try with these short things, and the greatest mercy to be able to do what one likes – no editors, no publishers, and only people to read who more or less like that sort of thing. (*L*. ii. 167–8).

In this letter, Woolf highlights the importance of experiment, of freedom, and of a sympathetic readership – the keys to the meaning of the Hogarth Press for her. She also opens up an issue that she was to debate throughout her writing life: the limits and possibilities of the novel form, and the need 'to invent a completely new form'. At this point in her writing career, the short story is an important genre, in both practical and literary terms. Short stories could be produced by the Woolfs on their own press, thus circumventing the 'middlemen' of publishing (and avoiding dealing with Woolf's half-brother Gerald Duckworth, whose publishing company had produced *The Voyage Out* and *Night and Day*), and they could be written 'all in one flight', remaining free of the burdens and constraints of plot and character 'development'.

Woolf's debates with fellow-writers in the 1920s revolve around the question of 'character in fiction'. In 'The Mark on the Wall', 'An Unwritten Novel', and, most strikingly, her third novel, *Jacob's Room*, there is an undercurrent of play on 'character' as a printing term and on the history of the word *character* as stemming from the Greek *kharratein*, to engrave. One of the subtexts of Woolf's early short stories is a definition of 'character' as (punctuation) mark and print type, a subversion of the received definitions of 'character' as psychological 'type' (often masquerading as a complex subjectivity) that runs throughout *Jacob's Room* and is largely responsible for its experimentalism and its complexity.

'The Mark on the Wall', like 'An Unwritten Novel', is a highly self-conscious meditation on the ways in which narratives are constructed. It stands at the edge of the 'stream of consciousness' so central to modernist narrative, so as to explore the extent to which identity and consciousness are separable and the points at which the 'stream' can be entered and perhaps diverted.[2] Not all lines or 'tracks' of thought are equally rewarding: 'I wish I could hit upon a pleasant track of thought', the narrator states, as she points to the indirect self-aggrandizement which makes daydreams so enjoyable. The mark on the wall both incites thoughts and acts as a full stop to end disagreeable ones; it is at one level a punctuation mark, beginning and ending trains of thought.

'The Mark on the Wall' explores the difference between the 'masculine' point of view – fact-bound, hierarchical, constraining – and a free-associative thinking which revels in the multiple imaginings opened up by freedom from the desire to find out what things 'really' are. Intentionally keeping a distance from the eponymous 'mark on the wall' while wondering about its identity, the narrator finds that perceptual undecidability allows the mind to wander freely, into and through history, pre-history, and post-history. The 'subconscious' mind, here as elsewhere in Woolf's writing, is inseparable from the primeval. The mark is identified by the male speaker who enters the room at the end of the story as a snail – a recurrent image in Woolf's writing of a fixed and carapaced identity, the shell serving as both home and 'psychic shield',[3] to be contrasted, as in her essay 'Street Haunting', with an unhoused, receptive, and wandering consciousness. The pinning-down of the 'mark on the wall' puts an end to the narrator's happy mental voyagings and identifications with the life of a tree: 'The song of birds must sound very loud and strange in June and how cold the feet of insects must feel upon it, as they make laborious progresses up the creases of the bark, or sun themselves upon the thin green awning of the leaves, and look straight in front of them with diamond-cut red eyes' (CSF 89).

Such images are central to Woolf's work, an aspect of, in Gillian Beer's words, her 'awareness of the simultaneity of the prehistoric in our present moment [which] absolves her from the causal forms she associates with nineteenth-century narratives'.[4] Woolf was to note some twenty years after the writing of the short story, when she was reading Freud: 'the point of view of any individual is bound to be not a birds eye view but an insects eye view, ... the view of an insect too on a green blade, which oscillates violently with local gusts of wind.'[5]

'Kew Gardens' brings together light, colour, and the insect's eye view. It takes up the imagery of 'The Mark on the Wall', removing the snail, as it were, from its anachronistic place on the sitting-room wall and returning it to the primeval realms of the flower bed, from where it conducts a snail's-horn response to the world. Different pairs and groups of people pass the flower bed, and their thoughts and dialogues are recorded: the first two 'conversations' are concerned with the raising of ghosts – in the first instance through memory; in the second, through spiritualism and telepathy. Where 'The Mark on the Wall' explores the workings of consciousness, 'Kew Gardens' addresses itself to communication of diverse and uncanny kinds. People take on the form, manner, and evanescence of insects as they move through the park, and their congress with each other is as meaningful or meaningless as the obscure relationship between the snail and the 'singular high-stepping angular green insect who attempted to cross in front of it'. The narrative is only interested in its 'characters' as they pass the flower bed in which the snail lives; it does not pursue them after they have moved on but turns its attentions to the next passers-by. Once they have passed the spot in which the snail, the flowers, and narrative consciousness are rooted, they seem to dissolve into the sunlight and shade, 'the green-blue atmosphere'. Woolf's experiments with 'point of view' led her to this use of the equivalent of a fixed camera – a technique she developed in *Mrs Dalloway*, in which Regent's Park becomes the site of a shifting and wandering narrative consciousness, a camera eye which follows first one individual and then another as he or she passes alongside. The principle of selection appears to be based on spatial and temporal contiguity and contingency rather than determined by the exigencies of plot or character development.

One of the earliest critical works on Woolf found in 'Kew Gardens' a clear example of 'cinematographic technique'. Winifred Holtby wrote in her 1932 study of Woolf:

> To let the perspective shift from high to low, from huge to microscopic, to let figures of people, insects, aeroplanes, flowers pass across the vision and melt away – these are devices common enough to another form of art. These are the tricks of the cinema. Mrs. Woolf had discovered the cinema. There is no reason why it should monopolise powers of expansion and contraction. In *Kew Gardens* the external figures appear and disappear with such brilliant clarity that we could almost photograph them from the words.[6]

To these devices Holtby added the scene-making method of *Jacob's Room*, with action 'indicated by the changing positions and gestures of the characters'. I discuss Woolf's uses of cinematic technique in more detail in Chapter 5; for the present, we might note the ways in which the shifting perspectives and the temporal and spatial 'expansion and contraction' central to *The Voyage Out* are subsequently incorporated into Woolf's more 'experimental' fictions and into the very rhythms of her prose.

UNWRITING THE NOVEL

As we face each other in omnibuses and underground
railways we are looking into the mirror; that accounts for
the vagueness, the gleam of glassiness, in our eyes. And the
novelists in future will realise more and more the
importance of these reflections, for of course there is not
one reflection but an almost infinite number; those are the
depths they will explore, those the phantoms they will
pursue, leaving the description of reality more and more
out of their stories, taking a knowledge of it for granted, as
the Greeks did and Shakespeare perhaps – but these
generalisations are worthless. The military sound of the
word is enough. It recalls leading articles, cabinet ministers
– a whole class of things which as a child one thought the
thing itself, the real thing, from which one could not depart
save at the risk of nameless damnation.

(CSF 85–6).

In this passage from 'The Mark on the Wall', the narrator moves
towards the formulation of an aesthetic – and then interrupts
herself. At the story's opening, she recalls a conversation with
the previous owner of her house in which 'he was in process of
saying that in his opinion art should have ideas behind it when
we were torn asunder, as one is torn from the old lady about to
pour out tea and the young man about to hit the tennis ball in
the back garden of the suburban villa as one rushes past in the
train' (CSF 83). Generalizations about the role and nature of art,
it would seem, invite interruption; Woolf was strongly aware of
the paradoxes involved in trying to fix, by fiat or manifesto, an
art which she values for its mobility and freedom from
convention. She suggests, in the passage quoted above, that
such conventions (General-isations) are part of a rigid, dis-
ciplinarian, masculine, and Victorian order.

Woolf's best-known essays from the late 1910s into the 1920s
are important attempts to shape and define a modern aesthetic,
often in the terms the narrator of 'The Mark on the Wall' begins
to explore. Woolf's sense of the contradictory nature of the task
remains acute, however; it has one outlet in the construction of
imaginary scenes and conversations in which different positions
and possibilities can be played out, without the need for
conclusions. Similar scenes appear and reappear in Woolf's
short stories, essays, and novels, cutting across the divide

between her fiction and non-fiction.

The observation of a fellow-traveller in a railway carriage is a favourite scenario. Woolf first elaborated it in 'An Unwritten Novel', in which her narrator imagines an identity and a life for the middle-aged woman who sits opposite her on a train. The empathy that ostensibly allows the narrator to enter 'Minnie's' world is ironically figured as the transfer of an itch between the shoulder blades:

> she [Minnie] had communicated, shared her secret, passed her poison; she would speak no more. Leaning back in my corner, shielding my eyes from her eyes, seeing only the slopes and hollows, greys and purples, of the winter's landscape, I read her message, deciphered her secret, reading it beneath her gaze. (*CSF* 114)

The narrator pursues Minnie in imagination to her sister-in-law's house in Eastbourne, furnishing it with potted palms and commercial travellers in a parody of an Arnold Bennett novel. Woolf 'unwrites' the naturalist novel as she goes along, breaking up its surfaces and its linearity by pointedly inserting gaps, parentheses, and ellipses in passages of description: 'But this we'll skip; ornaments, curtains, trefoil china plate, yellow oblongs of cheese, white squares of biscuits – skip – oh, but wait!' Realist detail, however 'saturated' (a favourite, Jamesian, term), cannot encompass complex realities: 'Have I read you right? But the human face – the human face at the top of the fullest sheet of print holds more, withholds more' (*CSF* 117). The juxtaposition of 'face' and 'sheet of print', which recurs throughout Woolf's writing (as in *Jacob's Room*, discussed below), again exploits the double meaning of 'character' as identity and as print type. It also suggests Woolf's complex understanding of 'the face' (the self's surface) as a parchment or palimpsest which, like the newspaper ('thin sheets of gelatine pressed nightly over the brain and heart of the world'), 'take[s] the impression of the whole' (*JR* 84).

At the close of 'An Unwritten Novel' and the end of the railway journey, 'Minnie' the lonely and tormented spinster dissolves as the woman in the carriage walks off with her son. The narrator's world temporarily collapses – until the process of building a story, creating the world anew, starts over: 'Mysterious figures! Mother and son. Who are you? Why do you walk down the street? Where the night will you sleep, and then, tomorrow? Oh, how it whirls and surges – floats me afresh! I start after them' (*CSF* 121). The 'unwriting' of one novel – the 'unwritten novel' of the title – opens up a space for other stories, other lives. Negation and creation are inextricably linked.

The novel 'unwritten' may also be *Night and Day*, as Woolf's letter to Ethel Smyth suggests: the house of fiction must be rebuilt in order for other, airier forms to emerge. The title of 'An Unwritten Novel' suggests something of the relationship between a structure which is all potential and one which must be undone, an instability faced by Woolf as she completed *Night and Day* when she wrote in her diary: '[As] the current answers don't do, one has to grope for a new one: & the process of discarding the old, when one is by no means certain of what to put in their place, is a sad one. Still, if you think of it, what answers do Arnold Bennett or Thackeray, for instance, suggest?' (*D*. i. 259). The regret Woolf expresses at 'discarding the old' literary forms is in marked contrast to the total rejection of tradition and convention espoused by many of her contemporaries.

MODERN FICTION

Woolf was acutely aware of writing at a transitional time in literature, and her self-criticisms of *Night and Day* suggest that she felt that she had not met the challenges newly posed to writers. In 1919 she published an essay on 'Modern Novels', a slightly modified version of which was published in *The Common Reader* (1925) as 'Modern Fiction', in which she referred to 'constructing our two and thirty chapters after a design which more and more ceases to resemble the vision in our mind' (*CDML* 8). (*Night and Day* has thirty-four chapters.) The essay contains Woolf's most famous, and frequently quoted, comments on fiction and the modernist aesthetic. It also forms part of a group of interlinked essays in which Woolf's critique of Arnold Bennett's Edwardian naturalism becomes a starting-point for new ways of thinking about the novel. Woolf's essay 'Mr Bennett and Mrs Brown', reworked and republished several times, is the most often cited of these.

In 'Modern Fiction' Woolf contrasts the 'materialism' of the Edwardian novelists H. G. Wells, Arnold Bennett, and John Galsworthy with the 'spiritualism' of the younger, 'Georgian' writers, most notably James Joyce. Her strongest criticisms of the 'materialists' are directed against Bennett, 'the worst culprit of the three, inasmuch as he is by far the best workman':

> He can make a book so well constructed and solid in its craftsmanship that it is difficult for the most exacting of critics to see through what chink or crevice decay can creep in. There is not so much as a draught between the frames of the windows, or a crack in the boards. And yet – if life should refuse to live there? (*CDML* 8)

Woolf's play with the Jamesian image of the 'house of fiction' is a key element in her essays and novels. Her writings on the modern novel owe much to Henry James's 'The New Novel' (1914), not least his reference to Bennett's *Clayhanger* as

> a monument not to an idea, a pursued and captured meaning, or in short *to* anything whatever, but just simply *of* the quarried and gathered material it happens to contain, the stones and bricks and rubble and cement and promiscuous constituents of every sort that have been heaped in it and thanks to which it quite massively builds itself up.[7]

In *Mr Bennett and Mrs Brown*, she writes of Bennett: 'he is trying to hypnotize us into the belief that, because he has built a house, there must be a person living there' (*WE* 80). Woolf's novels explicitly refuse such techniques. *Jacob's Room*, as we shall see later, presents us with an empty room ('no scaffolding; scarcely a brick to be seen', Woolf wrote in her diary of the novel's structure (*D*. ii. 13)), the space enclosing Jacob's absence, not his presence. *To the Lighthouse* takes as one of its central images an empty, crumbling house; light and darkness creep in at the keyholes and crevices and 'certain airs' enter through 'rusty hinges' to explore the process and duration of decay. In contrast to Bennett's solid and impermeable 'house of fiction', without chink or crevice, draught or crack, Woolf opens hers up to the elements in order to expose matter, 'material life', to time, to loss, to history, and to spirit.

Bennett's novels, Woolf argues in 'Modern Fiction', lead us to ask 'Is life like this? Must novels be like this?' Answering in the negative, she offers an account of consciousness and the novel which has been taken as her central credo for fiction-writing, and as a key 'manifesto' of literary modernism:

> Look within and life, it seems, is very far from being 'like this'. Examine for a moment an ordinary mind on an ordinary day. The mind receives a myriad impressions – trivial, fantastic, evanescent, or engraved with the sharpness of steel. From all sides they come, an incessant shower of innumerable atoms; and as they fall, as they

shape themselves into the life of Monday or Tuesday, the accent falls differently from of old; the moment of importance came not here but there; so that, if a writer were a free man and not a slave, if he could write what he chose, not what he must, if he could base his work upon his own feeling and not upon convention, there would be no plot, no comedy, no tragedy, no love interest or catastrophe in the accepted style, and perhaps not a single button sewn on as the Bond Street tailors would have it. Life is not a series of gig lamps symmetrically arranged; life is a luminous halo, a semi-transparent envelope surrounding us from the beginning of consciousness to the end. Is it not the task of the novelist to convey this varying, this unknown and uncircumscribed spirit, whatever aberration or complexity it may display, with as little mixture of the alien and external as possible? We are not pleading merely for courage and sincerity; we are suggesting that the proper stuff of fiction is a little other than custom would have us believe it.

It is, at any rate, in some such fashion as this that we seek to define the quality which distinguishes the work of several young writers, among whom Mr. James Joyce is the most notable, from that of their predecessors.   (*CDML* 8–9)

Woolf's views in 'Modern Fiction' provide, in Randall Stevenson's words, 'one of the most comprehensive and celebrated statements of the priorities of modernism'.[8] Foremost among these views is Woolf's injunction to 'look within'; 'life', she seems to suggest, is shaped by consciousness, and an 'aesthetic' is to be discovered in the place of subjectivity itself. The moderns, she argues later in 'Modern Fiction', are drawn to 'the dark places of psychology' – an allusion to a psychoanalytic understanding of complex human subjectivities. We need to remember, however, that Woolf maintained some considerable critical distance from Freud's theories at this time[9] and that, despite her 'look within', she tended to represent the encounter of self with self as very similar to that of self with other. Hence the *intersubjective* dimensions of the 'mirroring' relations she describes in 'The Mark on the Wall' – 'as we face each other < ... > we are looking into the mirror' – and the representation of both self and other as books to be read, their 'stories' already inscribed or 'impressed' upon the mind.

Woolf refers in the passage quoted above to the examination of 'an ordinary mind on an ordinary day', in part with James Joyce's one-day novel *Ulysses* in mind. Four of Woolf's novels – *Mrs Dalloway*, *To the Lighthouse*, *The Waves*, and *Between the Acts* – engage in something of this 'examination': a diurnal temporality or a 'dailiness' experienced by an intersecting group of consciousnesses takes the place of (or, in the case of *The Waves*, coexists with) the representation of individual life or lives over an extended period of time. The phrase further suggests the temporalities and the print techniques of the daily newspaper (a central image and paradigm in *Ulysses*), 'taking' (as well as 'receiving') 'impressions'. Woolf's account in 'Modern Fiction' of 'atoms' 'shap[ing] themselves into the life of Monday or Tuesday' is both a reference to this 'dailiness' and a playful allusion to her own collection of stories, *Monday or Tuesday*; experience, she suggests, shapes itself into the forms of her experimental and auto-printed writing.

The significant temporal unit for Woolf is not only the day but 'the moment'; this focus on the intensity of present time, the privileged moment taken, or even 'blasted', out of the historical continuum, is shared by many modernist writers. Woolf pursues this concept in a diary entry written a few years after 'Modern Fiction':

> The idea has come to me that what I want now to do is to saturate every atom. I mean to eliminate all waste, deadness, superfluity: to give the moment whole; whatever it includes. Say that the moment is a combination of thought; sensation; the voice of the sea. Waste, deadness, come from the inclusion of things that dont belong to the moment; this appalling narrative business of the realist: getting on from lunch to dinner: it is false, unreal, merely conventional. <...> I want to put practically everything in; yet to saturate. That is what I want to do in The Moths [*The Waves*]. It must include nonsense, fact, sordidity: but made transparent.   (*D*. iii. 209–10)

As Lyn Pykett notes, 'Woolf sought a fictional form which would replace the profusion of details found in the materialists (a saturation of details) with a saturation of the detail.'[10]

The 'Modern Fiction' passage also suggests Woolf's interest in creating non-linear narrative, a theme she addressed at the time of writing *Mrs Dalloway* in her correspondence with the painter Jacques Raverat and which she linked to visual and spatial forms of representation. Raverat contrasted the 'essentially linear' nature of writing with the radial patterns produced in the mind by words and their associations: 'There are splashes in the outer air in every direction, and under the surface waves that follow one another into dark and forgotten corners...'.[11] Woolf replied:

I rather think you've broached some of the problems of the writer's too, who are trying to catch and consolidate and consummate (whatever the word is for making literature) those splashes of yours; for the falsity of the past (by which I mean Bennett, Galsworthy and so on) is precisely I think that they adhere to a formal railway line of sentence, for its convenience, never reflecting that people don't and never did feel or think or dream for a second in that way; but all over the place, in your way. (*L.* iii. 136–6)

The letter suggests that Woolf viewed the techniques of nineteenth-century realism and naturalism (with their emphases on the accurate representation of an external world) as always having been inadequate to the complexities of 'reality', rather than merely now rendered obsolete by 'one of those little deviations which the human spirit seems to make from time to time'.

SURFACE AND DEPTH

Woolf does not fully endorse the 'impressionistic' method she describes in 'Modern Fiction' but largely ascribes it to Joyce, a writer towards whose work she was notoriously ambivalent, though undoubtedly indebted. While praising Joyce's ability to 'come so close to the quick of the mind', she also suggests that the Joycean method circumscribes the reader 'in a self which...never embraces or creates what is outside itself and beyond' (*CDML* 10). The line echoes a diary entry in which, planning the work that was to become *Jacob's Room*, she celebrates her discovery of a new form but expresses concern about the 'damned egotistical self; which ruins Joyce and [Dorothy] Richardson to my mind' (*D.* ii. 14).

In fact, in Joyce and Richardson much that is not the self penetrates, and indeed determines, consciousness and identity. Woolf's misreadings (based in substantial part on competitiveness) aside, the point is that she sought to develop fictional strategies other than those of 'stream-of-consciousness' techniques – techniques which attempt to represent the inner workings of the mind and to embody thought patterns by dispensing entirely with an omniscient narrator. By contrast, Woolf produced complex patterns of narration which, although specific to each of her novels, are united in combining 'the inner & the outer' (*D.* iii. 209) and in constructing a relationship between selves. Woolf's use of 'indirect discourse', 'the consciousness of the narrator married to the consciousness of the character and speaking for it', in J. Hillis Miller's words,[12] reduces the controlling power of a third-person narrator without confining the narrative to a single, monologic voice and consciousness. Erich Auerbach, in his unsurpassed essay on narrative method in *To the Lighthouse*, draws the distinction between a 'unipersonal subjective method', which 'admits only...one person's way of looking at reality' and a 'multipersonal representation of consciousness'.[13] In *To the Lighthouse* Mrs Ramsay is 'encircled by the content of all the various consciousnesses directed upon her (including her own)'. Woolf's method was also used to make the transition from one consciousness to another, often within a single sentence. Her techniques, as I have suggested, have the representation of the intersubjective as their aim.

In her review of Dorothy Richardson's novel *The Tunnel* (the fourth volume of her novel sequence *Pilgrimage*), Woolf commends Richardson for achieving 'a sense of reality far greater than that produced by the ordinary means', but goes on to ask 'which reality is it, the superficial or the profound?' Despite the breaking of the old forms, 'we still find ourselves distressingly near the surface' (*WE* 16). The comparisons Woolf draws between her own work and that of Joyce and Richardson are for the most part battled out over the issue of surface versus depth in the novel form. In suggesting that Richardson's reality is 'superficial', Woolf may well have been attempting to undercut the novelist May Sinclair's account of 'the sheer depth of [Richardson's] plunge',[14] wanting to claim 'depth' and 'plunge' (the latter a key term in *Mrs Dalloway*, as was the concept of 'tunnelling' in the novel's conception) for her own literary art.

In 'Women and Fiction' and *A Room of One's Own*, Woolf suggests that judgements over what is 'superficial' or 'profound', trivial or significant, are relative and reversible; there are no absolute values, and those that masquerade as universals usually conceal a strongly gendered bias. Yet in numerous essays Woolf asserts that it is the role of literature to create 'enduring' forms, and she invariably presents these through metaphors of depth. At times creativity is conceptualized in 'subterranean' terms – caves, inner chambers, the ocean floor – suggestive of a depth psychology. At others, Woolf refers to literary structure in terms drawn from geometry and architecture, and any account of her work as 'impressionistic' must be qualified by the extent to which Woolf, as Sue Roe notes, 'blocked her novels ... aligning subjective content with diagrammatic form'.[15]

To the Lighthouse, for example, reworks the artist and aesthetician Roger Fry's collocations of 'vision' and 'design'.[16] Woolf was clear about her 'design' for the novel ('2 blocks joined by a corridor'); the painter Lily Briscoe has a 'structural' model for her painting. Yet there is also a need for shapes and geometries to be given depth. Lily's desire for her painting – 'beautiful and bright it should be on the surface, feathery and evanescent, one colour melting into another like the colours on a butterfly's wing; but beneath the fabric must be clamped together with bolts of iron' (*TTL* 186) – echoes Woolf's description in her diary of Proust's writing, in which she comes closest, I would suggest, to defining her aesthetic ideal: 'as tough as catgut and as evanescent as a butterfly's bloom' (*D*. iii. 7).

These issues are in no way merely formal for Woolf but are intimately bound up with the modern novelist's negotiations with modernity and its fragmentary, fleeting, transient qualities. Woolf's writings on literature and modernity emphasize an 'ever-changing and turning world' – the phrase she uses in *A Room of One's Own* to describe the women's fiction of the future. In a number of her essays, Woolf not only points up but feminizes the fleeting, mutable nature of modern life which dominates the accounts of modernity given by the most significant social and cultural theorists of the early twentieth century: Georg Simmel, Siegfried Kracauer, Walter Benjamin.[17] Yet Woolf was also caught up in a paradoxical endeavour to 'build up out of the fleeting and the personal the lasting edifice which remains unthrown' (*ROO* 84) and to construct 'depth' behind the 'surface' of the modern.

The perceived tension between the permanence of art and the transience of the 'life' (or consciousness or time) it seeks to represent is, I would argue, one of the defining features of modernism. Throughout her essays Woolf appears to insist that, while writers may garner their materials from the surfaces of 'life', they must withdraw into the quieter and darker spaces of creativity in order to transmute their sensations and perceptions into art and to give a lasting foundation to their values.

In 'Life and the Novelist' (1926), a review of G. B. Stern's *A*

Deputy Was King, Woolf sets out such a two-stage model of literary creation.[18] The novelist, imaged as a diner in a restaurant or café, is first of all immersed in life and 'can no more cease to receive impressions than a fish in mid-ocean can cease to let the water rush through his gills'. For 'life' to be transformed into 'art', however, the writer must retire to 'some solitary room', exerting a stern discipline upon the 'froth' of life. Thus 'there emerges from the mist something stark, formidable and enduring, the bone and substance upon which our rush of indiscriminating emotion was founded' (*E.* iv. 401). The second stage of creation is in fact revealed to have pre-existed and underlain the first and to be the condition of its possibility. This circularity suggests the difficulty of giving priority either to the 'enduring' foundations or to the fleeting impressions.

As Rachel Bowlby has argued, in a discussion of Woolf's essays on modern culture:

> However much she may deplore the absence of solid, permanent values in theory, wherever this [dance of modern life] appears Woolf's essays seem to be carried away by its attractive movements, leaving behind the stable literary orders for the looser possibilities – pleasures and fears and risks – of changing identities, changing sights, changing places. (*CDML*, p. xxviii).

Woolf's ambivalent and paradoxical responses could be understood as the paradox of modernity itself which, in Charles Baudelaire's formulation, is 'the ephemeral, the fugitive, the contingent, the half of art whose other half is the eternal and the immutable'.[19]

CHARACTER IN FICTION

Woolf debated the question of 'character' in fiction in a number of essays written in the 1920s. In 'Modern Fiction', as we saw, she refers to the occurrence of 'little deviations in the human spirit' which need to be matched by changes in the novel form; human identity, the representation of character, and the writing of fiction thus become very closely aligned. She spelled this out in a letter to Gerald Brenan (Christmas Day 1922), responding, it would seem, to his suggestion that 'one must renounce' the novel genre:

I don't see how to write a book without people in it. Perhaps you mean that one ought not to attempt a 'view of life'? – one ought to limit oneself to one's own sensations – at a quartet for instance; one ought to be lyrical, descriptive: but not set people in motion, and attempt to enter them, and give them impact and volume? Ah, but I'm doomed! As a matter of fact, I think that we all are. It is not possible now, and never will be, to say I renounce. Nor would it be a good thing for literature were it possible. This generation must break its neck in order that the next may have smooth going. < . . . > The human soul, it seems to me, orientates itself afresh every now and then. It is doing so now. No one can see it whole, therefore. The best of us catch a glimpse of a nose, a shoulder, something turning away, always in movement. Still, it seems better to me to catch this glimpse, than to sit down with Hugh Walpole, Wells, etc. etc. and make large oil paintings of fabulous fleshy monsters complete from top to toe. Of course, being under 30, this does not apply to you. To you, something more complete may be vouchsafed.   (*L.* ii. 597–8)

Woolf continues, in response to Brenan's account of his difficulties with writing, with a reference to her attempts at suicide 'every 10 years, at 20, again at 30' (a startling anticipation of the poet Sylvia Plath's very similar claim[20]): 'Every ten years brings, I suppose, one of those private orientations which match the vast one which is, to my mind, general now in the race. I mean, life has to be sloughed; has to be faced: to be rejected; then accepted on new terms with rapture' (*L.* ii. 598–9).

Woolf suggests to Brenan that her primary reason for staying with the novel as a form was that it allowed her to move outside the limitations of 'one's own sensations' and to put other realities and identities 'in motion'. The letter also brings together writing and identity in complex and fascinating ways. Changes in the 'human soul' demand new forms of literary representation; periods of transition shatter literary form and psychological identity, both of which must be rebuilt 'on new terms'. 'Completeness', Woolf added in a postscript, may now be an impossible goal for the writer, but one that should be renounced only after it has been attempted. In her early letter to Clive Bell (quoted at the beginning of this chapter), Woolf defines her 're-form[ation]' of the novel as an attempt to 'capture . . . things at present fugitive' and to 'enclose the whole'. The challenge facing her was to capture these fugitive energies without thereby destroying them, 'to catch them', as she wrote in another context, 'before they become "works of art"' (*D.* iii. 102).

Woolf's letter to Brenan throws light both on her third novel, *Jacob's Room*, and on her essay 'Mr Bennett and Mrs Brown', first published as 'Character in Fiction'. In her diary Woolf described her plans for *Jacob's Room* in these terms:

> For I figure that the approach will be entirely different this time: no scaffolding: scarcely a brick to be seen; all crepuscular, but the heart, the passion, humour, everything as bright as fire in the mist. Then I'll find room for so much – a gaiety – an inconsequence – a light spirited stepping at my sweet will. Whether I'm sufficiently mistress of things – thats the doubt; but conceive mark on the wall, K[ew] G[ardens], & unwritten novel taking hands and dancing in unity. (*D*. ii. 13–14)

Jacob's Room (which I discuss in more detail in Chapter 5) was one of Woolf's most radical narrative experiments. Like the short stories I have discussed, *Jacob's Room* is a textual representation of incompletion – of narratives and of lives. Fragmentation is realized in the very layout of the novel. The white spaces Woolf used on the page, as John Mepham notes, are gaps which provide the reader with a sequence of separated scenes rather than a narrative and create new forms of connection.[21]

Like 'An Unwritten Novel', *Jacob's Room* unwrites established forms, including the *Bildungsroman* (the genre to which Woolf's first two novels were closest and the one in which her male contemporaries – James Joyce, E. M. Forster, D. H. Lawrence – had established their literary reputations) and biography. She read Lytton Strachey's biography of Queen Victoria during the writing of her novel and commented in her diary that it was a 'remarkably composed & homogenous book'. 'I doubt whether these portraits are true', she added '– whether that's not too much the conventional way of making history – But I think I'm coloured by my own wishes, & experimental mood' (*D*. ii. 65). In *Jacob's Room* Woolf eschewed a 'composed and homogenous' form, undermining narrative omniscience and pointing up the limitations of observation and/as narration, veering between a limited and omniscient narrative voice. It is not only that 'Jacob' is radically unknowable but that his 'biographer' can claim no certain knowledge of her subject.

Woolf gives us in Jacob the 'glimpse of a nose, a shoulder, something turning away, always in movement' which she describes in her letter to Brenan; the stress on the fugitive nature of the human subject echoes numerous moments in her essays in which she refers to 'life' escaping the novelist. Her emphasis on the physical form of 'characters' opens up the difficulties of reading the 'inside' from the 'outside'; it is also an aspect of the novel's self-conscious use of portraiture and statuary as forms of biography.

'An Unwritten Novel', as we have seen, sets its scene of character-(mis)reading in a railway carriage. In *Jacob's Room* Woolf uses the scene in reverse, as Jacob, going 'up to Cambridge', has his character 'read' over the top of a page of newspaper print by a Mrs Norman, a middle-aged woman sitting opposite him in the compartment. As Rachel Bowlby notes, the narrative shift to Mrs Norman (who appears for the first and the last time in this brief sequence) transfers attention away from Jacob during a major rite of passage (the young man going up to university), turning Jacob, the 'hero' of this (mock) *Bildungsroman*, 'into a mere type as seen from the place of Mrs Norman'.[22] Initially fearing for her safety – 'it is a fact that men are dangerous' – Mrs Norman applies 'the infallible test of appearance' to Jacob (an obsolete definition of 'character' is 'the face or features as betokening moral qualities' (*OED*)) and decides that he is 'like her own boy', whom, in this novel of mothers and sons, she is travelling to meet. 'One must do the best one can with her report', the narrative continues. 'It is no use trying to sum people up. One must follow hints, not exactly what is said, nor yet entirely what is done –' (*JR* 24). These last lines are repeated verbatim later in the novel, to introduce a discussion of attitudes towards 'character-mongering', thus linking the narrator with Mrs Norman, both of them women trying to 'read' and interpret Jacob 'from the outside'. The novel, however, at no point suggests that there is an 'inside' story which would open up to a different set of keys; rather, in Bowlby's words, 'that it is not possible to separate conventional signs, characters, stories and the reality which they structure and interpret'.[23] 'Characters' are always 'types'.

These terms were emphasized by Woolf's contemporary readers and critics. Rebecca West wrote that '*Jacob's Room* is not about individuals at all but types as seen through the refractions of commonplace observers' eyes' (M&M 101). The *Times Literary Supplement* reviewer felt that:

we should have to say that [*Jacob's Room*] does not create persons and characters as we secretly desire to know them. We do not know Jacob as an individual, though we promptly seize his type; perhaps we do not know anyone in the book otherwise than as a really intuitive person knows his acquaintances, filling in the blanks, if he is imaginative, by his imagination. (M&M 97)

This is surely a misreading: the 'blanks' in the novel remain unfillable, as Jacob remains unknowable. Yet it is striking that Woolf, in her responses to her readers, both insists upon the novel as an 'experiment' – 'too much of an experiment', 'nothing but an experiment', 'more an experiment than an achievement' (*L*. ii. 573, 581, 591) – and at times suggests that her decomposition of character was too radical. She wrote of the novel in her diary that '[Roger Fry] wishes that a bronze body might somehow solidify beneath the gleams & lights – with which I agree' (*D*. ii. 214). Certainly, in writing her next novel, *Mrs Dalloway*, she was concerned that her heroine's character should not be 'tinsely', and explored narrative techniques by which it could be given 'depth'.

Woolf's best-known discussion of 'character' emerged as a response to Arnold Bennett, who, in an article entitled 'Is the Novel Decaying', had argued that the creation of convincing characters was the most important aspect of the novel genre and had used *Jacob's Room* in his account of the new novelists 'who appear to be interested more in details than in the full creation of their individual characters' (M&M 113). Woolf retaliated in 'Mr Bennett and Mrs Brown', seeking to show that Bennett's very concept of 'character' was outmoded and inadequate. She hazards an assertion 'to the effect that in or about December 1910 human character changed'.[24]

> The first signs of it are recorded in the books of Samuel Butler, in *The Way of all Flesh* in particular; the plays of Bernard Shaw continue to record it. In life one can see the change, if I may use a homely illustration, in the character of one's cook. The Victorian cook lived like a leviathan in the lower depths, formidable, silent, obscure, inscrutable; the Georgian cook is a creature of sunshine and fresh air < ... > All human relations have shifted – those between masters and servants, husbands and wives, parents and children. And when human relations change there is at the same time a change in religion, conduct, politics and literature. Let us agree to place one of these changes about the year 1910. (*WE* 70–1)

The passage, like the essay (originally given as a lecture to a group of women students), is of course in part satirical. Woolf plays, for example, on the concept of giving a cook a 'character' ('a formal testimony given by an employer as to the qualities and habits of one that has been in his employ' (*OED*)), pointing up again not only that 'character' (the concept of the individual) has changed but that the term 'character' has multiple definitions, the failure to consider which has led to an endless reiteration of received opinions and literary clichés. Woolf may also have been hinting that Bennett – represented by her as the literary equivalent of a house-builder or, in 'Mr Bennett and Mrs Brown', a 'Northern businessman' – delineates 'characters' in his novels in ways which are more like (what we would now call) 'references' than they are representations of complex identities.

Woolf's examples of the cook and, in the same passage, of the married life of the Carlyles – 'the horrible domestic tradition which made it seemly for a woman of genius to spend her time chasing beetles, scouring saucepans, instead of writing books' – as representatives of a bygone Victorian age, have a further purpose. Historical turning-points are in large part marked in the essay as changes in the lives of women and Woolf allegorizes the ways in which the unreconstructed male novelist continues to use and abuse his female protagonists, embodied here in the figure of Mrs Brown.

Bennett's review of *Jacob's Room* was not the only context for the essay. In 1920, Woolf had reacted vigorously to Bennett's collection of essays *Our Women: Chapters on the Sex-Discord* and to a favourable review of the book by her friend Desmond MacCarthy. Her diary entry for 26 September 1920 records her 'making up a paper upon women, as a counterblast to Mr Bennett's adverse views reported in the papers' – a paper which, she suggests, is usurping the mental space she had been giving to the composition of *Jacob's Room* (*D*. ii. 69). The writing of her novel had suffered, she records, because of her loss of confidence, brought about in large part by T. S. Eliot's apparent indifference to her work and his praise for Joyce's *Ulysses*, the novel against which Woolf was always to measure her own experimentalism and originality. Her responses to Bennett, and in particular to his claim that 'intellectually and creatively man is the superior of woman', are thus in part informed by her anxieties about her work, and the seeming lack of support and appreciation coming from the male writers she knows and admires, at precisely the point at which she is trying to forge new and radical ways of writing fiction.

Woolf's 'paper on Women' seems to have taken initial form in her exchanges with MacCarthy, published in the *New Statesman*. MacCarthy, in presenting Bennett's views, certainly endorses his suggestion, which he represents as the reluctant admission of 'a convinced feminist', that 'Though it is true that a small percentage of women are as clever as clever men, on the whole intellect is a masculine speciality', and he does not dispute Bennett's view that women wish to be dominated. In her letters to the *New Statesman*, Woolf anticipates the arguments of *A Room of One's Own*:

> My difference with Affable Hawk is not that he denies the present intellectual equality of men and women. It is that he, with Mr Bennett, asserts that the mind of woman is not sensibly affected by education and liberty; that it is incapable of the highest achievements; and that it must remain for ever in the condition in which it now is. I must repeat that the fact that women have improved (which Affable Hawk now seeks to admit), shows that they might still improve; for I cannot see why a limit should be set to their improvement in the nineteenth century rather than in the one hundred and nineteenth. But it is not education only that is needed. It is that women should have liberty of experience; that they should differ from men without fear and express their differences openly (for I do not agree with Affable Hawk that men and women are alike). (*WE* 38)

Woolf pursued these issues at length in *A Room of One's Own* and I discuss them more fully in the next chapter. For the moment, we should note that, while generation (the explicit 'difference' explored in 'Mr Bennett and Mrs Brown') and class (the unspoken 'difference') are undoubtedly elements of the division Woolf constructs between the 'Edwardians' and herself, gender is the central issue and dynamic of the essay.

Woolf stages a scene in a railway carriage, in which she is witness to a strange encounter between the eponymous Mrs Brown, an elderly woman and most probably a widow, and one Mr Smith, assumed to be a Northern businessman, who seems to exert some form of power over her and, before he leaves the train, speaks to her 'in a bullying, menacing way'. Left alone in the carriage with Mrs Brown, the narrator is overwhelmed by 'the impression she made' ('character' as 'a distinctive mark impressed ... or otherwise formed' (*OED*)), which 'came pouring out like a draught, like a smell of burning', before the train stopped and Mrs Brown, 'very small, very tenacious; at once very frail and very heroic', disappears 'into the vast blazing station':

> The story ends without any point to it. <...>What I want you to see in it is this. Here is a character imposing itself upon another person. Here is Mrs Brown making someone begin almost automatically to write a novel about her. I believe that all novels begin with an old lady in the corner opposite. I believe that all novels, that is to say, deal with character, and that it is to express character – not to preach doctrines, sing songs, or celebrate the glories of the British Empire, that the form of the novel, so clumsy, verbose, and undramatic, so rich, elastic and alive, has been evolved. To express character, I have said; but you will at once reflect that the very widest interpretation can be put upon those words.<...> Thus Mrs Brown can be treated in an infinite variety of ways, according to the age, country, and temperament of the writer. (WE 74–5)

'Mrs Brown' thus becomes the figure of 'character' itself. Woolf, engaging in her own production of national 'types', constructs a model in which an English writer would represent Mrs Brown as a 'character' (that is, an eccentric) and a French writer as a 'type', subordinating the individual to 'give a more general view of human nature'. The Russian writer would interpret 'character' as 'soul'. In one paragraph, then, at least three different definitions of 'character' can be at work or in play.

Woolf 'take[s] the liberty of imagining a little party in the railway carriage – Mr Wells, Mr Galsworthy, Mr Bennett are travelling to Waterloo with Mrs Brown'. Wells and Galsworthy would barely see Mrs Brown, so busy would they be planning and representing their social utopias and dystopias respectively. Bennett, by contrast, 'would keep his eyes in the carriage', 'obser[ving] every detail with immense care'. But, as in his novel *Hilda Lessways*, the detail would wholly submerge the 'character', whether it be Woolf's Mrs Brown or Bennett's own Hilda, 'a girl with an eye for houses'.

The novels of all three, Woolf asserts, leave the reader with 'a strange feeling of incompleteness and dissatisfaction. In order to complete them it seems necessary to do something – to join a society, or, more desperately, to write a cheque'. By contrast, she argues:

> *Tristram Shandy* or *Pride and Prejudice* is complete in itself; it is self-contained; it leaves one with no desire to do anything, except perhaps to read the book again, and to understand it better. The

difference perhaps is that both Sterne and Jane Austen were interested in things in themselves; in character in itself; in the book in itself. Therefore everything was inside the book, nothing outside. But the Edwardians were never interested in character in itself; or in the book in itself. They were interested in something outside. Their books, then, were incomplete as books, and required that the reader should finish them, actively and practically, for himself. (WE 77)

As we shall see, Woolf came increasingly to fear and distrust what she saw as the polemical and didactic strain in fiction; this takes on a specific resonance in her writing of the 1930s, when it becomes specifically linked to male authoritarianism. In 'Mr Bennett and Mrs Brown', her criticisms of novelistic 'preaching' are undoubtedly couched in the language of Roger Fry's 'autonomy aesthetic' (itself part of a line that can be traced, in the modern period, from Flaubert to James), Woolf appearing to endorse Fry's argument that art 'presents a life freed from the binding necessities of our actual existence'.[25]

We need to see this, however, in the context of Woolf's passionate, if satirically expressed, advocacy of freedoms for women; there is nothing 'disinterested' about her gender politics or, in later texts, her pacifism. Aesthetic 'completeness', we might also note, is seen as an attribute of texts of the past and as something, as she had suggested to Brenan, that might no longer be achievable. Woolf's attitudes towards the 'incomplete' text are in many ways ambiguous, for she was not an advocate of narrative closure, exploring in her novels, as we have seen, different ways of writing beyond the ending. We can best understand her arguments, perhaps, if we pursue the concept of the 'shape that fits'. Woolf, as I argue in my discussions of A Room of One's Own and Three Guineas, saw 'excess' in the system (of value, of money, of power, of desire, even of meaning) as potentially corrupting. The 'shape' of a novel, she thought, should be fitted to what it represents (and its 'content' fitted to its 'shape'), and although her arguments might seem to repudiate any account of art's usefulness or social purpose in favour of an (aristocratic) ideal of aesthetic detachment, a concept of aesthetic 'utility' none the less resides in her model of 'fitness'.[26]

Woolf could also be hostile to an 'excess' of subjectivity. Hence her oddly unsympathetic responses to Charlotte Brontë in A Room of One's Own, in which Brontë's desire is said to exceed the text's shape, and her valorizations of Shakespeare (repeated throughout her work), whose life was wholly 'consumed' by his work, leaving 'no foreign matter unconsumed', and who neither offered his auditors and readers 'autobiography' nor generated any need for it. There are echoes here of T. S. Eliot's 'impersonality' thesis, outlined in his highly influential essay 'Tradition and the Individual Talent' (1919) in which he argues that the artist must undergo an act of self-extinction, a subsuming of self into the work of art. Woolf, however, was much less concerned with a transcendent subjectivity 'above' personality than with the expression of collective identities, 'the common life which is the real life' (*ROO* 102), the voice of 'Anon.'.

These last preoccupations are perhaps more central to Woolf's later essays and novels; at the time of writing 'Mr Bennett and Mrs Brown' Woolf is, as we have seen, primarily taken up with the breaking of literary conventions and with the pressing question of what should take their place, given that 'the tools of one generation are useless for the next'. Hers is the age and generation of 'breaking and falling, crashing and destruction', she writes, primarily linking this violence with the work of Joyce. Woolf, as in so many of her essays, recounts a story of narrative and historical rupture (a key trope of modernism, with its warcry 'Make it new') but searches out an alternative narrative of continuity and tradition; one which can also open up a space for women's histories and for the 'lives of the obscure'.

The essay does not explicitly discuss the place of the woman writer in the mêlée of the modern, whereas in *A Room of One's Own* Woolf makes gender rather than generation the central issue, using Galsworthy's work as an example of a 'self-assertive virility' useless to the woman reader and writer. Nor does she explore an aesthetic 'fitted' to women, as she does in *A Room of One's Own*, 'Women and Fiction' and 'Romance and the Heart'. In the latter essay she describes Dorothy Richardson's creation of 'the psychological sentence of the female gender', 'capable of stretching to the extreme, of suspending the frailest particles, of suspending the vaguest shapes' (*E*. iii. 365). But Woolf does suggest in 'Mr Bennett and Mrs Brown' that sexual conventions may be even harder to change than literary ones. While her narrator tells us that she threw Mr Bennett's 'ugly', 'clumsy' and 'incongruous' 'tool' out of the window, Joyce's 'indecency' may be no more enabling for women who, as Woolf writes elsewhere, have the full weight of social censorship and self-censorship proscribing their own 'writing about the body'

('Professions for Women' (*CDML* 105)). She does not spell these questions out, but she does tie together, here as elsewhere, the future of fiction and the future of women, in part by making 'Mrs Brown', 'the woman', fugitive and unaccountable as she is, the figure and embodiment both of 'literature' and of 'life itself'; 'we are trembling on the verge of one of the great ages of English literature. But it can only be reached if we are determined never, never to desert Mrs Brown' (*WE* 87).

3

Women and Writing:
A Room of One's Own

Virginia Woolf grew up with the suffrage feminism of the early years of the twentieth century, and the struggles and debates of this period influenced all her writing. In the second half of the twentieth century, the resurgent women's movement found significant expression in literary and cultural criticism and practice and Woolf was granted centre stage in the debates that began to revolve around such questions as the existence and nature of a separate female literary tradition; 'realist' versus 'modernist' writing as the most effective vehicle for a feminist politics; the place of feminist radicalism or 'anger' in aesthetic practice. It is striking that Woolf has been used by so many different critics to exemplify one or another of a variety of incommensurate positions and that such weight has been attached to establishing her commitment to whichever position she is held to represent. 'Feminism's Woolf', when followed through, might well provide the most detailed and vivid history of the preoccupations and values of post-war feminist literary and cultural criticism.

The recent 'historicist' turn in literary studies has also led to renewed interest in the nature of 'Woolf's feminism', and in particular to a rereading of those concepts of gender and sexuality which were highly influential in the early part of the century. In *Virginia Woolf and the Real World*, Alex Zwerdling argues that we will not fully understand Woolf's work until we see it as 'a response to some of the received ideas of her time about women and "the cause"'.[1]

He charts her earliest and short-lived involvement with the suffrage cause (she remained aloof, it should be noted, from the more militant suffragettes), an experience which found its way into the ironic depiction of suffrage workers in *Night and Day*. The near-total focus on the single issue of the vote in the early years of the century appeared both narrow and naïve to Woolf, who, in Zwerdling's words, believed that 'the psyche was much more resistant to change than the law' and knew that it would take more than the extension of the franchise to change the deep-seated psychological motives underlying masculine authoritarianism and women's collusion with their disempowerment. Woolf also believed that economic dependence played a crucial role in women's subordination; hence the relative indifference of the narrator of *A Room of One's Own* to the winning of the vote – which, she asserts, was of far less significance to her than her aunt's legacy, by which she came into possession of £500 a year.

Woolf appears in *A Room of One's Own* to attribute an aggressively masculinist 'sex-consciousness' in men's writing to the effects of the suffrage campaign – 'it must have roused in men an extraordinary desire for self-assertion' (*ROO* 89) – though the passage must surely be read in part ironically. The truly 'extraordinary' fact, Woolf hints, is that patriarchal privilege had formerly been so little challenged that 'a few women in black bonnets' could produce such extreme fear and anger. Woolf also recognized that, in the words of the sociologist Viola Klein, 'the exaggeration of sex differences is one of the unconscious techniques of the masculine mind to maintain its feeling of dominance undisturbed, when the ideology of feminine inferiority is losing its strength'.[2] The proliferation of scientific, psychological, philosophical, and sexological theories of sex and gender in the late nineteenth and early twentieth centuries is satirized in *A Room of One's Own*, as the narrator quails before the overwhelming volume of male writing on the topic of 'Women'.

'Woolf's particular contribution to the women's movement', Zwerdling argues, 'was to restore a sense of the complexity of the issues after the radical simplification that had seemed necessary for political action'.[3] In her novels, as in her discursive and polemical writing, she explores the psychology of gendered identities, the conflictual nature of the relations between the sexes and the unfreedoms of marriage. In *The Voyage Out* and *Night and Day*, the men in the novel are made angry and uneasy by the sense that the women with whom they are 'in love' have mental and imaginative 'spaces' which they cannot enter. *Jacob's Room* explores the unknowability of one sex by the other. *To the Lighthouse* is Woolf's most complex and extended fictional exploration of the historically constructed nature of masculinity and femininity; she both fought against and lived with its Victorian legacy throughout her life. In her last novel, *Between the Acts*, the impending European war has its counterpart in the war that is marriage.

In Chapter 7, I discuss Woolf's second extended feminist pamphlet, *Three Guineas*, written in the late 1930s, and its relationship to her pacifist beliefs. In this text Woolf elaborates themes and identities that preoccupied her throughout her life: women as 'outsiders', occupying a position and perspective which marginalizes them but which also offers less distorted and self-interested images of reality than are available from the centres of power; the relationship between the authoritarianisms exerted in the private home and those of the political state; the absurdity of masculine institutions and rituals. Woolf's pacifism was, in the years of the First World War, radically at odds with the stance of the suffragette activists, who for the most part adopted fiercely patriotic and pro-war beliefs. Her contempt for the distinctions and uniforms with which men in the institutions and professions reward and decorate themselves also led to an ambivalence towards what we could call 'equality' feminism, the belief that women should be allowed to enter society as it stands on equal terms with men. Woolf certainly endorsed entry into the professions for women, but in *Three Guineas* she outlines a scenario in which women – her 'society of outsiders' – 'would bind themselves not to continue making money in any profession, but to cease all competition and to practise their profession experimentally, in the interests of research and for love of the work itself, when they have earned enough to live upon' (*TG* 238). This vision suggests both a socialist utopianism and a concept of disinterestedness generally reserved for the privileged.

A Room of One's Own, which I discuss in detail in this chapter, has been most influential in the sphere of literary feminism. Woolf's construction of an independent female literary tradition, a separate story of women's literary development, has perhaps been the most significant model for feminist criticism this century, underlying the creation of presses dedicated solely to publishing women's writing and to the literary dimension of 'women's studies'. Woolf's assertion that 'we think back through our mothers if we are women' is, in the rhetorical contexts of *A Room of One's Own*, a more ambiguous claim than it would at first appear, but it has proved an immensely powerful model of literary matrilinearity none the less. Woolf also constructs a literary history around women's absence and exclusion, pointing to the gaps on the library shelves; this model of 'silences' has again been central to feminist accounts of women's writing.

Many of Woolf's essays were devoted to women writers; these essays, as Zwerdling notes, 'collectively attempt to describe the forces that encourage or inhibit a woman's literary vocation'.[4] From the early stages of her writing career, Woolf had been addressing, in reviews and essays, the issues of 'masculine' and 'feminine' writing and the nature of their differences, and the place of women in the literary tradition. The context was, more often than not, given by male critics deploring the 'feminization' of literature or reasserting the second-rate nature of women's writing. The early twentieth-century obsession with 'genius' informs much of this discussion and strongly influenced Woolf's responses; throughout her writing we find her arguing that 'genius' flourishes with nurture not neglect. Woolf's emphases on education and experience as the necessary conditions for women's cultural and intellectual life are also part of her sociology of culture, in which the environment and the social sphere become far more significant determinants of literary capacity and production than any concept of creativity as a purely personal property.

In 1928 Woolf gave two lectures to women students at Cambridge with the title 'Women and Fiction', and these formed the basis for *A Room of One's Own*, published the following year. The poet Kathleen Raine, then an undergraduate at Girton College, recorded one of the occasions in her autobiography, writing of Woolf's talk:

> I learned for the first time, and with surprise, that the problems of 'a woman writer' were supposed to be different from the problems of a man who writes; that the problem is not one of writing but of living in such a way as to be able to write. *A Room of One's Own* made claims on life far beyond mine: a room and a small unearned income were, to me, luxuries unimaginable.[5]

Raine captures both the sense that Woolf's was a élite view and the 'materialism' of Woolf's arguments – 'the problem is not one of writing but of living in such a way as to be able to write.'

The women's college was not merely the forum for the lecture, but a crucial imaginative arena for Woolf's feminism. Many of her novels attack the view that education is all-important for sons but not for daughters. In *Three Guineas* she writes of 'Arthur's Education Fund', that 'voracious receptacle' into which money for boys' education has been poured since the thirteenth century and which appears to 'educated men's daughters like petticoats with holes in them, cold legs of mutton, and the boat train starting for abroad while the guard slams the door in their faces' (*TG* 118–19). In *A Room of One's Own* she represents vividly the different histories and economies of the men's and women's colleges; the plenitude of the one, the poverty of the other. The histories of the colleges are, for Woolf, 'founding' narratives aligned with fathers and mothers and with the birth of civilizations; the text continually seeks to understand the history of the present by returning to (imagined) moments of origin, attempting to discover (as in the anthropological studies of patriarchal and matriarchal societies of her time) where the story of women's lives and women's fictions began.

Woolf retained the discursive form of the lecture; the book opens with a 'but', as if Woolf has intervened in the middle of a discussion with an apparent digression: 'But, you may say, we asked you to speak about women and fiction – what has that got to do with a room of one's own? I will try to explain' (*ROO* 3). As Woolf, or her narrator, points out, discussion of the 'two questions', 'women and fiction', could lead anywhere or nowhere; she has elected instead to begin with a conclusion – that 'a woman must have money and a room of her own if she is to write fiction' – and 'to develop in your presence as fully and freely as I can the train of thought which led me to think this'.

Emphasis is thus placed throughout the text on the process of, or journey taken, by thought; a foregone conclusion could imply a rigidly analytical or logical line of argument, but Woolf deliberately transgresses this, opting instead for a free-associative method, as in the psychoanalytic technique of exploring the unfolding of associations leading to an idea or a 'dream-thought'. Or, at least, this represents the textual ideal; in fact, Woolf dramatizes the ways in which the free, subliminal movement of thought is repeatedly broken into by a series of male 'censors', who interrupt the line, path, 'train' or 'current' taken by her associations and recall her to the 'reality principle' of her 'inferior' status as a woman. Her 'conclusion', moreover, is in no sense a neat summation of the text's arguments; *A Room of One's Own* both intrigues and frustrates critics and readers in large part because of its inconsistencies. For example, and as I discuss below, Woolf spends much of one chapter espousing the 'difference' of women's writing, values, and perspectives, only to argue (apparently) against 'difference' and for the unity of male and female as the ideal in the subsequent section.

The arguments of the text are situated in and shaped by specific times and spaces; a sumptuous lunch at a men's college in 'Oxbridge', an unpalatable dinner at a women's college, a trip to the British Museum Library to research the question of 'women and fiction', a view of a London street from an upper window. Woolf sets up relationships between walking or wandering and reading, writing and thinking. 'Trespassing' is both a physical crossing of an imposed boundary and an assertion of mental freedom. Throughout her life Woolf felt resentment at the fact that she had been denied a university education, but in *A Room of One's Own* she also reveals the productivity of departures from the straight and narrow, satirically referred to as 'training in a university' in the scene in the British Library. In *Three Guineas*, her second extended feminist pamphlet, Woolf proposes the creation of a 'Society of Outsiders', and in a *Room of One's Own* Woolf emphasizes the perspective of the 'outsider', working and writing in and on the margins.

Woolf's approach, that of 'show[ing] how one came to hold whatever opinion one does hold', also anticipates the emphasis in recent feminist theory on 'situated knowledge', the view that all knowledge is located in particular social contexts of experiencing and knowing; the aim is to undermine the claims to the absoluteness of fact and objectivity in much (male) theorizing. Thus Woolf begins by seeming to disavow the truth-claims of her arguments, or, at least, to suggest that 'fiction here is likely to contain more truth than fact':

> Therefore I propose, making use of all the liberties and licences of a novelist, to tell you the story of the two days that preceded my coming here – how, bowed down by the weight of the subject which you have laid upon my shoulders, I pondered it, and made it work in and out of my daily life. I need not say that what I am about to describe has no existence; Oxbridge is an invention; so is Fernham; 'I' is only a convenient term for someone who has no real being. Lies

will flow from my lips, but there may perhaps be some truth mixed up with them; it is for you to seek out this truth and to decide whether any part of it is worth keeping. (*ROO* 4)

Woolf thus uses fictional strategies to talk about fiction and about 'women and fiction'; 'fiction' becomes a form of identity, a style and a concept, subject and object simultaneously, and not merely a genre or theme. She also represents the intertwining of fiction and history, both writing and inventing 'women's history' through fictional characters who stand for, and stand in for, the absences in historical narrative. Woolf's fable of Shakespeare's sister, who wanted to be a poet like her brother but committed suicide after finding herself pregnant with the child of the theatre manager who seduced her, is the most striking of her fictional histories.

In the quotation above, Woolf refers to making the topic of her lecture 'work in and out of my daily life'. This not only suggests the breaking-down of divisions between mental life and daily life, mind and embodied experience; the fluidity of movement 'in and out' is also a flouting of the structures of inclusion and exclusion that Woolf saw as fundamental to patriarchal society and its treatment of women: 'I thought how unpleasant it is to be locked out; and I thought how it is worse perhaps to be locked in' (*ROO* 21). On her visit to 'Oxbridge', Woolf's narrator finds herself repeatedly 'locked out', excluded from chapel, library, and even the turf of the college quadrangle; not only is her way physically barred, but these barriers interrupt her thoughts, sending them into hiding. Physical experience, material conditions, Woolf is arguing, are in no way separate from intellectual and creative life, but shape its very possibilities.

The 'barring' of the narrator's way recurs throughout the text, culminating in Woolf's account of the typical contemporary male novel, full of sex and male ego, in which 'a straight dark bar, a shadow shaped something like the letter "I"' seems to lie across the page, blocking the sky. This novel is one manifestation of 'that very interesting and obscure masculine complex <...> that deep-seated desire not so much that *she* shall be inferior as that *he* shall be superior, which plants him wherever one looks, not only in front of the arts, but barring the way to politics too.' (*ROO* 50). Just as the reader of Mr A's novel finds herself 'dodging this way and that' in order to catch a glimpse of the female character and of the landscape behind the ego-phallic 'I' of the male narrator, so the multiple perspectives and different narrative strands of *A Room of One's Own* entail a 'dodging this way and that' in an attempt to gain a sighting of women and of the sky, an unimpeded view of which Woolf uses to represent women's freedom of thought and action.

Vanessa Bell's design for the dust jacket of the Hogarth Press edition of the text centred upon a clock face, making 'time' the desideratum for women's creativity. Woolf's conceptual play in the text is, however, predominantly spatial; she links in particular the space of the room with that of the mind or brain. Satirizing biologistic concepts of the different structures and capacities of the male and female brain, Woolf shows how the narrative 'I', and 'Woman' as a concept, become 'a thought' in the great dome of the British Library Reading Room, imaged by Woolf as a 'huge bald forehead', in which she finds, when researching on the question of 'women', such texts as Professor von X's monumental work *The Mental, Moral and Physical Inferiority of the Female Sex*.

Woolf's play with the links between rooms, thought, and identity suggests that *A Room of One's Own* is, at one level, a satirical reworking of one of the key texts of European philosophy, Descartes's *Discourse on Method*. Descartes's ability to construct 'a method' derives, he writes, from his keeping to the straight road of reason and reflection: 'those who go forward only very slowly can progress much further if they always keep to the right path, than those who run and wander off it.'[6] ('Method' derives from the Greek *hodos*, road or way.) Woolf, as we have seen, charts her meanderings and the progression of her 'trains of thought' along roads and routes that are far from straight: 'For truth...those dots mark the spot where, in search of truth, I missed the turning up to Fernham <...> I spare you the twists and turns of my cogitations, for no conclusion was found on the road to Headingley, and I ask you to suppose that I soon found out my mistake about the turning and retraced my steps to Fernham' (*ROO* 14).

The *Discourse* situates the story of Descartes's search for epistemological certainty (something, as we have seen, that *A Room of One's Own* radically disrupts) in a *poêle* ('stove-heated room'), a place, in John Sturrock's words, 'at once warm, secure and solitary, in which he can reflect without distraction'.[7] In this enclosed and inward space, markedly different from the shared sitting rooms in which Woolf's nineteenth-century women writers attempt to create a space for writing, the self not only confirms its substantiality but makes the transition from the autobiographical 'I' to the universal 'I' of epistemology, the Cogito. The question we could then pose to *A Room of One's Own* is that of the nature of the (female) 'I' which will, at some future date, find itself in the eponymous room.

In fact, concepts of both the 'I' and 'a room' are called into question. Woolf desubstantializes the 'I' throughout the text; '"I" is only a convenient term for somebody who has no real being'; thoughts 'think' the narrator and 'had me entirely at their mercy' (a reversal, surely of the 'I think, therefore I am' of the Cartesian Cogito). She repeatedly invokes 'Anon.', 'who wrote so many poems without signing them' and who, she speculates, 'was often a woman'. 'I like their anonymity', Woolf writes of women at the close of the text. Woolf's imaginings of a future for women include neither their assertion of autonomous ego nor their extrapolations of a universal from a singular 'I'. Her model is rather that of the 'I' emerging out of the collectivity: 'For masterpieces are not single and solitary births; they are the outcome of many years of thinking in common, of thinking by the body of the people, so that the experience of the mass is behind the single voice' (*ROO* 60–1).

The 'life' Woolf celebrates in *A Room of One's Own* is in large part the life of the streets; she suggests that women have spent too long in rooms, though rarely, of course, in rooms of their own, and, in addition, that rooms are as different from each other as women. In a lengthy and complex passage, she points to the ways in which 'great men' have entered women's rooms, 'drawing-room or nursery', in order to be 'fertilized' by 'some different order and system of life' and 'a natural difference of opinion': 'the sight of her creating in a different medium from his own would so quicken his creative power that insensibly his sterile mind would begin to plot again, and he would find the phrase or the scene which was lacking when he put on his hat to visit her' (*ROO* 78–9). Male 'creativity' depended, it would seem, on the 'difference' affirmed in the interior of the women's room, a point made more savagely in *To the Lighthouse*:

> into this delicious fecundity, this fountain and spray of life, the fatal sterility of the male plunged itself, like a beak of brass, barren and bare. He wanted sympathy. He [Mr Ramsay] was a failure, he said. <...> It was sympathy he wanted, to be assured of his genius, first of all, and then to be taken within the circle of life, warmed and

soothed, to have his senses restored to him, his barrenness made fertile, and all the rooms of the house made full of life – the drawing-room; behind the drawing-room the kitchen; above the kitchen the bedrooms; and beyond them the nurseries; they must be furnished, they must be filled with life. (*TL* 42–3).

The 'difference' between the two orders of 'creativity', literary and procreative, male and female, intellectual and domestic, must be maintained at all costs, even as the proliferating and burgeoning reproductive metaphor 'quickens' everything around it, the male included. 'Difference' itself proliferates, however, to the point where the binary system of 'male' and 'female' can no longer be maintained, when it is a woman who enters the women's room:

one has only to go into any room in any street for the whole of that extremely complex force of femininity to fly in one's face. How should it be otherwise? For women have sat indoors all these millions of years, so that by this time the very walls are permeated by their creative force, which has, indeed, so overcharged the capacity of bricks and mortar that it must needs harness itself to pens and brushes and business and politics. But this creative power differs greatly from the creative power of men. And one must conclude that it would be a thousand pities if it were hindered or wasted, for it was won by centuries of the most drastic discipline, and there is nothing to take its place. It would be a thousand pities if women wrote like men, or lived like men, or looked like men, for if two sexes are quite inadequate, considering the vastness and variety of the world, how should we manage with one only? Ought not education to bring out and fortify the differences rather than the similarities? For we have too much likeness as it is <...> (*ROO* 79)

Whereas the structure of male and female, male versus female, reproduces the sameness of difference, the encounter of women with women produces not more 'likeness' but an explosion of the 'differences' within the categories of 'woman' and the 'women's room', 'differences' with the power to destroy the opppressive system of sexual difference. In this system, 'woman' has been created in and through men's idealizations of 'womanhood', while 'women have served all these centuries as looking-glasses possessing the magic and delicious power of reflecting the figure of man at twice its natural size'. If the 'looking-glass vision' is taken away, 'man may die, like the drug fiend deprived of his cocaine', while, in a hundred years, 'women will have ceased to be the protected sex' and may well 'die off so much younger, so much quicker, than men that one will say, "I saw a woman to-day", as one used to say "I saw an aeroplane"' (*ROO* 36). Woolf's point, presumably, is not that the human species will be extirpated, but that conceptions of 'man' and 'woman' are as relative and historically contingent as any other system of values and that the forms that gender identity will take in the future are as yet unimaginable.

The relativity of 'values' is a central concept in Woolf's writing. 'It is probable', she writes in 'Women and Fiction' 'that both in life and in art the values of a woman are not the values of a man' (*WW* 49). She elaborates this claim at length in *A Room of One's Own*:

> it is obvious that the values of women differ very often from the values which have been made by the other sex; naturally, this is so. Yet it is the masculine values that prevail. Speaking crudely, football and sport are 'important'; the worship of fashion, the buying of clothes 'trivial'. And these values are inevitably transferred from life to fiction. This is an important book, the critic assumes, because it deals with war. This is an insignificant book because it deals with the feelings of women in a drawing-room. A scene in a battle-field is more important than a scene in a shop – everywhere and much more subtly the difference of value persists. (*ROO* 67)

As in *Three Guineas*, Woolf plays with the relationships between money and value. In *A Room of One's Own* she insists that women must have money if they are to be educated, if they are to create works of value, and if they are to have 'freedom to think of things in themselves'. The model of a female literary tradition given in *A Room of One's Own*, highly influential for subsequent feminist critics, constructs the development of women writers as a journey along a road whose most significant turn is taken by the Restoration novelist and dramatist Aphra Behn, a middle-class woman who wrote for money: 'here begins the freedom of the mind, or rather the possibility that in the course of time the mind will be free to write what it likes' (*ROO* 58). Behn's legacy was to make it possible for women to live by the pen, to make enough to live on. As in *Three Guineas*, Woolf suggests that women should aspire to economic sufficiency but not excess. Women's 'accumulation' is defined in energetic terms: the 'accumulation of unrecorded life', the walled-up and potentially explosive creative energy of women (implicitly contrasted with the accumulations of 'the stockbroker and the great barrister' who turn their backs on the spring sunshine, 'going indoors to make money and more money and more money' (*ROO* 35)), both is the substance of female creativity and, Woolf argues, should provide the women novelists of the future with their materials.

If at one level Woolf celebrates 'the accumulation of unrecorded life' and its potentially transgressive energies, at another she implies that it requires containment through transformation into art. She constructs a complex symbolic relationship between words, values, desires, and money, and suggests that excess in the system is potentially corrupting and distorting. She argues of Jane Austen, in her account of nineteenth-century women writers in *A Room of One's Own*, that 'her gift and her circumstance matched each other completely' (*ROO* 62). By contrast, and as I discussed in the previous chapter, Charlotte Brontë was for Woolf 'at war with her lot', her desires exceeding her circumstances: 'She left her story, to which her entire devotion was due, to attend to some personal grievance' (*ROO* 66).[8]

Woolf has been taken to task by numerous feminist critics for her apparent denigration and, indeed, repression of women's righteous anger; her view that anger has no place in art. This repression has been seen as precisely the kind of subservience to male sensibilities that Woolf satirizes in *A Room of One's Own* and/or as an apolitical, formalist insistence that art should be free of polemic and politics, a position that certainly entered into Woolf's thinking at times. In *A Room of One's Own* Woolf is, in fact, arguing that it is women's confinement, the source of their anger and frustration, that corrupts and distorts their 'free' expression and the 'natural' shape of their writing, rather than anger itself. Tensions do remain, however, between Woolf's appeals for women's stories to be told and her insistence that 'personal grievance' has no place in art. These relate to her complex and ambivalent relationship to autobiography, to the sense of self-exposure that accompanied the production and publication of her overtly feminist writings, and to her view that the lability of fictions should not be 'distorted' by the rigidities of anger.

As we have seen, Woolf drew very close links between the future of women and the future of fiction. In a key passage in *A Room of One's Own*, she extends the issue of the gendered 'difference of value', effecting the substitution of the shop for the battlefield:

All these infinitely obscure lives remain to be recorded, I said, addressing Mary Carmichael as if she were present; and went on in thought through the streets of London feeling in imagination the pressure of dumbness, the accumulation of unrecorded life, whether from the women at the street corners with their arms akimbo, and the rings embedded in their fat swollen fingers, talking with a gesticulation like the swing of Shakespeare's words; or from the violet-sellers and match-sellers and old crones stationed under doorways; or from drifting girls whose faces, like waves in sun and cloud, signal the coming of men and women and the flickering lights of shop windows. All that you will have to explore, I said to Mary Carmichael, holding your torch firm in your hand. Above all, you must illumine your own soul with its profundities and its shallows, and its vanities and generosities, and say what your beauty means to you or your plainness, and what is your relation to the ever-changing and turning world of gloves and shoes and stuffs swaying up and down among the faint scents that come through chemists' bottles down arcades of dress material over a floor of pseudo-marble. For in imagination I had gone into a shop; it was laid with black and white paving; it was hung, astonishingly beautifully, with coloured ribbons. Mary Carmichael might well have a look at that in passing, I thought, for it is a sight that would lend itself to the pen as fittingly as any snowy peak or rocky gorge in the Andes. And then there is the girl behind the counter too – I would as soon have her true history as the hundred and fiftieth life of Napoleon or seventieth study of Keats and his use of Miltonic inversion which old Professor Z and his like are now inditing.   (*ROO* 81–2)

Woolf is not suggesting that the owners of the 'obscure lives' begin to tell their own stories; she imagines only that they will be 'recorded' by the educated women she is addressing. None the less, hers is a striking vision of the city as a public sphere of women who are neither confined to the private house nor attracting opprobrium for their walking of the streets. As in *Orlando*, the department store signifies a feminized modernity. The new 'palaces of consumption', as Judith Walkowitz notes, 'offered women an opportunity to become leisurely spectators in a new urban landscape.'[9] Woolf's imaginings of the spaces of the 'new' novel are at one with the new spaces of the department stores, both arenas speaking to women's desires.

The 'girl behind the counter', the 'shopgirl', was a central protagonist for a number of male Naturalist writers of the late nineteenth century, including Émile Zola and George Gissing.[10] In presenting the shopgirl as the heroine of the new women's fiction, Woolf may have been implying that it would take a woman writer to tell her 'true' story. At another level, the fact that Woolf's imaginings of the women's novel of the future centres upon a character who had already entered so fully into fiction should alert us to the difficulty of 'thinking forward' through our daughters and of prescribing new literary subjects and forms. The syntax of that part of the passage above in which the narrator addresses 'Mary Carmichael' – 'say what is your relation to the world of gloves and shoes and stuffs swaying up and down among the faint scents that come through chemists' bottles down arcades of dress material over a floor of pseudo-marble' – endlessly defers (echoing as it does the opening of the 'A Game of Chess' section of T. S. Eliot's *The Waste Land*[11]) the emergence of the female subject which the sentence, and the women's writing of the future, is supposed to be constructing. More broadly, we are alerted to the difficulty of imagining, not to speak of producing, a writing fitted and shaped to and by women.

'Mary Carmichael' is the name Woolf gives to the author of her 'representative' women's contemporary novel, which she entitles *Life's Adventure*. The novel, flawed as it is, Woolf's narrator tells us, marks a turning-point as significant as that taken by Aphra Behn:

> I turned the page and read ... I am sorry to break off so abruptly. Are there no men present? Do you promise me that behind that red curtain over there the figure of Sir Chartres Biron is not concealed? We are all women you assure me? Then I may tell you that the very next words I read were these – 'Chloe liked Olivia ...' Do not start. Do not blush. Let us admit in the privacy of our own society that these things sometimes happen. Sometimes women do like women.
>
> 'Chloe liked Olivia,' I read. And then it struck me how immense a change was there. Chloe liked Olivia perhaps for the first time in literature. (*ROO* 74)

The turning-point is the representation in fiction of relationships between women, 'light[ing]' a torch in that vast chamber where nobody yet has been' (*ROO* 76). The narrator becomes a silent spectator, watching 'to see how Mary Carmichael set to work to catch those unrecorded gestures, those unsaid or half-said words, which form themselves, no more palpably than the shadows of moths on the ceiling, when women are alone, unlit by the capricious and coloured light of the other sex'. Mary Carmichael, herself a silent, concealed spectator of the women in the women's room, must use 'words that are hardly syllabled yet'. Woolf uses an evolutionary, allegorical language reminiscent of much 'New Woman' literature – Olive Schreiner's *Dreams* is a central example[12] – as Olivia, at once biologist and biological specimen, reaches out from 'under the shadow of a rock' (shades of *The Waste Land*) towards the light. The scene represents the making, watching, and playing out of fantasies: of the shape of women's desires, undistorted by male values; of a language fitted to those desires; of being there 'at the beginning' to witness the emergence of the 'new' woman.

The reference to Sir Chartres Biron spying on the women's room in the passage quoted above is a playful invocation of the obscenity trial proceeding against Radclyffe Hall's *The Well of Loneliness*, with its representation of erotic love between women, at the time when Woolf was giving her Cambridge lectures; Biron was the magistrate in the trial. The manuscript version of *A Room of One's Own* makes direct reference to the trial, courting its own prosecution:

> 'Chloe liked Olivia: they shared a —' the words came at the bottom of the page; the pages had stuck; while fumbling to open them there flashed into my mind the inevitable policeman; the summons <…> There the pages came apart. Heaven be praised! It was only a laboratory. Chloe and Olivia. They were engaged in mincing liver which is apparently a cure for pernicious anaemia.[13]

Again, Woolf points to the spaces hollowed out by repression, censorship, and self-censorship.

'I shall be attacked for a feminist & hinted at for a Sapphist,' Woolf predicted before the publication of *A Room of One's Own* (*D*. iii. 262). Her biography-novel *Orlando*, a very public 'love-letter' to Vita Sackville-West (discussed in detail in Chapter 6), was published in the week prior to Woolf's Cambridge lectures. Winifred Holtby discussed *A Room of One's Own* and *Orlando* in the same chapter of her study of Woolf, under the heading 'Two in a Taxi', arguing that both books are concerned with 'literature, time and sex', and that '*Orlando* dramatises the theories stated more plainly in the essay. The essay makes clear the meaning of the allegory.' In linking the two texts, Holtby seems to hint that Woolf's use of the concept of 'androgyny', so fiercely debated and contested by more recent feminist critics, is allied to theories of bisexuality and homosexuality.[14] If we pursue this hint, *A Room of One's Own* ceases to perform, in Elaine Showalter's phrase, a 'flight into androgyny', a 'strategic retreat' from a troubled feminism.[15] Both models – that of the androgynous mind and that of the separate space of women's culture – become different ways of representing women's desire for each other, 'asymmetrically feminizing the concept of androgyny', in Elizabeth Abel's words.[16]

The cultural links between 'androgyny' and 'homosexuality' are also affirmed, though in rather different ways, in the sexological discourse which Woolf both deploys and satirizes in *Orlando*, and which Vita Sackville-West used without irony in her writings. In a radio debate on 'Marriage', broadcast in 1929, Sackville-West and her husband Harold Nicolson proposed as the marital ideal that the man should develop his womanly qualities and the woman her manly qualities, the union of the manly woman and the womanly man providing a complementarity which mirrors the combination of male and female attributes within the single self. (Both Sackville-West and Nicolson, it should be noted, had predominantly homosexual relationships outside their marriage, and Sackville-West certainly saw herself as 'feminine' in relation to her husband, 'masculine' in relation to her women lovers.[17]) Sackville-West's model, which draws on Otto Weininger's highly contentious and, arguably, heavily misogynist *Sex and Character* (1903),[18] recalls Woolf's lines in *A Room of One's Own*:

One has a profound, if irrational, instinct in favour of the theory that the union of man and woman makes for the greatest satisfaction, the most complete happiness. But the sight of the two people getting into the taxi and the satisfaction it gave me made me also ask whether there are two sexes in the mind corresponding to the two sexes in the body, and whether they also require to be united in order to get complete satisfaction and happiness? And I went on amateurishly to sketch a plan of the soul so that in each of us two powers preside, one male, one female; and in the man's brain the man predominates over the woman, and in the woman's brain the woman predominates over the man. The normal and comfortable state of being is that when the two live in harmony together, spiritually co-operating. If one is a man, still the woman part of the brain must have effect; and a woman also must have intercourse with the man in her. Coleridge perhaps meant this when he said that a great mind is androgynous. It is when this fusion takes place that the mind is fully fertilized and uses all its faculties. Perhaps a mind that is purely masculine cannot create any more than a mind that is purely feminine, I thought. (*ROO* 88–9)

At one level, the concept of 'androgyny' clearly did hold power and resonance for Woolf as a myth of creativity, operating as a perfect balancing of sexual characteristics which neutralizes excess. It is a further aspect of the aesthetic 'fitness' to which I referred earlier; all is fused, all is consumed, into and by the act of 'creation'. Yet the 'over-sexualization' of the language (and the dirty joke – 'the woman also must have intercourse with the man in her') does suggest that we should not take Woolf's model of creative, harmonious, sex-transcendent androgyny entirely at face value. The elaborated metaphors of sexual intercourse and reproduction refer us back to the male writer's need to be 'fertilized' by woman's 'different' creativity (child-birth rather than bookbirth). The language of sex-transcendence is in fact couched in the language of sex, as if there were no escape from its terms: 'some collaboration has to take place in the mind between the woman and the man before the art of creation can be accomplished. Some marriage of opposites has to be consummated' (*ROO* 94). The metaphors of consummation and fertilization at one level reinforce the conventional equations between childbirth and male literary creativity which Woolf had earlier satirized.

The fact of childbirth and child-rearing also acts as one of the barriers intercepting the narrator's imaginings of a different lot for women:

> If only Mrs Seton and her mother and her mother before her had learnt the great art of making money and had left their money <...> to the use of their own sex <...> We might have been exploring or writing; mooning about the venerable places of the earth; sitting contemplative on the steps of the Parthenon <...> Only, if Mrs Seton and her like had gone into business at the age of fifteen, there would have been – that was the snag in the argument – no Mary. <...> Making a fortune and bearing thirteen children – no human being could stand it. (*ROO* 19–20)

Victorian mothers were engaged in the production of children; the nineteenth-century women writers Woolf names were linked, she notes, by their childlessness. The text offers the modern woman no 'solution' to the problem of reconciling the incompatible demands of and for books and babies. Instead, it uses the strategies (rather than the explicit arguments) of either non-consummation or of substitute gratification; sublimation, auto-eroticism ('The writer, I thought, once his experience is over, must lie back and let his mind celebrate his nuptials in darkness'(*ROO* 94), and the narrative equivalent of *coitus interruptus*, as 'trains' of thought are stopped in their tracks or, rather, derailed.

'Androgyny', like the space of 'women alone', is further staged as fantasy in *A Room of One's Own*, both as sexual fantasy (that of the perfection of pairing) and as a nostalgic longing, harking back to 'the illusion' of romance 'which inspired Tennyson and Christina Rossetti to sing so passionately about the coming of their loves' (*ROO* 14), an illusion shattered by the outbreak of the First World War. Woolf explores this further in *To the Lighthouse*, as I discuss in Chapter 5. The framing of sexual roles and identities, masculine and feminine, in the language of poetry (Tennyson/Rossetti) alerts us to the fact that identities are bound by words. Both *A Room of One's Own* and *Three Guineas* explore the need for new words or, at least, for a redefinition of old words. In the earlier text, Woolf focuses on the woman writer's struggles with a 'masculine' language unfitted for her use. Women's language, like women's desires, is defined in the terms of repression, 'illegitimacy', proscription, the 'unsaid or half-said'. At times in Woolf's writing it seems to be the elusiveness and waywardness of the language and the desires that is their attraction; at others 'repression' is envisaged as one of those masculine bars or barriers that women must struggle to overcome. The first sentence, and the last, that Mary Beton writes, 'crossing over to the writing-table and taking up the page headed Women and Fiction', is that 'it is fatal for anyone who writes to think of their sex', an assertion, as Rachel Bowlby notes, that could be taken not as the text's 'message' but as a further proscription, another bar across the page.[19]

The complexities and ambiguities of Woolf's representations of sexual difference emerge strikingly when compared with those of Sackville-West, whose review of *A Room of One's Own* contained a no-nonsense supposition of the fixed attributes of masculinity and feminity: 'I know of no writer who fulfils this condition [of the 'natural fusion' of masculine and feminine] more thoroughly than Mrs Woolf herself. She enjoys the feminine qualities of, let us say, fantasy and irresponsibility, allied to all the masculine qualities that go with a strong, authoritative brain' (M&M 258). Winifred Holtby, a far more subtle critic, though one rather despised by Woolf, notes, by contrast:

looking round upon the world of human beings as we know it, we are hard put to it to say what is the natural shape of men or women, so old, so all-enveloping are the moulds fitted by history and custom over their personalities. We do not know how much of sensitiveness, intuition, protectiveness, docility and tenderness may not be naturally 'male', how much of curiosity, aggression, audacity and combativeness may not be 'female'.[20]

Sackville-West assumes an unproblematic knowledge of what is 'male' and what is 'female'. Holtby understands Woolf to be saying that we cannot 'yet' give an answer to the question 'what is a woman?'. She also reinforces Woolf's models of cultural and historical distortion, whereby the 'natural shape' of men and woman is twisted by patriarchy's insistence upon the inferiority of women, 'for if they were not inferior, they would cease to enlarge' (*ROO* 32). At one level Woolf's 'androgynous vision' derives, despite the ambiguities and paradoxes I have noted, from an unambiguous yearning for a way out of, or beyond, the confines of sexual difference and the intense 'sex-consciousness' of her times. Woolf's fear of the 'unmitigated masculinity' making itself felt in Fascist Europe (and in much of the modernist literature and manifesto-making of her time) was both real and prescient. Her model of 'androgyny' as a counter to 'self-assertive virility' could also be understood as a political vision, in a broader sense than that of gender politics, and one which she would explore, though from a different starting-point, in *Three Guineas*.

The later text is anticipated in many important ways by *A Room of One's Own*; most crucially, perhaps, in the passage in which Woolf describes 'a sudden splitting off of consciousness'. This follows the allegory of 'two people getting into a cab' as a model of 'unity':

What does one mean by 'the unity of the mind'? I pondered, for clearly the mind has so great a power of concentrating at any point at any moment that it seems to have no single state of being. It can separate itself off from the people in the street, for example, and think of itself as apart from them, at an upper window looking down on them. Or it can think with other people spontaneously, as, for instance, in a crowd waiting to hear some piece of news read out. It can think back through its fathers or through its mothers, as I have said that a woman writing thinks back through her mothers. Again if one is a woman one is often surprised by a sudden splitting off of consciousness, say in walking down Whitehall, when from being a natural inheritor of that civilization, she becomes, on the contrary, outside of it, alien and critical. Clearly the mind is always altering its focus, and bringing the world into different perspectives. (*ROO* 87–8)

The passage names a number of 'stories'; of the founding narratives of generation and of literary heritage (mothers *or* fathers); of urban modernism (the perspectives of 'the man of the crowd' or of the detached observer at the upper window or on the balcony). The discussion is ostensibly about 'states of mind', a prelude to Woolf's discussion of creative 'androgyny'. Yet it marks a political as much a psychological position, its uneasy pronouns ('it', 'one', 'she') suggesting the uneasiness of the woman's position in a culture, a nation, which she cannot fully call her own. In the passage from *A Room of One's Own* this angle of vision takes the female subject by surprise. In *Three Guineas* it is a willed political stance, that of the woman who takes up her place as outsider.

4

Writing the City: 'Street Haunting' and *Mrs Dalloway*

In recent years, there has been substantial exploration of the relationships between *modernism* as a literary and artistic movement and *modernity* as a state of human history and social relations, whose beginning is variously dated, but usually taken to precede modernism. The work of Virginia Woolf is of particular significance here. In her writing we find those features associated with literary modernism – fluid character-izations and explorations of subjectivity, experiments with temporality – in conjunction with the depiction of aspects of modernity – the centrality of the city as metropolis and an acute and often uneasy awareness of time and historicity.

The modern city is of particular significance for a number of reasons. Most importantly for literature, the city came to function as a metaphor for the trajectories of narrative itself. Its new forms of transport and the chance encounters it sustains also provided powerful metaphors for human relationships. For women, specifically, entry into the public spaces of the city was used to mark their liberation from enclosure in the private, domestic sphere. Dorothy Richardson's novel sequence *Pilgrim-age* is in part a celebration of Miriam Henderson, her protagonist and *alter ego*, journeying in and around London, finding opportunities, despite economic hardship, for self-creation and relationships denied to the heroine of the nineteenth-century novel. Woolf's second novel, *Night and Day*, is enacted against the backdrop of London. In *Jacob's Room* the mapping of the city becomes an analogue for the exploration of human 'character'. In *The Years* Woolf charts the changing relationships of her protagonists to the city over half a century. London is central to *Flush* (Woolf's 'biography' of Elizabeth Barrett Browning's spaniel) and to *Orlando*.

Woolf also recorded and dramatized her relationship to London in her diaries. The following entry was written in January 1919, while she was at work on *Night and Day*:

> Here I was interupted on the verge of a description of London at the meeting of sunset & moon rise. I drove on top of a Bus from Oxford St. to Victoria station, & observed how the passengers were watching the spectacle: the same sense of interest & mute attention shown as in the dress circle before some pageant. A Spring night; blue sky with a smoke mist over the houses. The shops were still lit; but not the lamps, so that there were bars of light all down the streets; & in Bond Street I was at a loss to account for a great chandelier of light at the end of the street; but it proved to be several shop windows jutting out into the road, with lights on different tiers. Then at Hyde Park Corner the search light rays out, across the blue; part of a pageant on a stage where all has been wonderfully muted down. The gentleness of the scene was what impressed me; a twilight view of London. Houses very large & looking stately. Now & then someone, as the moon came into view, remarked upon the chance for an air raid. We escaped though, a cloud rising towards night. (*D*. i. 111)

Woolf's depiction of London as spectacle and theatrical setting also permeates *Night and Day* (the 'meeting of sun set & moon rise' is the point where day meets night), though in the diary entry she incorporates the lighting effects of the theatre of war (the man-made searchlight and the 'natural' moon) which the novel resolutely excluded, leading Katherine Mansfield to refer to it as 'a lie in the soul'.[1]

The view from the top of the omnibus recurs throughout Woolf's novels, often as a contrast or counterpoint to the sensations and impressions of the walker in the city. At the close of *Night and Day* Ralph and Katherine 'mount to the very front seat' of an omnibus and are 'borne on, victors in the forefront of some triumphal car, spectators of a pageant enacted for them, masters of life' (*ND* 466). Such hubris is later echoed in *Mrs Dalloway*, in which Mrs Dalloway's daughter imagines her future as she rides atop a bus navigating its way down the Strand. London is 'spectacle', but Woolf is also fascinated by the relationship between consciousness or 'states of mind' and the city. In *Night and Day* Katherine's decision to walk on by the

Strand or by the Embankment 'was not a simple question, for it concerned not different streets so much as different streams of thought'. Woolf never fully embraced the 'stream-of-consciousness' techniques which become one of the primary narrative vehicles for representing city consciousness in modernist fiction, consciousness in motion, but *Night and Day* is permeated by the connections between walking, thinking, and daydreaming, and between the circulation of traffic and people through the city and the relationships of its central characters: 'Here was the fit place for their meeting, [Katherine] thought; here was the fit place for her to walk thinking of [Ralph]' (*ND* 408), as she watches 'the great torrent of vans and carts sweeping down Kingsway'. When Katherine's purpose is clear, London is a broad river; her uncertainties find spatial form in the city as labyrinth.

In a diary entry written towards the end of 1918, Woolf writes: 'I keep thinking of different ways to manage my scenes; conceiving endless possibilities; seeing life, as I walk about the streets, an immense opaque block of material to be conveyed by me into its equivalent of language' (*D*. i. 214). 'Scene-making' was central to Woolf's art, her 'natural way of marking the past' (*MB* 142), a mode of perception and organization of her material far more sympathetic to her than plot. In this diary entry she links it to the city and to her walking about the street; other entries reveal her walking through London 'making up stories' (*D*. i. 270).

Woolf often used her diaries to 'rehearse' scenes that would later make their appearance in her essays and novels; this is perhaps most strikingly the case with her writing about London. In 1925 she wrote the following entry:

> Happiness is to have a little string onto which things will attach themselves. For example, going to my dressmaker in Judd Street, or rather thinking of a dress I could get her to make, & imagining it made – that is the string, which as if it dipped loosely into a wave of treasure brings up pearls sticking to it.<...> And my days are likely to be strung with them. I like this London life in early summer – the street sauntering and square haunting<...> (*D*. iii. 11)

The lines are echoed in one of Woolf's most vivid essays, 'Street Haunting: A London Adventure', first published in 1927, in which she writes of the pleasures of 'rambling the streets of London' in winter. As Rachel Bowlby has argued, this essay offers one of the most striking accounts of the *flâneuse*, the female version of the *flâneur* (stroller) whose significance for urban life was described by Charles Baudelaire and, following and interpreting him, Walter Benjamin.[2] In Woolf's essay, the narrator, the walker in the city, 'shed(s) the self our friends know us by and becomes part of that vast republican army of anonymous trampers'. When we leave the shelter of the home, in which the objects and possessions that surround us fix us in our own pasts, 'the shell-like covering which our souls have excreted to house themselves<...> is broken, and there is left of all these wrinkles and roughnesses a central oyster of perceptiveness, an enormous eye' (*CDML* 71).

'Street Haunting' both extols the pleasures of this purely spectatorial and aestheticizing 'eye', which replaces the singular 'I' of identity, now become fluid, multiple, and uncarapaced, and suggests its limitations. The 'eye', 'gliding smoothly on the surface', sees pure beauty, pure colour, receiving the sights of the modern city as works of art: 'the glossy brilliance of the motor omnibuses; the carnal splendour of the butcher's shops with their yellow flanks and purple steaks; the blue and red bunches of flowers burning so bravely through the plate glass of the florists' windows' (*CDML* 72). Woolf echoes Marcel Proust's account of Venice as both 'crystallized matter' and dream city; the eye, Woolf writes, resting only on beauty, 'breaks off little lumps of emerald and coral as if the whole earth were made of precious stone'. And yet:

> the thing it cannot do (one is speaking of the average unprofessional eye) is to compose these trophies in such a way as to bring out the more obscure angles and relationships. Hence after a prolonged diet of this simple, sugary fare, of beauty pure and uncomposed, we become conscious of satiety. We halt at the door of the boot shop and make some little excuse, which has nothing to do with the real reason, for folding up the bright paraphernalia of the streets and withdrawing to some duskier chamber of the being where we may ask, as we raise our left foot obediently upon the stand: 'What, then, is it like to be a dwarf?' (*CDML* 72)

This surprising question introduces (calls into being) the entry of a female 'dwarf' into the boot shop, accompanied by two 'normal size' women, looking like 'benevolent giants' beside her. These shifts of scale are encapsulated in the dwarf's foot, the 'shapely, perfectly proportioned foot of a well-grown woman <...> Seeing nothing but her feet, she imagined perhaps that the rest of her body was of a piece with those beautiful feet'. Woolf's deliberate introduction of 'the grotesque' into the formerly aestheticized scene is mirrored in her account of the way in which the dwarf 'had called into being an atmosphere which, as we followed her out into the street, seemed actually to create the humped, the twisted, the deformed. <...> [she] had started a hobbling grotesque dance to which everybody in the street now conformed.' And, even as 'we' begin to feel assurance that this 'maimed company' is in step with the dance and does not grudge 'us' our prosperity:

> suddenly, turning the corner, we come upon a bearded Jew, wild, hunger-bitten, glaring out of his misery; or pass the humped body of an old woman flung abandoned on the step of a public building with a cloak over her like the hasty covering thrown over a dead horse or donkey. At such sights the nerves of the spine seem to stand erect; a sudden flare is brandished in our eyes; a question is asked which is never answered. Often enough these derelicts choose to lie not a stone's throw from theatres, within hearing of barrel organs, almost, as night draws on, within touch of the sequinned cloaks and bright legs of diners and dancers. (CDML 74)

These destitute figures both shock the 'eye' out of its complacency and allow it to continue on its 'adventure'. The aesthetic of the modern city in fact lies in its surreal and shocking contrasts, and its own nervous motion, in which extremes of wealth and poverty, beauty and ugliness, lie, quite literally in this passage, side by side. Thus, although the Jew and the old woman ask a question which is neither answered, nor, indeed, posed, the 'shock' of the encounter does not halt the narrator, who is able to incorporate it into the 'spectacle' of the city, and even to incorporate 'these derelicts' who 'choose' to lie next to theatres and shop windows and thus to make with their bodies one extreme of the city's contrasts. The 'eye' can thus move on, 'passing, glimpsing'; the extremes of the city become part of identity itself, not 'composed of one thing only' but 'streaked, variegated all of a mixture; the colours have run'.

Woolf's contrast between the surface perceptions of the 'enormous eye' and the 'duskier chamber of the being', opened up through entry into other lives and other selves, is also closely allied to her meditations on the respective merits of visual and verbal forms. In particular, it anticipates her essay on the paintings of Walter Sickert. Here she constructs an imaginary conversation in which the human response to colour is likened by one speaker to that of 'certain insects <...> in whom the eye is so developed that they are all eye <...> When I first went into

Sickert's show, said one of the diners, I became completely and solely an insect – all eye. I flew from colour to colour, from red to blue, from yellow to green' (*CDB* 173–4). The other diners suggest that this is an exaggerated account; human beings have evolved out of the insect's-eye view and have lost 'the microscopic eye'. Sickert's paintings are not pure colour, pure visuality; they are also the life histories of their subjects and sitters. The visual has 'evolved' into verbal, narrative, and biographical forms. Throughout Woolf's work we find an ambivalence towards what Jonathan Crary has called 'the sheer optical attentiveness of modernism' and a need to reincorporate those elements which 'pure' perception excludes; language, history, memory, sexuality.[3]

In 'Street Haunting', the 'eye'/'I' periodically withdraws from the 'bright paraphernalia' of the streets into interior or liminal spaces, imagined or real. Pearls in a jeweller's window give access to a self in pearls leaning over a balcony in June (the pearl-strung treasure of the imagination which Woolf describes in her diary entry, next to her pleasure in 'street sauntering and square haunting'). Imaginary rooms can be furnished, dismantled, and refurbished freely from the 'treasure' of the furniture stores; the 'house of fiction' releases its occupants into flux and mobility. In one sense, the city is democratic; it offers its spectacle to those 'with no thought of buying', and, indeed, with no thought of buying, 'the eye is sportive and generous'. Aesthetics and commerce are both twinned and opposed; the unpossessed commodities in the shops, unlike those purchased, do not fix the self into its biography but allow it to make and remake itself. Similarly, the books in the second-hand bookshop 'are wild books, homeless books; they have come together in vast flocks of variegated feather, and have a charm which the domesticated volumes of the library lack. Besides, in this random miscellaneous company we may rub against some complete stranger who will, with luck, turn into the best friend we have in the world' (*CDML* 77).

In the literature of the city, the city itself becomes a text to be read and interpreted. Woolf emphasizes the graphic and textual elements of the city as well as its visual and cinematic qualities. In the passage quoted above, the anonymous stranger, the most significant figure in representations of modern urban life, is translated into a book. 'Reading', in this context, is likened to the fleeting encounter which characterizes social relations in the city:

one is forced to glimpse and nod and move on after a moment of talk, a flash of understanding, as, in the street outside, one catches a word in passing and from a chance phrase fabricates a lifetime <...> here, at the street corner, another page of the volume of life is laid open by the sight of two men consulting under the lamp-post. (*CDML* 78)

The lines echo *Jacob's Room*, in which we seek Jacob through city scenes and in city faces on which stories seem to be written: these city-dwellers are 'rude illustrations, pictures in a book whose pages we turn over and over as if we should at last find what we look for <...> What do we seek through millions of pages – oh, here is Jacob's Room' (*JR* 84). The stories that we make up are already inscribed on the world.

In 'Street Haunting' the books in the second-hand book-shops, we are also told, are 'wild books, homeless books', to be contrasted with the 'domesticated volumes of the library'. They are thus like the lodgers or even the 'derelicts' of the city, of no fixed abode. Homelessness is a key concept, which could be rethought in this context as 'unhomeliness' or the 'unhomely', a literal translation of the German word for 'uncanny', Freud's *Das Unheimliche*.[4] The uncanny, as Walter Benjamin noted, was born out of the rise of the great cities, in which human beings are strangers to each other and to themselves. The 'uncanniness' of Woolf's essay is figured in the 'haunting' of its title, in its question 'which is never answered', and in its 'ghostly' encounters with split-off parts of the self, not all of whom are gathered in at dusk when the self recomposes itself for its entry into the home.

Yet in Woolf's narrative the 'complete stranger' (the book) may then turn into the 'best friend'. This is one aspect of the continual interplay between strangeness and familiarity in her writing, and of the structure of 'shock', which can be a response either to the unfamiliar or to something which (like the 'uncanny' for Freud) 'we had known before' ('The Art of Biography' (*CDML* 151)). Her art is that of 'scene-making', which 'fabricates a lifetime' from 'a word in passing', making up stories and histories which then appear as if they had been lived through. This is her way of proceeding in walking and in writing; the encounter with the stranger in the city halts the pace and must be circumscribed, but the 'scene-making', the imaginative entry into other lives and stories, is also a way of carrying on.

The years of *Mrs Dalloway*'s inception, planning, and writing – late 1922–1924 – were ones in which the Woolfs made the decision to leave suburban Richmond and return to London. Virginia Woolf's diary entries for 1923 and 1924 intersperse reflection on *Mrs Dalloway* (or, rather, *The Hours*, the novel's working title) with her increasing excitement at the prospect of living in London again. Shortly after the Woolfs moved to Tavistock Square in Bloomsbury, Woolf records:

> London is enchanting. I step out upon a tawny coloured magic carpet, it seems, & get carried into beauty without raising a finger. The nights are amazing, with all the white porticoes & broad silent avenues. And people pop in & out, lightly, divertingly like rabbits; & I look down Southampton Row, wet as a seal's back or red & yellow with sunshine, & watch the omnibus going & coming, & hear the old crazy organs. One of these days I will write about London, & how it takes up the private life & carries it on, without any effort. Faces passing lift up my mind; prevent it from settling, as it does in the stillness at Rodmell.
>
> But my mind is full of The Hours.<...> And I like London for writing it<...> (*D.* ii. 301–2)

The ambiguous final phrase of this passage suggests both that London is a desirable place in which to write the novel and that the city is itself actively caught up in the process of writing.

Of Woolf's 'city' novels, *Mrs Dalloway* maps most closely onto 'modernist' images of the metropolis. It shares with Joyce's *Ulysses* (which Woolf read during the period in which she was writing *Mrs Dalloway*) the structure of the 'one-day novel', anticipating by a few years the most famous avant-garde 'day-in-the-life-of-a-city' films, Walter Ruttman's *Berlin: Symphony of a Great City* (1927) and Dziga Vertov's *The Man with the Movie Camera* (1928). Both Joyce and Woolf use perambulation and locomotion around the city – Joyce's Dublin, Woolf's London – as narrative routings and play with the new devices of the cinema: flashbacks, montage, tracking shots. The 'one-day' structure also allowed for the exploration of 'an ordinary mind on an ordinary day' which Woolf had made central to the 'new' literature in her essay 'Modern Fiction'.

Mrs Dalloway is in part divided between the secluded, interior space of the Dalloways' house and the city streets, as well as between memories of Clarissa Dalloway's girlhood home, the country house Bourton, and London in June 1923, five years after the end of the First World War. The London parks which play such a prominent part in the novel create a space for *rus in urbe* – the country in the city – so that the country/city divide is both established and transgressed.

In the opening section of the novel, the life of the city is celebrated, in part through Mrs Dalloway's consciousness:

> In people's eyes, in the swing, tramp, and trudge; in the bellow and the uproar; the carriages, motor cars, omnibuses, vans, sandwich men shuffling and swinging; brass bands; barrel organs; in the triumph and the jingle and the strange high singing of some aeroplane overhead was what she loved; life; London; this moment of June. (*MD* 6)

In this symphony of a city pedestrians and vehicles alike become caught up in the rhythms of urban existence, 'the crowded dance of modern life', as a phrase from Woolf's essay 'Life and the Novelist' has it. From her early essay 'Street Music' (1905) onwards, Woolf had used the imagery of dance and rhythm to describe the orchestration of movement within the city (*E*. i. 31). The relationship between the apparently disordered maelstrom of the city and the syncopation of the urban rhythms bears not only on the ways in which 'art' gives formal order to the flux and welter of perceptions and mental impressions, but is linked to the relationship between individual and group consciousness and motion which Woolf explores in *Mrs Dalloway*.

Modernist writing on the city of the late nineteenth and early twentieth centuries was substantially caught up in representations, often negative, of the urban mass or crowd as well as in the paradox, familiar from Romanticism's representations of the city, that the individual is at his or her most isolated and anonymous in the midst of the crowd. (Loneliness, in the sociologist Georg Simmel's more positive account of 'The Metropolis and Mental Life', is the condition of freedom.[5]) Woolf, like Joyce, emphasizes the diversity of the constituents and modes of locomotion of the urban population, so that it never becomes an undifferentiated mass. She explores, in the opening sections of the novel, communication and circulation in the city and the forces that disrupt or halt its dance or symphony.

The narrative 'vehicles' she uses to explore this process are symbols of modernity – the motor car and the aeroplane. Elsewhere in her writing Woolf uses the experience of these forms of transport and movement as a way of exploring the multiplicity of identities that make up what we think of as 'the self' – travel and transport in car and plane open up the fragmented nature of individual being. In *Mrs Dalloway* the car and the aeroplane represent, or bring in their wake, those forms of social organization – the state and commerce respectively – which both cement and disrupt social consciousness and collective life. They are also deeply implicated in the modes of acknowledgement and denial made by a society in the aftermath of world war.

Mrs Dalloway's garland-gathering is disrupted by a loud bang which is taken to be a pistol shot in the street outside the flowershop but turns out to be the exploding tyre of a large car, carrying a passenger whose 'face [was] of the very greatest importance'. The stationary car brings the circulation of traffic and pedestrians to a standstill while putting rumours into circulation (*MD* 17), rumours which subdue and unify 'faces which a second before had been utterly disorderly':

> But now mystery had brushed them with her wing; they had heard the voice of authority; the spirit of religion was abroad with her eyes bandaged tight and her lips gaping wide. But nobody knew whose face had been seen. Was it the Prince of Wales's, the Queen's, the Prime Minister's? Whose face was it? Nobody knew.
>
> Edgar J. Watkiss, with the roll of lead piping round his arm, said audibly, humorously of course: 'The Proime Minister's kyar.'
>
> Septimus Warren Smith, who found himself unable to pass, heard him. (*MD* 17)

The car and its occupant symbolize state, country, nation – stirring up in passers-by a pride and patriotism towards which the narrative reveals its ambivalence and, indeed, its contempt through its personifications. The image of religion in the passage above suggests, as Maria DiBattista notes, 'a kind of communal blindness and idiocy'.[6] The car passes on, leaving behind it

> a slight ripple which flowed through glove shops and hat shops and tailors' shops on both sides of Bond Street. <...>in all the hat shops and tailors' shops strangers looked at each other and thought of the dead; of the flag; of Empire.<...>For the surface agitation of the passing car as it sunk grazed something very profound. (*MD* 21)

The 'something very profound' is suggestive less of depth as complexity than of burial and sedimentation. The emotions and sentiments stirred up by the 'passing of greatness' – and the phrase suggests not only a passing-through but a passing-away – lead Woolf to elaborate an image of the present seen from the perspective of the future and become archaic, prehistoric; its symbols of state and majesty known as we know those of ancient cultures, enduring because embalmed and hence protected from the workings of time:

> the enduring symbol of the state which will be known to curious antiquaries, sifting the ruins of time, when London is a grass-grown path and all those hurrying along the pavement this Wednesday morning are but bones with a few wedding rings mixed up in their dust and the gold stoppings of innumerable decayed teeth. The face in the motor car will then be known. (*MD* 19)

The shift of temporal perspective enacted here suggests the anachronism of the representatives of power and all that they stand for: Englishness, Empire, Monarchy – the legacy of Victorianism in a society intent on denying the wounds of the First World War and the irrecoverability of the old order.

The episode, which opens with a sound like a pistol-shot (an echo, perhaps, of the pistol-shot which killed Archduke Franz Ferdinand in 1914, as he travelled in his car through Sarajevo, inaugurating the political crisis which led into World War One), was anticipated by a diary entry written in the first years of the War:

> We went up to London – L. to the London Library, I to Days [bookshop]. I walked with him across the Green Park. In St James Street there was a terrific explosion; people came running out of Clubs; stopped still and gazed about them. But there was no Zeppelin or aeroplane – only, I suppose, a very large tyre burst. But it is really an instinct with me, & most people, I suppose, to turn any sudden noise, or dark object in the sky into an explosion, or a German aeroplane. And it always seems utterly impossible that one should be hurt (D. i. 32. 1 Feb. 1915).

The return of this 'explosion' in the post-war world of *Mrs Dalloway* is an indication of the extent to which the novel is caught up with the after-shocks of war. At the novel's opening, Clarissa's repetition of the fact that the War is over is interwoven with the knowledge that the mourning is not:

> For it was the middle of June. The War was over, except for some one like Mrs Foxcroft at the Embassy last night eating her heart out because that nice boy was killed and now the old Manor House must go to a cousin; or Lady Bexborough who opened a bazaar, they said, with the telegram in her hand, John, her favourite, killed; but it was over; thank Heaven – over. (MD 6–7)

As the novel veers between the modes of ecstasy and despair, so it plays out the knowledge that the 'victory' of celebration ('it was over') can only be achieved by means of denial and repression. The passage quoted above brings to centre stage the mourning of mothers for their dead sons; *Mrs Dalloway* shares many of the elegiac dimensions of *Jacob's Room*, and is profoundly shaped by post-war consciousness. The temporal mode that has come to define the effects of trauma, including war, and 'shell-shock' in particular, on the human psyche and organism is 'belatedness' or 'deferral'. Writing of Septimus Smith, the returned soldier in the novel, Bernard Blackstone asserted: 'Deferred shell-shock is Sir William Bradshaw's diagnosis of Septimus's malady; deferred war-shock might, perhaps, be our account of the total motif of *Mrs Dalloway*'.[7]

As Hermione Lee has noted,[8] the first version of Mrs Dalloway, which Woolf began writing in June 1923, opened with a procession of the sons of dead officers laying a wreath on the Cenotaph (which translates from the Greek as 'empty tomb'), the war memorial designed by Sir Edwin Lutyens in 1919 and completed in 1920, war-memory thus taking priority over Clarissa Dalloway's experience of 'this moment in June'. In the final version of the novel, Woolf included a later scene in which a line of boy-soldiers, embodiments of the processes of memorialization itself and surrogates for the dead, lay a wreath upon 'the empty tomb', or Cenotaph:

> Boys in uniform, carrying guns, marched with their eyes ahead of them, marched, their arms stiff, and on their faces an expression like the letters of a legend written round the base of a statue praising duty, gratitude, fidelity, love of England... as if one will worked legs and arms uniformly, and life, with its varieties, its irreticences, had been laid under a pavement of monuments and wreaths and drugged into a stiff yet staring corpse by discipline. (MD 57)

The London of *Mrs Dalloway* is, as David Bradshaw has argued, mapped by its statues and its monuments.[9] The Cenotaph is obliquely figured in the sky-writing scene of the novel, which comes in the wake of the passing vehicle of state and monarchy. The gathering of people in the Mall, and the descent of an 'extraordinary silence and peace' as 'bells struck eleven times', is almost certainly an allusion to Armistice Day, and to the introduction of the two minute silence on the first anniversary of the armistice, when, at eleven a.m. on the eleventh of

November 1919, all movement and activity came to a standstill. Yet if the collective consciousness of the crowd is focused upon, or created by, the demands of memorialization, it is also centred upon the workings of advertising and commerce. Woolf wrote the aeroplane scene soon after the first use of sky-writing in 1922 to advertise the *Daily Mail* newspaper. G. K. Chesterton may have felt that, in the use of smoke-writing, man had vulgarized infinity, but the paper was immensely proud of the fact that the spectacle was not only seen by millions of people at once but that, according to report, the multitude burst into a chorus of 'Daily Mail' as soon as the first letters were transcribed on the air.

Woolf's message in the sky is less easily deciphered:

> Dropping dead down, the aeroplane soared straight up, curved in a loop, raced, sank, rose, and whatever it did, wherever it went, out fluttered behind it a thick ruffled bar of white smoke which curled and wreathed upon the sky in letters. But what letters? A C was it? an E, then an L? Only for a moment did they lie still; then they moved and melted and were rubbed out up in the sky, and the aeroplane shot further away and again, in a fresh space of sky, began writing a K, and E, a Y perhaps?   (*MD* 23–4)

Woolf offers and then effaces the 'KEY' to the sky-writing's message and meaning. The members of the crowd who, a moment before, were 'let[ting] rumours accumulate in their veins and thrill the nerves in their thighs at the thought of Royalty looking at them', in a fantasy of the awe-struck gaze reversed, are now gazing, awe-stricken, at the sky, as if waiting for a divine message. This is advertising as transcendence – ' "It's toffee," murmured Mr Bowley.' In the closing passage of the scene, religion and advertising become intertwined: the 'seedy-looking man' carrying religious pamphlets decides to enter St Paul's Cathedral and place them 'before an altar, a cross, the symbol of something which has soared beyond seeking and questing and knocking of words together and has become all spirit, disembodied, ghostly – why not enter in? he thought, and while he hesitated out flew the aeroplane over Ludgate Circus' (*MD* 32–3).

Smoke letters and clouds merge, so that the cultural and the natural become indistinguishable, and the clouds as emblems of mutability and flux become imbued with a purposiveness without known purpose, a signification both urgent and arbitrary: 'The clouds to which the letters, E, G, or L had attached themselves moved freely, as if destined to cross from East to West on a mission of the greatest importance which would never be revealed, and yet certainly so it was – a mission of the greatest importance' (*MD* 24). The irony Woolf explores is that the public messages of advertising, which function by their appeal to ostensibly private dreams, are read by Septimus Smith as a signal to him alone – not of a purchasable commodity but of the provision, freely and in perpetuity, of values without price – beauty, charity, goodness. Septimus does indeed read the sky-writing as a divine message, although one he cannot interpret, but Woolf also seems to be satirizing the promises made by consumer culture of unconditional and limitless pleasure.

Sky-writing emphatically breaks words up into their individual letters. Septimus 'hears' these letters as physical sensations: ' "K... R..." said the nursemaid, and Septimus heard her say "Kay Arr" close to his ear, deeply, softly, like a mellow organ, but with a roughness in her voice like a grasshopper's, which rasped his spine deliciously and sent running up into his brain waves of sound which, concussing, broke' (*MD* 25). The sounds 'Kay Arr' chime with the 'kyar' of the prime minister; connections are thus made via the materiality of language.

One of the central questions for Woolf, as *Mrs Dalloway* developed out of its original structure of discrete episodes (it was originally composed as a series of separate stories, collectively entitled *Mrs Dalloway's Party*) was how to forge the links between the different parts of the narrative and between characters. It was a question that was to emerge again in her next novel, *To the Lighthouse*, in which, as we shall see, the artist Lily Briscoe's attempts to bring the two halves of her painting into relationship are mirrored by the broader issue of the novel's structure itself. Of *Mrs Dalloway* she wrote: '[it] has branched into a book; and I adumbrate here a study of insanity and suicide; the world seen by the sane and the insane side by side – something like that' (*D*. ii. 207). The novel explores the relationship between Clarissa and Septimus Smith, who never meet, but between whom profound connections none the less develop. Through the shell-shocked Septimus, damaged not only by the war but by the alienating effects of city space, Woolf also suggests the madness and the uncanniness of connection, between words, things, and people, the troubling and irrational aspects of E. M. Forster's dictum, 'Only connect':

But they beckoned; leaves were alive; trees were alive. And the leaves being connected by millions of fibres with his [Septimus'] own body, there on the seat, fanned it up and down; when the branch stretched he, too, made that statement. <...> Sounds made harmonies with premeditation; the spaces between them were as significant as the sounds. A child cried. Rightly far away a horn sounded. All taken together meant the birth of a new religion – (*MD* 26)

Woolf uses her structural devices to point up both narrative connection and dispersal or diffusion. Her narration follows Clarissa Dalloway on her walk, moving into her consciousness and then out again; the narrative is then transported onwards by the car on its way to Buckingham Palace. The car is succeeded by the aeroplane as narrative vehicle and linking device; as the plane passes over Regent's Park, it is observed by Lucrezia Warren Smith, who points it out to Septimus, and we move between Septimus' and Rezia's thoughts, a move which emphasizes the gap between them. The narrative voice is then passed on to incidental figures in the park, whose consciousnesses we enter briefly; they are linked only by the chance encounter and the novel will not pursue them further. (Parks, as in 'Kew Gardens', were for Woolf key sites for encounters which are both fleeting and yet psychically invested.) Then, as a woman in the park looks upwards, we are returned to the passage of the aeroplane. The omniscience of its aerial view makes it into a parodic version of the omniscient narrator; finally liberated from any semblance of this narrative task, it is released into ecstatic emissions of 'pure delight' before it, and Woolf, finally abandon the scene.

The next city scene follows Clarissa's former suitor, Peter Walsh, just returned from India, along the London Streets, after his visit to Clarissa. The preceding section of the novel explores Clarissa Dalloway's sense of herself as a middle-aged woman – 'narrower and narrower would her bed be' – and a rethinking of the sexual and social choices she made as a girl, which have led her to her current position as Mrs Richard Dalloway. Her identity fragmented, it has to be recollected, assembled, gathered together, like the torn dress she intends to wear to her party that evening.

Peter Walsh is largely defined, and defines himself, through his relations to women – relations which, Woolf suggest, depend upon fantasy and projection:

But she's extraordinarily attractive, he thought, as, walking across Trafalgar Square in the direction of the Haymarket, came a young woman who, as she passed Gordon's statue, seemed, Peter Walsh thought (susceptible as he was), to shed veil after veil, until she became the very woman he had always had in mind; young, but stately; merry, but discreet; black, but enchanting.

Straightening himself and stealthily fingering his pocket-knife he started after her to follow this woman, this excitement, which seemed even with its back turned to shed on him a light which connected them, which singled him out, as if the random uproar of the traffic had whispered through hollowed hands his name, not Peter, but his private name which he called himself in his own thoughts. 'You,' she said, only 'you', saying it with her white gloves and her shoulders. Then the thin long cloak which the wind stirred as she walked past Dent's shop in Cockspur Street blew out with an enveloping kindness, a mournful tenderness, as of arms that would open and take the tired —

But she's not married; she's young: quite young, thought Peter, the red carnation he had seen her wear as she came across Trafalgar Square burning again in his eyes and making her lips red. But she waited at the kerbstone. There was a dignity about her. She was not worldly, like Clarissa; not rich, like Clarissa. Was she, he wondered as she moved, respectable? Witty, with a lizard's flickering tongue, he thought (for one must invent, must allow oneself a little diversion), a cool waiting wit, a darting wit; not noisy.

She moved; she crossed; he followed her. To embarrass her was the last thing he wished. Still if she stopped he would say 'Come and have an ice,' he would say, and she would answer, perfectly simply, 'Oh yes'.

But other people got between them in the street, obstructing him, blotting him out. He pursued; she changed. There was colour in her cheeks; mockery in her eyes; he was an adventurer, reckless, he thought, swift, daring, indeed (landed as he was last night from India) a romantic buccaneer, careless of all these damned proprieties, yellow dressing-gowns, pipes, fishing-rods, in the shop windows; and respectability and evening parties and spruce old men wearing white slips beneath their waistcoats. He was a buccaneer. On and on she went, across Piccadilly, and up Regent Street, ahead of him, her cloak, her gloves, her shoulders combining with the fringes and the laces and the feather boas in the windows to make the spirit of finery and whimsy which dwindled out of the shops on to the pavement, as the light of a lamp goes wavering at night over hedges in the darkness.

Laughing and delightful, she had crossed Oxford Street and Great Portland Street and turned down one of the little streets, and now, and now, the great moment was approaching, for now she slackened, opened her bag, and with one look in his direction, but not at him, one look that bade farewell, summed up the whole situation and dismissed it triumphantly, for ever, had fitted her key, opened the door, and gone! Clarissa's voice saying, Remember my party, sang in his ears. The house was one of those flat red houses with hanging flower-baskets of vague impropriety. It was over.

Well, I've had my fun; I've had it, he thought, looking up at the swinging baskets of pale geraniums. And it was smashed to atoms – his fun, for it was half made up, as he knew very well; invented, this escapade with the girl; made up, as one makes up the better part of life, he thought – making oneself up; making her up; creating an exquisite amusement, and something more. But odd it was, and quite true; all this one could never share – it smashed to atoms. (*MD* 59–61)

Here Woolf dramatizes and satirizes the 'fleeting encounter' which characterizes the literature of the city and of modernity. Peter Walsh takes on the guise of the *flâneur*, 'botanizing on the asphalt', as the critic Walter Benjamin famously phrased it.[10] Woolf also hints at the more sinister aspects of Peter Walsh's pursuit, as he fingers his pocket-knife and follows the woman he has selected for his 'excitement'.

Woolf explores both the ways in which fantasies are projected onto the outside world, and the ways in which the visible world, and specifically the modern city, give shape to, or indeed construct, those fantasies and desires. At the beginning of this scene, Peter's identity itself is mediated through, or made by, the reflective surfaces of modernity: 'And there he was, this fortunate man, himself, reflected in the plate-glass window of a motor-car manufacturer in Victoria Street.' The windows of the Regent Street shops also enable Peter to 'dress' the woman he pursues in 'the fringes and the laces and the feather boas' that define femininity through their, and its, excesses – 'femininity as masquerade' – and which, in this passage, are contrasted with the 'respectable', socially 'proper', and emphatically unerotic male accoutrements of dressing-gowns and pipes and fishing-rods. Earlier in the passage, Peter's gaze acts as the mirror or glass onto which the image of the young woman's red carnation is projected, 'burning again in his eyes', and then refracted back to make her lips invitingly red.

In this scene Woolf explores the construction of private dreams in public spaces. In an echo of Septimus Smith's belief that the sky-writing aeroplane is signalling to him alone, and, later in the novel, that Nature, as a woman, 'breathe[s] through her hollowed hands Shakespeare's words, her meaning' (*MD* 154). Peter's fantasy is of being singled out from the crowd. The woman, who is his desire and his excitement, and the rhythms of the city seem to combine and speak to him: 'as if the random uproar of the traffic had whispered through hollowed hands his name, not Peter, but his private name which he called himself only in his own thoughts. "You" she said, only "you", saying it with her white gloves and her shoulders.'

Woolf's use of the terms 'hollowed out' (*MD* 55), 'hollowness' (*MD* 193), 'hollowed hands' (*MD* 59, 154) is significant, and Woolf was further to explore the 'hollowing out' of the world in the 'Time Passes' section of *To the Lighthouse*. In *Mrs Dalloway* the 'hollowed hands' through which the city, personified in the shape of the young woman, speaks, suggest both the ways in which a space is created, in modernity and the modern city, for private dreams, which serve, in Peter Walsh's case, to fill the 'hollowness' of identity, as well as the 'hollowed-out' aspect of these dreams, so readily filled with desire and so easily 'smashed to atoms'. The young woman firmly shuts the door on Peter and his fantasies: 'It was over.'

Solipsistic and even onanistic as Peter Walsh's 'fun' appears, he, like Clarissa, uses the city to create 'life', narrative, and identity. His escapade with the girl is 'made up, as one makes up the better part of life, he thought – making oneself up; making her up' (*MD* 61), the lines echoing the opening paragraphs of the novel, in which Clarissa, thinking of life and London, pursues the idea of 'making it up, building it round one, tumbling it, creating it every moment afresh'. The novel celebrates but also satirizes the 'creativity' of such imaginings, and suggests the 'fictional' dimensions of all human identities and the inseparability of 'selves' and 'stories'.

The five years Peter Walsh has spent away from England are also the measure of the five years between the end of the War and the present of the novel. On his walk, Peter Walsh passes Septimus and Rezia Smith; for Septimus there can be no end of the War, so entrapped is he in the aftermath of its agonies and in the world of the dying and the dead, and as Peter comes towards him, he sees him as 'the dead man in the grey suit'. Peter misreads Rezia's despair as the outcome of a lover's quarrel, and incorporates it into his narratives of the 'amusing' novelty of what he imagines to be his sharpened perceptions, and of the changes brought about during his time in India: 'Every woman, even the most respectable, had roses blooming under glass; lips cut with a knife; curls of Indian ink, there was design, art, everywhere; a change of some sort had undoubtedly taken place' (*MD* 80).

Peter projects a world which he populates with desiring and nurturing women. His fantasies and dream-states intersect with, and are ironized by, the novel's own dream-like apprehensions of a post-war world of ghostly women mourners, 'spectral presences' whose insubstantiality and motility exist in a realm other to the official sphere of concrete monuments and time-bound acts of memorialization, and who function, indeed, as counter-monuments, or counter-memorials.

> Such are the visions. The solitary traveler is soon beyond the wood; and there, coming to the door with shaded eyes, possibly to look for his return, with hands raised, with white apron blowing, is an elderly woman who seems (so powerful is this infirmity) to seek, over the desert, a lost son; to search for a rider destroyed; to be the figure of the mother whose sons have been killed in the battles of the world. (*MD* 65)

The third, key 'city scene' of the novel moves the narrative focus to Mrs Dalloway's daughter Elizabeth, who, at 18 (Mrs Dalloway's age in the 'flashback' at the opening of the novel) and on the brink of 'womanhood', represents a new set of choices for women, implicitly and explicitly contrasted with those made by her mother. Elizabeth and her governess Miss Kilman, despised by Clarissa for her ugliness, her clumsiness, her self-pity, have been taking tea at the Army and Navy Stores in Victoria. The department store, with 'trunks specially prepared for taking to India', is suitably chosen in a novel in which colonialism and Britain's imperial mission inform a number of the character's lives, though the Empire is crumbling.

Escaping with relief from Miss Kilman's clutches, Elizabeth decides to take an omnibus up Whitehall:

> Suddenly Elizabeth stepped forward and most competently boarded the omnibus, in front of everybody. She took a seat on top. The impetuous creature – a pirate – started forward, sprang away; she had to hold the rail to steady herself, for a pirate it was, reckless, unscrupulous, bearing down ruthlessly, circumventing dangerously, boldly snatching a passenger, or ignoring a passenger, squeezing eel-like and arrogant in between, and then rushing insolently all

sails spread up Whitehall. And did Elizabeth give one thought to poor Miss Kilman who loved her without jealousy, to whom she had been a fawn in the open, a moon in a glade? She was delighted to be free. (*MD* 150)

Peter Walsh imagined himself a 'romantic buccaneer', adventuring up Regent Street. Elizabeth is at once pirate, at one with the omnibus, pirate ship, rider, figurehead and a piece of statuary, part of the novel's sphere of monuments and memorials: 'the heat gave her cheeks the pallor of white painted wood; and her fine eyes, having no eyes to meet, gazed ahead, blank, bright, with the staring, incredible innocence of sculpture.' The shifting subject of the sentences –'She took a seat on top. The impetuous creature – a pirate – started forward, sprang away; she had to hold the rail to steady herself < ... >' (*MD* 150) – and the extensive use of present participles, here, as elsewhere in the novel, give a fluidity to subject–object relations which allows for unexpected identifications and personifications.

Elizabeth's decision to take the bus on to the Strand – 'Oh, she would like to go a little farther' – becomes linked with her thoughts as she travels onwards about professions for women and what she might become: 'She would become a doctor, a farmer, possibly go into Parliament if she found it necessary, all because of the Strand' (*MD* 151). Woolf thus explicitly links women's freedom of the city and of the public sphere with the new possibilities open to them: 'For no Dalloways came down the Strand daily; she was a pioneer, a stray, venturing, trusting' (*MD* 152).

'Law, medicine, politics, all professions are open to women of your generation, said Miss Kilman' (*MD* 144). The line anticipates Woolf's essay 'Professions for Women', given as a lecture in 1931, in which Woolf famously introduced the figure of the 'Angel in the House', that symbol of Victorian femininity and rectitude whom the woman writer must destroy in order to write freely: 'Had I not killed her she would have killed me. She would have plucked the heart out of my writing.' The Angel dead, the 'young woman had only to be herself.' 'Ah', the narrator continues,

> but what is 'herself'. I mean, what is a woman? I assure you, I do not know. I do not believe that you know. I do not believe that anybody can know until she has expressed herself in all the arts and professions open to human skill. < ... > Even when the path is

nominally open – when there is nothing to prevent a woman from being a doctor, a lawyer, a civil servant – there are many phantasms and obstacles, as I believe, looming in her way. (*CDML* 103–5)

The questions 'what is a woman?', 'what might a woman become?', are, as Rachel Bowlby notes, implicit throughout *Mrs Dalloway*.[11] In this section of the novel, the boldness of the omnibus's journeying is allied with Elizabeth's plans for her future, but her more tentative walk 'just a little way towards St Paul's' reveals her dreams as potentialities not yet to be realized:

> And it was much better to say nothing about it. It seemed so silly. It was the sort of thing that did sometimes happen, when one was alone – buildings without architects' names, crowds of people coming back from the city having more power than single clergymen in Kensington, than any of the books Miss Kilman had lent her, to stimulate what lay slumbrous, clumsy, and shy on the mind's sandy floor, to break surface, as a child suddenly stretches its arms; it was just that, perhaps, a sigh, a stretch of the arms, an impulse, a revelation, which has its effects for ever, and then down again it went to the sandy floor. She must go home. She must dress for dinner. But what was the time? – where was a clock? *MD* 151–2)

Elizabeth's reaching out – childish, hubristic, revelatory – towards a future is interrupted by the imposition of present time, the clock time that chimes throughout the novel, marking that public and official time which Woolf contrasts not only with subjective time and memory but with the complex presentness of the novel's opening, 'this moment in June'.

In *Mrs Dalloway* clock time 'shreds and slices' through the continuum of life. Patriarchal authority (Monarchy, State, Empire) does not merely hold up the traffic; it 'rules' time, imposing upon it, as does Sir William Bradshaw, the physician who 'treats' (or, rather, destroys, Septimus Smith), the law of 'proportion'. It is also deeply collusive with commerce, so that time itself becomes a commodity.

> Shredding and slicing, dividing and subdividing, the clocks of Harley Street nibbled at the June day, counselled submission, upheld authority, and pointed out in chorus the supreme advantages of a sense of proportion, until the mound of time was so far diminished, that a commercial clock, suspended above a shop in Oxford Street, announced, genially and fraternally, as if it were a pleasure to Messrs Rigby and Lowndes to give the information gratis, that it was half-past one. (*MD* 113)

In his brilliant study *Time and Narrative*, Paul Ricoeur uses *Mrs Dalloway* as one of his 'tales about time'.[12] The passing of the day as it progresses is punctuated by the tolling of Big Ben – 'the leaden circles dissolved in the air' – and other bells. As Ricoeur notes, the strokes of Big Ben are part of the characters' experience of time and of its 'fictive refiguration' in the novel. As the numerous 'events' of the day progressively accumulate, pulling the narrative ahead, it is simultaneously pulled backwards by excursions into the past. 'By giving a temporal depth to the narrative', Ricoeur argues, 'the entanglement of the narrated present with the remembered past confers a psychological depth on the characters without, however, giving them a stable identity, so discordant are the glimpses the characters have of one another and of themselves'.[13] Here he echoes Woolf's own diary commentary on the construction of Mrs Dalloway, in which she writes of her discovery of 'what I call my tunnelling process, by which I tell the past by instalments as I need it. How I dig out beautiful caves behind my characters; I think that gives exactly what I want; humanity, humour, depth. The idea is that the caves should connect and each comes to daylight at the present moment' (*D*. ii. 263). In a diary entry written a few months later, she added, 'It took me a year's groping to discover what I call my tunnelling process, by which I tell the past in instalments' (*D*. ii. 272).

The striking of Big Ben and the other bells and clocks, ringing out the hours, represents chronological time; what is significant, Ricoeur notes, is the relation that the protagonists establish with these marks of time. The proximity between the 'caves' constitutes an underground network that *is* the experience of time in *Mrs Dalloway*. This experience, Ricoeur argues, 'confronts, in a complex and unstable relationship, monumental time, itself resulting from all the complicities between clock time and the figures of authority'.[14] In Ricoeur's analysis, 'monumental history' (a category he takes from Nietzsche) secretes a 'monumental time' which has its audible expression in chronological time. Hence the complicity of clock time with the figures and institutions of authority and power in the novel – the medical profession, commerce, state, monarchy, Empire, war – located at the heart of the imperial city. Septimus Smith is both the hero and the victim of the radical discordance between personal time and monumental time: 'monumental history, everywhere present in London, and the various figures of authority, epitomized in the medical profession, [give] to clock time the train of power that transforms time into a radical threat.'[15] The horror of time rises up from the depths of monumental history – the Great War – bringing back from the dead the ghost of Septimus' war comrade, Evans.

Clarissa, while sharing Septimus' experience of the terror of time, is 'saved' by her ability to plunge 'into the very heart of the moment' and by a relationship with time which is both collusive and subversive. Her 'time', 'women's time', the time of Clarissa as 'hostess' ('remember my party', she repeats) is sounded by the bells of St Margaret's. These come in the wake of the 'great booming voice' of the 'masculine' Big Ben, 'like a hostess who comes into her drawing-room on the very stroke of the hour and finds her guests there already'. Like Mrs Ramsay at her dinner party in *To the Lighthouse* ('unveiling each of these people <...> without effort like a light stealing under water' (*TL* 116)), the sound of St Margaret's (which is, Peter Walsh thinks, 'Clarissa herself'), 'glides into the recesses of the heart'. But Clarissa's heart is weak, unlike 'the pulse of a perfect heart' of prosperous London which Peter glimpses soon after his 'fling' (*MD* 61), and her time (the time of St Margaret's) returns us again to the imbrication of time and death.

Time plays a crucial role in modernist representations. As Randall Stevenson notes, hostility to clocks in modernist fiction is fuelled not only by hatred of the regulatory structures of modern, urban, and industrial existence (as in D. H. Lawrence's novels) but also by novelists' hostility to chronological sequence[16] – what Woolf called 'the appalling narrative business of the realist: getting on from lunch to dinner' (*D*. ii. 209). Woolf's investigations into time are also part of the modernist fascination with the relationship between, in the terms given in *Orlando* (in which the striking of clocks is one of the 'shocks' of modernity), 'time on the clock and time in the mind', subjective time and the time of events (*O*. 68). In *To the Lighthouse* and *Mrs Dalloway*, as in Proust's great work, 'memory' constructs a temporality outside chronology, and a way of moving backwards and forwards through time and space. And, in both of Woolf's novels, the time of memory is most often associated with 'women's time', with love between women – Mrs Dalloway's memories of her 'first' love, that of and for Sally Seton, broken into by the marriage plot: Lily Briscoe's desire for 'her' Mrs Ramsay. I take up these questions and representations in the next chapter.

5

The Novel as Elegy: *Jacob's Room* and *To the Lighthouse*

> I am making up 'To the Lighthouse' – the sea is to be heard all through it. I have an idea that I will invent a new name for my books to supplant 'novel'. A new — by Virginia Woolf. But what? Elegy?
>
> (*D.* iii. 34)

'The people are ghosts,' Leonard Woolf commented of *Jacob's Room* (*D.* ii. 186). In three of her novels – *Jacob's Room*, *To the Lighthouse* and *The Waves* – Woolf constructed her narrative around a central absence: Jacob, Mrs Ramsay, Percival. All three novels are, in their different ways, elegies for the dead. *To the Lighthouse* was, Woolf wrote, a means of laying the ghosts of her parents to rest. Both *Jacob's Room* and *The Waves* address, obliquely, the loss of her brother Thoby. Woolf wrote to Vanessa Bell in 1929: '& then Thoby's form looms behind – that queer ghost. I think of death sometimes as the end of an excursion which I went on when he died. As if I should come in & say well, here you are. And yet I am not familiar with him now, perhaps. Those letters Clive read made him strange and external' (*D.* iii. 275). Strangeness, externality, and ambivalence in fact characterize the narrative relationship to Jacob; the narrative position is unstable, veering or 'vacillating' (a key term for Woolf) between internal and external perspectives, past and present, pathos and satire. Woolf's 'elegiac' novels were, at one level, elegies for the conventions of the novel itself.

Vanessa Bell's illustration for 'A Haunted House' in *Monday or Tuesday* is a sketch of a large, empty armchair, behind which is a portion of a window framed by a tied-back curtain. The sketch is characteristic of the artist: as Roger Fry wrote of Bell, 'her rooms are empty and her landscapes lonely'.[1] It prefigures one of the dominant images of *Jacob's Room*, contained in the sentence which occurs near the beginning of the novel and is repeated verbatim at the end: 'Listless is the air in a empty room, just swelling the curtain; the flowers in the jar shift. One fibre in the wicker armchair creaks, though no one sits there' (*JR* 31), the repetition blurring the distinction among the absent between, in Gillian Beer's words, 'those who are dead and those who are away'.[2]

Neither *Jacob's Room* nor *The Waves* attempts to 'recapture' the lost brother. *Jacob's Room*, in particular, rejects the conventions of Victorian biography and Victorian modes of mourning and memorialization. In the weeks immediately following Julia Stephen's death, Leslie Stephen wrote the volume which came to be known in the Stephen family as *The Mausoleum Book*. Intended as a private document, written for his children, it tells the story of Stephen's two marriages and of his grief at the deaths of his wives. He paints a portrait of Julia as a beautiful saint, distinguished primarily by good works and 'the holy and tender love' she felt for her children. The title by which the volume came to be known is a significant one: a mausoleum is a stately burial place. While Stephen the atheist could not hope for an afterlife for his beloved wife, he strove against the sense of an ending through, in Alan Bell's words, 'a continuing immanence of memory', a prolongation of life through lasting influence.[3] Yet his tome is also a tomb, burying the subject whose 'life' it recounts.

Jacob's Room is replete with funerary architecture – graves, tombstones, epitaphs, mourning emblems – but none of it is able to enclose Jacob, who eludes memorialization, as he escapes conventional forms of 'characterization'. Rooms are central to the novel, although the abiding image is of an empty room; Jacob's room does not contain him. Woolf also points up 'Jacob's gloom', a melancholia which bears a complex relationship to the novel's explorations of modernity and of mourning. The rhyme 'Jacob's room', 'Jacob's gloom' also hints at a third possibility: 'Jacob's tomb'. This is the text Woolf does not write; hers will not be another 'mausoleum book'.

Near the beginning of the novel, we hear of the widowhood of Jacob's mother, Betty Flanders:

Seabrook lay six foot beneath, dead these many years; enclosed in three shells; the crevices sealed with lead, so that, had earth and wood been glass, doubtless his very face lay visible beneath, the face of a young man whiskered, shapely, who had gone out duck-shooting and refused to change his boots.

'Merchant of this city,' the tombstone said; though why Betty Flanders had chosen so to call him when, as many still remembered, he had only sat behind an office window for three months, and before that had broken horses, ridden to hounds, farmed a few fields, and run a little wild – well, she had to call him something. An example for the boys.

Had he, then, been nothing? An unanswerable question, since even if it weren't the habit of the undertaker to close the eyes, the light so soon goes out of them. At first, part of herself; now one of a company, he had merged in the grass, the sloping hillside, the thousand white stones, some slanting, others upright, the decayed wreaths, the crosses of green tin, the narrow yellow paths, and the lilacs that drooped in April, with a scent like that of an invalid's bedroom, over the churchyard wall. Seabrook was now all that; and when, with her skirt hitched up, feeding the chickens, she heard the bell for service or funeral, that was Seabrook's voice – the voice of the dead. (JR 10-11)

Seabrook, Jacob's father, is safely entombed – almost embalmed. Yet it is unclear who or what has been preserved, when even his epitaph is inaccurate. The 'unanswerable question' of his identity or nonentity is indeed answered by a non-answer, a response at a tangent, though one that alludes to the lack of identity between the living and the dead.

The work of mourning, as Freud described it, entails the gradual detachment of the ego from the lost object.[4] Failure to sever attachment results in the kind of 'encrypting' of the dead person revealed in Leslie Stephen's construction and internalization of a 'mausoleum' for his wife. Woolf would seem to be describing the processes of 'normal mourning' in Betty Flanders's externalization of Seabrook. Yet the movement from an individual and internalized to a collective and external relationship to the dead man has a broader meaning; it marks the shift from individual loss to collective mourning for the war dead. The term 'company', with its military connotations, and the 'thousand white stones' hint at the massed graves of Flanders fields. Jacob's patronym marks a destiny already reached, a death already undergone – Jacob's doom.

As Winifred Holtby noted, *Jacob's Room* is Woolf's war book, though it 'never mentions trenches, camps, recruiting officers, nor latrines'. It rather asks what is lost when a young man is killed in war: 'What lost by him? What was lost by his friends? What exactly was it that had disappeared?'[5] The questions echo those asked by Woolf herself in her 1918 review of Edward Marsh's *Memoir* of the young poet Rupert Brooke, who had died in 1916 and was one of the models for Jacob: 'One turns from the thought of him, not with a sense of completeness and finality, but rather to wonder and to question still: what would he have been, what would he have done?' (*E*. ii. 281–2) The biography of the life fulfilled is an inadequate form for these lives which were still in the making; the past tense gives way to the past conditional.

The novel transcribes Jacob's absence and circumscribes his loss but does not represent his death. He is not granted a position or an ending from which to speak, or to have spoken for him, the fiction of a completed life and a coherent selfhood. When Betty Flanders and her friend Mrs Jarvis take an evening walk to a Roman camp, they again hear and read the voices of the dead: 'Yet even in this light the legends on the tombstones could be read, brief voices saying, 'I am Bertha Ruck', 'I am Tom Gage'. And they say which day of the year they died, and the New Testament says something for them, very proud, very emphatic, or very consoling' (*JR* 116). As John Mepham notes, *Jacob's Room* could be read as Woolf's answer to Wordworth's 'Essays upon Epitaphs'.[6] Where Wordsworth argues that epitaph is based on the conviction that 'every man has a character of his own to the eye that has skill to perceive it' and that the writer of epitaph must have command of 'the universal language of humanity', Woolf shows how 'utterly unknown' are other human beings and how illusory 'general' truths and values: 'It is no use trying to sum people up. One must follow hints, not exactly what is said, nor yet entirely what is done'.

Woolf would also appear to be undermining the belief that names are coterminous with identities, and naming people with knowing them. *Jacob's Room* gives a name to virtually every figure who passes through its pages, however fleetingly; the currency of naming as characterization is thus devalued. Yet the calling or crying-out of Jacob's name throughout the novel – 'Jacob! Jacob!' – is also a powerful image of loss, linked to the epitaphic figure of 'prosopopeia', defined by Paul de Man as 'the fiction of an apostrophe to an absent, deceased or voiceless entity, which posits the possibility of the latter's reply and confers upon it the power of speech'.[7] Ironically, it is 'Flanders' – a name, a place, and a way of dying – which renders Jacob absent, deceased, and voiceless; the name both grants identity and cancels it out. *Jacob's Room* dramatizes Woolf's ambivalent relationship to 'character in the novel'. 'It is no use trying to sum people up' is one of the novel's refrains. The novel demolishes the view held by the realist or naturalist novel that character is knowable and representable. As Woolf was to write to Vita Sackville-West: 'This proves, what I could write reams about – how little we know anyone, only movements and gestures, nothing connected, continuous, profound' (*L*. iii. 204-5) Yet it is also, and literally, murderous not to seek to differentiate. Young men are sent to die by powerful men who view an interest in 'character' as gossip and as women's work. The war machine, the modern way of death, is an aspect of mass society which effaces individual differences. The novel itself vacillates between two polarized positions on 'character' and 'we are driven back' and forth from one to another:

> So we are driven back to see what the other side means – the men in clubs and Cabinets – when they say that character-drawing is a frivolous fireside art, a matter of pins and needles, exquisite outlines enclosing vacancy, flourishes and mere scrawls.
>
> The battleships ray out over the North Sea, keeping their stations accurately apart. At a given signal all the guns are trained on a target which (the master gunner counts the seconds, watch in hand – at the sixth he looks up) flames into splinters. With equal nonchalance a dozen young men in the prime of life descend with composed faces into the depths of the sea; and there impassively (though with perfect master of machinery) suffocate uncomplainingly together. Like blocks of tin soldiers the army covers the cornfield, moves up the hillside, stops, reels slightly this way and that, and falls flat, save that, through field-glasses, it can be seen that one or two pieces still agitate up and down like fragments of broken match-stick. (*JR* 136)

War is a boy's game; the 'men in clubs and Cabinets' are still playing with their 'tin soldiers'. The brutality of the passage is also Woolf's, of course; she will not heroize the dead of a war to which, as a lifelong pacifist, she was profoundly opposed. The soldiers dying 'impassively' and 'uncomplainingly' have become indivisible from the war-machine; they are viewed through the new technological filters, as if in cinematic long-shot or from an aerial perspective.

Jacob's Room mourns Jacob but it also satirizes his melancholia. 'Jacob's gloom' is a function both of his youth and of modernity itself: 'this gloom, this surrender to the dark waters which lap us about, is a modern invention. Perhaps, as Cruttendon said, we do not believe enough. Our fathers at any rate had something to demolish' (*JR* 121). Yet this is probably too simple an account: 'there has never been any explanation of the ebb and flow in our veins – of happiness and unhappiness', 'Jacob's gloom', a source of puzzlement to his friends and the cause of much of their musing about his 'character', is an ironic counterpoint to his doom: 'And he [Jacob] sighed again, being indeed so profoundly gloomy that doom must have been lodged in him to cloud him at any moment, which was odd in a man who enjoyed things so, was not much given to analysis, but was horribly romantic, of course, Bonamy thought, in his rooms in Lincoln's Inn' (*JR* 122). Jacob, sailing with his college friends in Cornwall, responds at one moment with ecstasy, at the next with an 'overpowering sorrow', to the sight of 'the white sand bays with the waves breaking unseen by any one': 'But imperceptibly the cottage smoke droops, has the look of a mourning emblem, a flag floating its caress over a grave. The gulls, making their broad flight and then riding at peace, seem to mark the grave' (*JR* 39). As Jacob veers between opposed emotions, so those who know him 'vacillate eternally between <...> two extremes' (*JR* 135–6) in attempting to characterize him, a 'vacillation' insepar- able from the novel's indeterminate and ambivalent stance towards the question of 'character-drawing' in fiction. We cannot say whether the 'characteristic' of 'moodiness' is part of Jacob himself, constructed by the 'vacillations' of those who seek to define him, bound into the narrator's uncertainties about her subject, or produced by the novel's uncertainties over the merits and demerits of 'character-drawing'. The impossi- bility of objective knowledge about a character (such as the traditional novel is able to assume) is dramatized at every level.

Jacob is at his most mercurial in Greece, where the culture itself appears to be pulled between its past and its present, between the enduring and the ephemeral: 'Athens is still quite capable of striking a young man as the oddest combination, the most incongruous assortment. Now it is suburban, now immortal' (*JR* 129). 'No form can he set on his sensations', Woolf writes of Jacob at this point. The phrase echoes an earlier passage in the novel, in which 'form' becomes linked to the 'novel of formation', the *Bildungsroman*. The elements of Jacob's life to date, the episodes of the novel, are thrown up 'upon what we are; <...> – "I am what I am, and intend to be it," for which there will be no form in the world unless Jacob makes one for himself' (*JR* 28). The novel asks how it is that discrete, arbitrary and fragmentary elements and experiences can combine to create 'a young man of substance' – a question that has clear implications for the construction of character in fiction – and finds that the making of a form, the process of formation, is very much helped by the 'steady certainty' of a Cambridge spring, a privilege claimed and maintained.

Woolf uses the idea of Greece in *Jacob's Room* to explore the paradoxes and ironies of our concepts of civilization, particularly in relation to war; she anticipates Freud's title (*Civilization and its Discontents*) in her exploration of civilization and Jacob's discontents. She also takes a distance from the neo-classicism that marks so much modernist writing. 'The Greeks' are the property of the educated and arrogant young men of the novel: 'Civilizations stood round them like flowers ready for picking. Ages lapped at their feet like waves fit for sailing. And surveying all this, looming though the fog, the lamplight, the shades of London, the two young men decided in favour of Greece' (*JR* 64). Women, excluded from the privileges granted by a 'classical education', are the prizes, not the sharers, of this vision: 'She had called him Jacob without asking his leave. She [Florinda] had sat upon his knee. Thus did all good women in the days of the Greeks' (*JR* 64). Most 'Greek' of all is Jacob's friend Bonamy, who 'couldn't love a woman and never read a foolish book' and who 'was fonder of Jacob than of anyone in the world'. Woolf alludes here to the ways in which 'the Greek way of life' encoded male homosexuality in the late nineteenth and early twentieth centuries, an eroticism which again excludes women.

If the war death of a young man requires us to ask 'what would he have been, what would he have done?', these questions could also be posed of the unfulfilled lives of young women like Clara Durrant, whose existence is 'squeezed and emasculated within a white satin shoe' (*JR* 133). The focus on women's lives in the novel undercuts the romantic heroization of Jacob, and contributes to the narrative's ambiguous stance towards its central figure, whose 'elusiveness' is both ontological and sexual. The women who love him can no more pin him down than can the narrator-as-biographer, who asks the reader to consider:

the effect of sex – how between man and woman it hangs wavy, tremulous, so that here's a valley, there's a peak, when in truth, perhaps, all's as flat as my hand. Even the exact words get the wrong accent on them. But something is always impelling one to hum vibrating, like the hawk moth, at the mouth of the cavern of mystery, endowing Jacob Flanders with all sorts of qualities he had not at all – for though, certainly, he sat talking to Bonamy, half of what he said was too dull to repeat; much unintelligible (about unknown people and Parliament); what remains is mostly a matter of guess work. Yet over him we hang vibrating. (*JR* 61)

There is a sexual charge to the biographer's, and the reader's, desire to know, or indeed create, his or her subject, as Woolf was to play up to great effect in *Orlando*. The shifting pronouns and narrative voice in this passage – 'my', 'one', 'we' – are part of the novel's complex and ambiguous representations of identification and desire, which circulate between author, narrator, characters, and readers and, in the process, 'make up' Jacob. The narrator-biographer, who at one point notes her 'difference', of sex and of age, from her 'subject', is, moreover, an 'outsider', excluded, as in *A Room of One's Own*, from many of the institutions to which Jacob belongs or has access and hence from knowledge of the world he occupies.

Sexuality and gender are strongly linked to the novel's veering between 'omniscient' and 'limited' narration. One of Betty Flanders's letters sits on Jacob's hall table, passed over by Jacob as he moves to the bedroom with Florinda:

The sitting-room neither knew nor cared. The door was shut; and to suppose that wood, when it creaks, transmits anything save that rats are busy and wood dry is childish. These old houses are only brick and wood, soaked in human sweat, grained with human dirt. But if the pale blue envelope lying by the biscuit-box had the feelings of a mother, the heart was torn by the little creak, the sudden stir. Behind the door was the obscene thing, the alarming presence, and terror would come over her as at death, or the birth of a child. Better, perhaps, burst in and face it than sit in the antechamber listening to the little creak, the sudden stir, for her heart was swollen, and pain threaded it. My son, my son – such would be her cry, uttered to hide her vision of him stretched with Florinda, inexcusable, irrational, in a woman with three children living in Scarborough. (*JR* 79)

Having foresworn omniscience, at least for the moment, the narrative contemplates sending emissaries into Jacob's London bedroom, that second room of Jacob's which is not narratively realized – 'no doubt the bedroom was behind' (*JR* 58) – and whose door remains closed until Betty Flanders bursts it open at the end of novel. The passage focuses the novel's exploration of narrative repression, of what is not shown and not said and cannot be owned up to or indeed owned; who or what, for example, is imagining, or refusing to imagine, the bedroom scene? The 'stir' and 'creak' of the sexual encounter also find their echo in the novel's most resonant line: 'Listless is the air in an empty room, just swelling the curtain; the flowers in the jar shift. One fibre in the wicker armchair creaks, though no one sits there' (*JR* 155). Mothers, whose desire for their sons is certainly prohibited, would, if they could, write to their sons: 'come back, come back, come back to me' (*JR* 77); as it is, the purportedly 'intimate' writing of the epistolary tends to conceal more than it reveals.

Letters are one among many of the forms and instruments of communication, spoken and written, on which the novel is centred – gossip, diaries, maps, typewriters, telephones, telegrams, newspapers, books, engravings, imprintings, and inscriptions of various kinds. As we have seen, Woolf plays with the derivation of 'character' from *kharattein* – 'to engrave' – and the concept of reading character as one would read a map or navigate a city. She also explores the ways in which voice and writing, detached and sent forth from speakers and writers, become deployed as instruments of power and propaganda: 'The voice continued, imprinting on the faces of the clerks in Whitehall (Timothy Durrant was one of them) something of its own inexorable gravity, as they listened, deciphered, wrote down. Papers accumulated, inscribed with the utterances of Kaisers <...> (*JR* 151). Letters are also 'phantom[s] of ourselves', 'speech attempted': 'Venerable are letters, infinitely brave, forlorn and lost' (*JR* 79). Literary men, when they write to their friends, 'have turned from the sheet that endures to the sheet that perishes'; women are for the most part confined to 'the sheet that perishes'. Yet, even so, letters extend the self, taking the mind where the body cannot go. The question of what survives us, of how and on what we make our mark, inscribe our 'character', is central to *Jacob's Room*, as it is to *Mrs Dalloway*, *To the Lighthouse*, and *The Years*, and culminates in the novel's last lines, when Betty Flanders asks: " 'What am I to do with these, Mr Bonamy?" She held out a pair of Jacob's old shoes.'

Alex Zwerdling suggests that this moment is clarified by an anecdote about Woolf recounted by one of her friends: 'The only other remark I remember from that afternoon was when she was talking about the mysteries of 'missing' someone. When Leonard was away, she said, she didn't miss him *at all*. Then suddenly she caught sight of a pair of his empty shoes, which had kept the position and shape of his feet – and was ready to dissolve into tears instantly.'[8] The anecdote is important in its focus on the ways in which the body makes its mark, but it may also suggest too neat a 'fit' between the shoes and their owner, symbol and meaning. The stilling or silencing of Jacob's footsteps, which we have followed throughout the novel, is appropriately embodied in the empty shoes, though it is one of the novel's paradoxes that it figures absence in more substantial terms than presence. The synecdochical nature of the shoes – they 'stand in' for the absent Jacob – is again appropriate in a novel in which 'character' has been represented in flashes and fragments. Yet the presentation of Jacob's 'old shoes' and the query as to their fate remains an enigmatic gesture. The question 'what am I to do with these?' could as properly be posed by the reader, confronted with a further undecipherable sign in a text the empty centre of which is a 'character' which cannot be read.

It is significant, however, that it is Jacob's mother who poses the question and makes the gesture which keep the ending of the novel in perpetual suspension, the scene freeze-framed, as the words of her letter open the novel *in medias res*: ' "So of course," wrote Betty Flanders, pressing her heels rather deeper in the sand, "there was nothing for it but to leave" ' (*JR* 3). The mother is there at the beginning, digging her heels in, and at the end of *Jacob's Room*, reminding us, as Rachel Bowlby suggests, that, while it may be biographers who record lives, it is mothers who bring them into being.[9]

The problem of achieving and of letting go is a problem shared by mothers and artists, Gillian Beer notes.[10] It is closely related to the issues of surviving and relinquishing which run throughout *Jacob's Room*, *Mrs Dalloway*, and *To the Lighthouse* and to elegy itself, which both perpetuates and relinquishes the lost object, turning 'loss into language'. Betty Flanders survives Jacob and is confronted by what is left over, what 'survives' him, although in a novel which has so radically 'uncreated' character death may entail no more of a dispersal of the self and its effects than 'life'. Mrs Ramsay 'opens' *To the Lighthouse*, brings it into being, with her words to her youngest and best-loved son James, but lets go through death; the novel's 'resolution' coincides with that of Lily Briscoe the artist, not the mother. Yet after Mrs Ramsay's death the book, in Beer's words, 'continues to explore what lasts (how far indeed has she let go or will others let her go?)'.[11]

> 'The flight of time & the consequent break of unity in my design. That passage < ... > interests me very much'.
>
> (D. iii. 36)

> 'One has to have a central line down the middle of the book to hold the design together'
>
> (Letter to Roger Fry, 27 May 1927 (L. iii. 385))

These quotations, in which Woolf plans or describes the 'shape' of *To the Lighthouse*, find their form in the novel's two most significant structures, the design and temporality of the narrative itself and Lily Briscoe's painting, which 'frames' the whole novel, with its line down the centre enacting a simultaneous joining and division of the two sides of the canvas, a 'break of unity' and a 'hold[ing] together'. The temporality of *To the Lighthouse* is that of two days separated by a gap or 'passage' of ten years. In the first part of the novel, 'The Window', the Ramsay family and assorted guests are depicted during a day on the Hebridean island which is their summer home. In the novel's central section, 'Time Passes', Mrs Ramsay dies and the First World War fractures history and reality. In the novel's final section, 'The Lighthouse', Lily completes the painting whose 'vision' had formerly eluded her and Mr Ramsay and his two youngest children, James and Cam, reach the lighthouse, having finally made the journey planned with the first words of the novel. The title of the novel suggests its dual temporality and status as elegy and as quest-narrative – 'to' the lighthouse.

Woolf turned to the new scientific theories of time, space, and relativity to explore the complex workings of memory and of memory traces which have both spatial and temporal aspects. In her diary she writes of a discussion which 'was passing my limits – how if Einstein is true, we shall be able to foretell our own lives' (D. iii. 68); the complexity of past–future relationships runs throughout *To the Lighthouse*. Woolf also constructs a 'passage' in the novel through which the past travels to the present and the present to the past. This 'passage' is of profound importance for Woolf; it is given spatial form and temporal duration in the central 'Time Passes' section of the novel. She explores the 'passage' between experience and representation: she writes of Lily Briscoe that 'It was in that moment's flight between the picture and her canvas that the demons set on her who often brought her to the verge of tears and made this passage from conception to work as dreadful as any down a dark passage for a child' (*TL* 23). The 'passage' is also the corridor along which Mr Ramsay stumbles after Mrs Ramsay's death: '[Mr. Ramsay stumbling along a passage stretched his arms out one dark morning, but, Mrs. Ramsay having died rather suddenly the night before, he stretched his arms out. They remained empty]' (*TL* 140).

In her diaries, her letters, and her memoir 'A Sketch of the Past', Woolf emphasizes that the writing of *To the Lighthouse* was a way of laying to rest her past and, in particular, the 'continuing presences' of her parents. Woolf's diaries and memoirs are full of references to the ghosts of her past, chief among them her mother, and she often describes the hold of Victorian ideals of femininity as a haunting: 'haunted by great ghosts, we insisted that to be like mother, or like Stella, was to achieve the height of human perfection' (*MB* 62). In 'A Sketch of the Past', written in 1939, as a relief from her work on Roger Fry's biography ('May 15th 1939. The drudgery of making a coherent life of Roger has once more become intolerable, and so I turn for a few days respite to May 1895'), Woolf described 'the influence of my mother' as the most significant of the 'invisible presences', amongst which she includes social and cultural as well as psychological realities, which define her:

> My mother obsessed me, in spite of the fact that she died when I was thirteen, until I was forty-four. Then one day walking round Tavistock Square I made up, as I sometimes make up my novels, *To the Lighthouse*; in a great, apparently involuntary, rush. One thing burst into another. Blowing bubbles out of a pipe gives the feeling of the rapid crowd of ideas and scenes which blew out of my mind, so that my lips seemed syllabling of their own accord as I walked. What blew the bubbles? Why then? I have no notion. But I wrote the book very quickly; and when it was written, I ceased to be obsessed by my mother. I no longer hear her voice; I do not see her.
>
> I suppose that I did for myself what psychoanalysts do for their patients. I expressed some very long felt and deeply felt emotion. And in expressing it I explained it and then laid it to rest. (*MB* 94)

In *The Mausoleum Book* Leslie Stephen turned to Julia Margaret Cameron's photographs of Julia Stephen 'to give an impression to her children of what she really was. ... Her beauty ... was the complete reconciliation and fulfilment of all conditions of feminine beauty.... Her loveliness thrills me to the core, whenever I call up the vision'.[12] During the writing of *To the Lighthouse* Woolf produced an introduction to a collection of Cameron's portraits (Cameron was her great-aunt), which the Hogarth Press published as *Victorian Photographs of Famous Men and Fair Women*, a title which ironically resonates throughout the novel, as Woolf dissects Victorian conceptions and conventions of masculinity and femininity. In the novel, Mrs Ramsay is seen through the filter of 'beauty', a 'vision' encapsulated as in Cameron's romantic stagings. For Virginia Woolf, 'beauty', in the memoir as in *To the Lighthouse*, is, paradoxically, an effacement or defacement: 'She [Julia Stephen] was not so rubbed out and featureless, not so dominated by the beauty of her own face, as she has since become' (*MB* 99). The line echoes Lily Briscoe's meditations in the novel, as she tries to recall Mrs Ramsay. The ghost of Mrs Ramsay, the woman in grey – 'the shape of a woman' in grey – came readily enough. Yet this is the 'vision' of beauty, of 'feminine' perfection, not the one for which Lily seeks: 'beauty came too readily, came too completely. It stilled life – froze it. One forgot the little agitations <...>which made the face unrecognisable for a moment and yet added a quality one saw for ever after' (*TL* 193). *To the Lighthouse* struggles over the 'vision' of Mrs Ramsay, both before and after her death – a struggle between the 'vision' of beauty, the feminine ideal, the lady in grey who comes all too readily – and Lily's desire for 'her' Mrs Ramsay, who does finally appear: 'There she sat' (*TL* 219).

Woolf herself was explicit about the autobiographical dimension of the novel, and the intense interest in all aspects of Woolf's life, fuelled by the publication of her diaries, letters, and memoirs, means that *To the Lighthouse* has received a great deal of critical and biographical attention. The figure of Mrs Ramsay is most often at the centre of discussion, and where earlier critics tended to celebrate her creativity in human relations (the 'spinsterish' Lily's passion for her art being seen as a lesser form of creativity), recent critics have seen the portrait of Mrs Ramsay as less positive. Feminist critics have pointed to the ways in which she upholds systems of marriage and a 'separate-spheres'

ideology of masculinity and femininity which severely dis-
advantages women; psychoanalytic critics have focused on the
ambivalence towards the mother figure which fuels Lily's drive
to represent her. The work of art (Lily's painting and Woolf's
novel) has been read as an act of symbolic matricide; laying the
mother to rest is also a way of ensuring (or, at least, attempting
to ensure) that she will not return.

Woolf's last novel, *Between the Acts*, explicitly thematizes and
dramatizes the 'new' concept of 'ambivalence', as I show later.
To the Lighthouse is also caught up in the pull between, and
coexistence of, 'love' and 'hate'. In a novel in which 'states of
mind' and thoughts are made visible, Lily Briscoe's ambivalent,
divided, contradictory feelings are repeatedly articulated: 'Such
was the complexity of things. For what happened to her,
especially staying with the Ramsays, was to be made to feel
violently two opposite things at the same time.' (*TL* 111) The
objects of these contradictory passions and feelings are almost
always the state of 'being in love' and/or of marriage.[13] Rejecting
marriage for herself – 'she need not undergo that degradation' –
Lily is none the less 'intoxicated' by the passion invoked by 'in
love', even when it arises as a ten-year-old memory, attached to
'the Rayleys', a young man and woman subject to Mrs Ramsay's
'mania' for marriage, now no longer 'in love' but part of the
cynical present. Contradictory feelings are imaged throughout
as an alternation between 'looking up' and 'looking down', and
between rising and falling: 'the load of her accumulated
impressions of him [William Bankes] tilted up, and down
poured in ponderous avalanche all she felt about him. That was
one sensation. Then up rose in a fume the essence of his being.
That was another' (*TL* 29). The state of being torn between, or of
simultaneously entertaining, contradictory feelings is linked
directly, though by contrast, to the fixed 'system' of male and
female, to sexual difference and to marriage.

In *A Room of One's Own*, the narrator refers to 'a sort of
humming noise' that could be heard before the war, a noise that
translates into the Victorian love poetry of Tennyson and
Christina Rossetti and is echoed in the harmonies of 'two
different notes, one high, one low' which is Mrs Ramsay's image
of marriage. Woolf encodes a complex set of responses to the
Victorian past and to its conception of masculinity and
femininity, perceived as obsolete and yet possessing their own
beauty. Woolf clearly stated that *To the Lighthouse* was 'about' her

parents – 'to have father's character done complete in it; & mother's; & St Ives; & childhood' (*D*. iii. 18) – but the figures of Mr and Mrs Ramsay also represent a division into male and female identities – 'the symbols of marriage, husband and wife' (*TL* 80) – from which the novel takes a critical distance. In particular, as we saw in the discussion of *A Room of One's Own*, men's demand for nurture, reassurance, and 'sympathy' from women is represented as an aggressive force, both sexual and infantile, that exhausts women and that, for Mrs Ramsay, 'diminished the entire joy, the pure joy, of the two notes sounding together ['two different notes, one high, one low'], and let the sound die on her ear now with a dismal flatness' (*TL* 44–5).

There is a striking photograph of the 10-year-old Virginia Stephen, taken at Talland House, the holiday home at St Ives on which the Hebridean house at the centre of *To the Lighthouse* is based. Virginia's face is visible in a corner of a sitting room; she is looking at her parents, who occupy the foreground of the photograph, reading on a sofa. She could be said to be in the position of a second camera eye or acting as a mirror image of the photographer. The photograph asserts the centrality of the parents but inserts the child looking at them, so that the central pair – mother and father – is triangulated by the watching child. This structure and its variants (in particular, mother and child looked at by father) are enacted in numerous scenes throughout *To the Lighthouse*; it is, in one sense, the structure of the novel itself, in which the daughter 'looks at' the figures of her parents and in which 'point of view' is transmuted into the observation of perception itself, looking at people looking and being looked at.

Erich Auerbach, in his account of narration and duration in the novel, wrote that 'there is an attempt to approach [Mrs Ramsay] from many sides as closely as human possibilities of perception and expression can succeed in doing'.[14] The statement picks up on Lily's thoughts about Mrs Ramsay at the novel's close: 'One wanted fifty pairs of eyes to see with she reflected. Fifty pairs of eyes were not enough to get round that one woman with, she thought.' As in a cubist painting, multiple perspectives recompose the outer shapes of objects into new 'inner' visual rhymes and associations. The 'enveloping' and interpenetrating effects of multiple consciousnesses are achieved through Woolf's radical uses of 'indirect speech' (she wrote of the novel that 'it is all in *oratio obliqua* (*D*. iii. 106)) and of 'indirect interior monologue', in which the narrative consciousness speaks in and through the mental language of its characters, without becoming wholly identified with it. She also represents thoughts and images which are not clearly attributable either to a fictional subject or to a narrative voice, and effects transitions between one consciousness and another, often within the same sentence or paragraph, and between characters as objects and as subjects of perception. When one character moves into the perceptual field of another, for example, there will often be a transition, a relaying, of narrative consciousness from one to the other, so that the former 'object' of perception becomes the perceiving 'subject'.

The novel is above all about looking, perspective, distance, its organization an extraordinarily complex interplay of eye lines and sight lines. In 'The Window', characters are repeatedly shown 'looking at' Mrs Ramsay. Some twenty pages into the novel we are told that, from its opening, Mrs Ramsay has been sitting for Lily Briscoe's painting, framed in the eponymous 'window' of the novel's first and longest section. Lily's perceptions of Mrs Ramsay are contrasted with those of the men who see and 'reverence' her:

> Looking along the level of Mr. Bankes' glance at her, she thought that no woman could worship another woman in the way he worshipped; they could only seek shelter under the shade which Mr. Bankes extended over them both. Looking along his beam she added to it her different ray, thinking that she was unquestionably the loveliest of people (bowed over her book); the best perhaps; but also, different too from the perfect shape which one saw there. (*TL* 55)

As Françoise Defromont writes: 'There is no definitive truth; each character has his/her own truth which the reader can surprise across the transparency of another look. The consciousness of each serves a kind of mirror-function.'[15] The refracting and reflecting 'beam' and 'ray' of human perception, which are the instruments of knowing as well as of seeing other people, have their counterpoint in the light from the lighthouse, which, like the spaces of darkness between the strokes of light, is identified with Mrs Ramsay herself. Alone for a brief moment, Mrs Ramsay feels herself 'shrunk, with a sense of solemnity, to being oneself, a wedge-shaped core of darkness <...> this self having shed its attachments was free for the strangest adventures'; the narrative, briefly, gives us Mrs Ramsay, at other times so intensely surrounded and interpellated by the needs and desires of other, *for herself*.

The lines echo many passages in Woolf's writing in which 'the self' is freed from the constraints of personality and relationship into diffuse identities. Here the 'I' becomes 'eye', mirroring the light from the lighthouse: 'She looked up over her knitting and met the third stroke and it seemed to her like her own eyes meeting her own eyes' (*TL* 70). The 'adventure', and the danger, is that this 'core of darkness' is so radically at odds with Mrs Ramsay's social and familial self that it can appear as a negation of identity.

This is both reinforced by Lily's painting (abstraction outside familiar/familial representations) and ameliorated (she is brought out of darkness into the sphere of representation). The relationships between 'shape', identity, and desire run throughout Woolf's writing, her own version of the complex and solid geometries of visual modernisms. Mrs Ramsay appears in two shapes for Lily: 'the shape of a dome', linked throughout Woolf's writing to love between women, and the 'purple triangular shape' of her painting, a delineation which corresponds to Mrs Ramsay's own sense of herself as 'a wedge-shaped core of darkness'. This 'shape' forges a unity between Mrs Ramsay as the subject (her self-image) and the object (Lily's representation) of perception and knowledge, and suggests that women's autonomy, their selves for themselves, have something of the shape and rhythm of 'modernist' forms. We might also note the metonymic relationship of Lily's painting to Woolf's novel as a whole, and the role of the novel in giving 'shape' to the inwardness of Mrs Ramsay.

Lily's painting is 'of' Mrs Ramsay and James, though it is abstract: the mother-and-child pairing is conventionally coded for William Bankes and for Mr Ramsay, for whom it becomes an image or 'illustration' of a tenderness which gives him succour and then of a vulnerability which demands his protection:

> He stopped to light his pipe, looked once at his wife and son in the window, and as one raises one's eye from a page in an express train and sees a farm, a tree, a cluster of cottages as an illustration, a confirmation of something on the printed page to which one returns, fortified and satisfied, so without his distinguishing either his son or his wife, the sight of them fortified him and satisfied him and consecrated his effort to arrive at a perfectly clear under-standing of the problem which now engaged the energies of his splendid mind. (*TL* 38–9)

Circling the garden, 'thinking up and down', Mr Ramsay uses the image of his wife and child to ground his intellectual endeavours as he inscribes his cerebrations, conceptual and textual, on the external world: 'seeing his wife and child, seeing again the urns with the trailing red geraniums which had so often decorated processes of thought, and bore, written up among their leaves, as if they were scraps of paper on which one scribbles notes in the rush of reading – he slipped, seeing all this, smoothly into speculation' (*TL* 48). In 'Time Passes' death and the violence unleashed by war litter 'leaves' (the word play is on the 'leaves' of plants and books) around the garden and break the 'treasures' of eye and mind – 'the hare erect; the wave falling; the boat rocking' (*TL* 139) (images very close to those used by Woolf in her essay 'The Cinema' to encapsulate the innocence, beauty, and naïvety both of the pre-war world and the aesthetic of the early cinema) – so 'that it seems impossible that their calm should ever return or that we should ever compose from their fragments a perfect whole or read in the littered pieces the clear words of truth' (*TL* 140). The world can no longer be confidently read or interpreted.

Where Mr Ramsay's concern is that his reputation and his books should 'last', Mrs Ramsay hopes for continuation through other people's marriages, her children, and their memories of her: 'It flattered her, where she was most susceptible of flattery, to think how, wound about in their hearts, however long they lived she would be woven' (*TL* 123). The novel, as I suggested above, explores the question of what lasts, through time and memory and despite death and negation. 'Time Passes' represents the dissolution or unravelling of the substantial world built up in the first part of the novel, leaving 'a centre of complete emptiness'.

> So with the house empty and the doors locked and the mattresses rolled around, those stray airs, advance guards of great armies, blustered in, brushed bare boards, nibbled and fanned, met nothing in bedroom or drawing-room that wholly resisted them but only hangings that flapped, wood that creaked, the bare legs of tables, saucepans and china already furred, tarnished, cracked. What people had shed and left – a pair of shoes, a shooting cap, some faded skirts and coats in wardrobes – those alone kept the human shape and in the emptiness indicated how once they were filled and animated; how once hands were busy with hooks and buttons; how once the looking-glass had held a face; had held a world hollowed

out in which a figure turned, a hand flashed, the door opened, in came children rushing and tumbling; and went out again. Now, day after day, light turned, like a flower reflected in water, its clear image on the wall opposite. Only the shadows of the trees, flourishing in the wind, made obeisance on the wall, and for a moment darkened the pool in which light reflected itself; or birds, flying, made a soft spot flutter slowly across the bedroom floor. (*TL* 140–1)

Light no longer meets Mrs Ramsay's mirroring 'eye'/'I'. Flowers continue to grow around the house but blindly: 'the flowers standing there, looking before them, looking up, yet beholding nothing, eyeless, and so terrible' (*TL* 147).

This last phrase is echoed in Woolf's diaries, in which she describes the process of beginning the second part of the novel:

> I cannot make it out – here is the most difficult abstract piece of writing – I have to give an empty house, no people's characters, the passage of time, all eyeless & featureless with nothing to cling to: well, I rush at it, & at once scatter out two pages. Is it nonsense, is it brilliance? Why am I so flown with words, & apparently free to do exactly what I like? (*D*. iii. 75–6)

The 'eyeless' ('I'-less) writing is central to what Woolf, in a diary entry written when she began to envisage *The Waves* (later described as 'an abstract mystical eyeless' book (*D*. iii. 203)), called 'the thing that exists when we aren't there' (*D*. iii. 114). This both recalls Andrew Ramsay's explanation to Lily of his father's philosophical work on 'subject and object and the nature of reality' – ' "Think of a kitchen table then", he told her, "when you're not there" ' (*TL* 28) – and echoes 'The Cinema', written at the same time as the novel, in which Woolf attempts to define the 'reality' of the images of early film: 'We behold them as they are when we are not there. We see life as it is when we have no part in it. As we gaze we seem to be removed from the pettiness of actual existence, its care, its conventions' (*CDML* 55). The arguments of the essay in fact suggest that Woolf is critical of this position; the potential of the cinema will be achieved, Woolf argues, when the spectator's faculties cease to be 'detached from use' and move to seize sense impressions at the moment of their fleeting unity and 'convert their energy into art'. These lines are echoed in *To the Lighthouse*, in which Lily fights against 'beautiful phrases' in her painting: 'what she wished to get hold of was that very jar on the nerves, the thing itself before it has been made anything. Get that and start afresh' (*TL* 209).

Suzanne Raitt's account of the relationship between 'The Cinema' and *To the Lighthouse* focuses on the question of the cinematic 'gaze' and the representation of Mrs Ramsay as its object.[16] To this I would add the ways in which Woolf's Platonism is linked to the cinematic elements of light and projection, anticipating the assertion of the classicist Francis Cornford (with whose work Woolf was familiar) that: 'A modern Plato would compare his Cave to an underground cinema, where the audience watch the play of shadows thrown by the film passing before a light at their backs.' [17]

From its inception, cinema has also been linked to the realm of the unconscious and to dreams and what Freud called the 'dream-work', the representation of ideas and impulses in images. In 'The Cinema', Woolf refers to the ways in which, through the medium of film, the 'dream architecture' of 'cascades falling and fountains rising, which sometimes visits us in sleep or shapes itself in half-darkened rooms, could be realized before our waking eyes' (*CDML* 58). In 'Time Passes', the passage of ten years is also the passing of one night, from the midnight hour when the lights are extinguished to the breaking of dawn and of the veil on the sleepers' eyes. The narrative oscillates during this night between absolute quiescence and stillness and the eruptions of nightmare, in which the world tosses and turns.

In 'Time Passes', we see Woolf attempting to produce an equivalent to the cinematic aesthetic in the novel or, rather, exploring the possibilities of a future or potential cinema. She is critical of the cinema when it attempts to usurp what she perceives as the ground of the other arts; her interest lies in abstract film, in which thoughts and emotions could be made visible, 'like smoke pouring from Vesuvius'. In the absence of 'plot' in 'Time Passes', Woolf produces a form of experimental cineplay, using visual images to express emotions and animating objects into non-human life. In the following passage, sound is incorporated – 'folded' – into silence (the silence of the cinema), while the unfolding of Mrs Ramsay's shawl (a highly cinematic image, as the fold of the shawl swings to and fro) becomes an image of historical rupture:

> Nothing it seemed could break that image, corrupt that innocence, or disturb the swaying mantle of silence which, week after week, in the empty room, wove into itself the falling cries of birds, ships hooting, the drone and hum of the fields, a dog's bark, a man's

shout, and folded them round the house in silence. Only once a board sprang on the landing; once in the middle of the night with a roar, with a rupture, as after centuries of quiescence, a rock rends itself from the mountain and hurtles crashing into the valley, one fold of the shawl loosened and swung to and fro. Then again peace descended; and the shadow wavered; light bent to its own image in adoration on the bedroom wall. (*TL* 141–2)

Mrs Ramsay, whose medium is light, 'appears' after her death as in a film or slide projection on a wall: 'and faint and flickering, like a yellow beam or the circle at the end of a telescope, a lady in a grey cloak, stooping over her flowers, went wandering over the bedroom wall, up the dressing-table, across the wash-stand' (*TL* 149). In the first part of the novel, scenes are caught, framed, as if in a box camera: '[Lily] nicked the catch of her paint-box to, more firmly than was necessary, and the nick seemed to surround in a circle for ever the paint-box, the lawn, Mr Bankes, and that wild villain, Cam, dashing past' (*TL* 60); in 'Time Passes' and 'The Lighthouse' Woolf explores the concept of memory as projection.

The unfolding of the shawl in the passage quoted above is also an undoing of Mrs Ramsay's maternal love and work; the second loosening of the shawl is linked to the war death of Andrew Ramsay, killed by an exploding shell. In 'The Window' Mrs Ramsay wrapped the shawl around a boar's skull to appease both James and Cam – James wanted the skull to remain on the wall, while Cam was frightened by it – the skull is thus both absent and present. She also wove words round it, and into Cam's memory: 'that it was like a beautiful mountain <...> with valleys and flowers <...> that she must shut her eyes and go to sleep and dream of mountains and valleys and stars falling' (*TL* 124–5). The mountains and the valleys return in the passage from 'Time Passes', but as components of the scene of violence and rupture: 'a rock rends itself from the mountain and hurtles crashing into the valley' (*TL* 142). In the final section of the novel Cam recalls the words as her mother spoke them; the narrative thus seeks to repair the damage to the mother's work of love, although Cam is woken from the dream that the words accompany to her father's 'Come now' and to the adventure of the trip to the lighthouse that he leads. In this sense, Cam, like the narrative itself, is pulled forward and away from the past which the mother inhabits.

The stark fact of Mrs Ramsay's death is narrated, in the square brackets which punctuate the second and third sections of the novel, near the opening of 'Time Passes'. At one level, the bracketing of those elements which traditionally form the substance of novels (childbirth, marriage, death) and the giving-over of the narrative to 'unnarratable' events, such as the passing of time and the decay of matter, is a conscious reversal of the priorities and the preoccupations of the 'conventional' novel. At another, the words between brackets become more, not less, significant, framed by the brackets as if by a window. There is no death bed scene in *To the Lighthouse*; we are told of Mrs Ramsay's death in double retrospect: '[Mr. Ramsay stumbling along a passage stretched his arms out one dark morning, but, Mrs. Ramsay having died rather suddenly the night before, he stretched his arms out. They remained empty]' (*TL* 140). The reference could hardly be briefer or more understated, and yet the death of Mrs Ramsay pervades the rest of the novel. In particular, we could read the 'Time Passes' section, with its intense focus on the physical processes of the crumbling, rotting house (the house with which Mrs Ramsay is so closely associated in 'The Window'), as a way of representing the corrosive effects of time on the mother's dead body.

In the absence of the living body, the narration veers between the extremes of matter and spirit, physical process and metaphysical questionings, often in the language of Woolf's late Victorian 'fathers'. She echoes Matthew Arnold's 'Dover Beach' in her representations of dreamers and walkers pacing the shore (as spectral as the 'solitary traveller' in *Mrs Dalloway*), searching for absolute meanings which can no longer be assumed or assured, and combing the beach in search of 'some absolute good, some crystal of intensity, remote from the known pleasures and familiar virtues, something alien to the processes of domestic life, single, hard, bright, like a diamond in the sand, which would render the possessor secure' (*TL* 144). The language (here and in the novel as a whole) is also Paterian, not only in its representations of 'moments' extracted from the flux of existence, or of 'ecstasy' (a word associated with Mrs Ramsay) as, in Walter Pater's terms, a 'burning' with a 'hard gem-like flame', but in its 'imaginations of the strangest kind – of flesh turned to atoms which drove before the wind, of stars flashing in their hearts, of cliffs, sea, cloud, and sky brought purposely together to assemble outwardly the scattered parts of the vision within'.[18] Pater opened the 'Conclusion' to *The Renaissance* with an account of the ways in which the processes and elements of our physical life are 'broadcast' in the natural world: 'Like the elements of which we are composed, the action of these forces extends beyond us: it rusts iron and ripens corn ... birth and gesture and death and the springing of violets from the grave are but a few out of ten thousand resultant combinations'.[19] 'Birth and gesture and death' (we recall Mr Ramsay's 'gesture' as he stretches out his empty arms) are the punctuation marks of 'Time Passes'; if we follow the Paterian account, this section of the novel becomes an assertion of human life and death as a continuum in 'perpetual motion'. Hence also the representation of 'decay' as process and productivity, rather than as the negation of life, though 'flesh turned to atoms' is a starker reminder of the effects of war.

Woolf's 'cineplay' in 'Time Passes' is predicated upon the fact of reverberations across and through time, space, and matter; the war is heralded by 'ominous sounds like the measured blows of hammers dulled on felt, which, with their repeated shocks still further loosened the shawl and cracked the tea-cups' (*TL* 145). As in *Jacob's Room*, Woolf is laconic about the death of young men in war: '[A shell exploded. Twenty or thirty young men were blown up in France, among them Andrew Ramsay, whose death, mercifully, was instantaneous]' (*TL* 145). It is this explosion, however, which cannot be contained fully in and by the brackets, which finally shatters the dream of symmetry and the mirror-relationship between the external world and what Pater called 'the inward world of thought and feeling',[20] between subject and object, art and nature: 'the mirror was broken' (*TL* 146).

The questers on the shore thus belatedly discover what the house has 'known' since Mrs Ramsay's death – the emptiness of the mirror and the 'eyelessness' of the world. At this point they are evacuated from the narrative, which records the extreme point of a destructiveness in which Nature and Culture have colluded: 'it seemed as if the universe were battling and tumbling, in brute confusion and wanton lust aimlessly by itself' (*TL* 147). From here until the end of 'Time Passes', the space of the narrative is the empty house, and the focus is turned towards the final stages of its dissolution, overrun by the monstrous fecundity of nature, from which it is pulled back at the turning point: 'One feather, and the house, sinking, falling, would have turned and pitched downwards to the depths of darkness' (*TL* 151).

The agents of its repair are two charwomen who, groaning and creaking, 'got to work' [and] 'stayed the corruption and the rot' (*TL* 151). At one level Woolf represents these working-class characters as forms of life so primitive that they cannot act as centres of consciousness, so that Mrs McNab leers sideways at the mirror and, despite her presence, the house remains 'eyeless'. At another, it could be suggested that it is in part her ministrations which enable the house to remain a house of light. It is her memory of Mrs Ramsay which 'projects' her faint image upon the wall and she is associated with light (though not, like Mrs Ramsay, as its reflector), throughout 'Time Passes': 'the sun so striped and barred the rooms and filled them with yellow haze that Mrs. McNab, when she broke in and lurched about, dusting, sweeping, looked like a tropical fish oaring its way through sun-lanced waters' (*TL* 145).

Hermione Lee suggests that Woolf was recording the fact that the secure upper-middle-class world of the Ramsays is blown away by the war, while 'the class that survives is that low form of life that brings the house back from the brink of ruin: Mrs McNab and Mrs Bast and her son George'.[21] They are, of course, operating under instruction and the relationship of mistress to servant remains apparently unchanged: 'one of the young ladies wrote: would she get this done; would she get that done; all in a hurry <...> expected to find things as they had left them' (*TL* 151). The work required of Mrs McNab and Mrs Bast is physical but its function is to 'make good' loss and destruction. The repair to the fabric of the house is also a reparation of what has been destroyed and, in some ways, a denial, a covering-over, of the workings of time and of the processes that have taken place in the family's absence: 'expected to find things as they had left them.' The expectation is an echo of Mrs Ramsay's overwhelming desire that life itself should hold still, should not change in her absence.

Woolf's intense desire for a return to Talland House and St Ives was expressed at intervals throughout her life. At one level, the novel was a wish-fulfilment for Woolf. The house is repaired; the family return. The Stephens' holiday home was given up after Julia Stephen's death and, Woolf wrote in 'A Sketch of the Past', 'St Ives vanished for ever' (*MB* 136). In the memoir, she describes the vividness of her memories of St Ives: 'I can reach a state where I seem to be watching things happen as if I were there' (*MB* 77). This is the other aspect of 'the thing that exists when we aren't there', and in fact it shows up the fantasy aspect of the world represented as if without a perceiving conscious-ness, as in 'Time Passes': the fantasy is of being there to watch things happen as if one were not there.

The Stephen children returned to Cornwall in 1905, though not to Talland House. The diary Virginia kept at this time is written in a mannered and consciously 'archaic' and elegiac prose, as if to mark stylistically the return to the past:

> It was with some feeling of enchantment that we took our places yesterday in the Great Western train. This was the wizard who was to transport us into another world, almost into another age. We would fain have believed that this little corner of England had slept under some enchanter's spell since we last set eyes on it ten [eleven] years ago, & that no breath of change had stirred its leaves, or troubled its waters. There, too, we should find our past preserved, as though through all this time it has been guarded & treasured for us to come back to one day – it matters not how far distant. <...>
>
> Ah, how strange it was, then, to watch the familiar shapes of land & sea unroll themselves once more, as though a magicians hand had raised the curtain that hung between us, & to see once more the silent but palpable forms, which for more than ten years we had seen only in dreams, or in the visions of waking hours. (PA 281)

Like Mrs Ramsay, the young Virginia Stephen seeks continua-tion; the diary is full of re-encounters with villagers on whom the family had left a lasting impression, despite 'mind[s] not naturally sensitive to receive it': 'It was a pleasure to see the blank respectful face of the woman behind the counter in the eating shop glow with sudden recognition when she spoke our name' (PA 286). The diary is certainly both naïve and patron-izing, but its pathos lies in the way that these accounts of delighted recognition clearly function as compensations for Virginia's feelings of invisibility, and the break in continuity, in the place of real attachment, the house. Creeping up to Talland House in the dark, they see the house and its garden looking 'as if we had but left it in the morning. But yet, as we well knew, we could go no further; if we advanced the spell was broken. The lights were not our lights; the voices were the voices of strangers. We hung there like ghosts in the shade of the hedge, & at the sound of footsteps we turned away' (PA 282).

In To the Lighthouse Woolf reweaves 'the spell': the Ramsay family return to the house. Yet the novel resists the simple lure of this re-enchantment. 'Time Passes' has fractured time and narrative; there is no returning to the old forms, familial or literary. 'The Lighthouse' is a continual process of negotiation with the past, not a reliving of it. The house is not, in a sense, reoccupied; the narrative moves swiftly outside, shifting between Lily painting on the lawn and Mr Ramsay, James, and Cam sailing to the lighthouse. Both activities are highly complex in their meanings; they are repetitions as well as new departures; fulfilments too belated to be meaningful; returns to the past and a way of 'laying it to rest'.

> 'So much depends then, thought Lily Briscoe <...>upon distance.'
>
> (TL 207)
>
> 'Distance lends enchantment to the view.' ... we shall wish to discover the exact distance at which enchantment begins.'[22]

Woolf wrote in her diary of 'casting about for an end' to the novel, the phrase nicely entwining Mrs Ramsay's knitting and Mr Ramsay's mackerel-fishing on the trip to the lighthouse. She was concerned with the problem of bringing Lily and Mr Ramsay together: 'what becomes [of] Lily and her picture' if the novel closes with Mr Ramsay climbing onto the lighthouse rock:

> Should there be a final page about her & Carmichael looking at the picture & summing up R's character? In that case I lose the intensity of the moment. If this intervenes between R. & the lighthouse, there's too much chop and change, I think. Could I do it in a parenthesis? so that one had the sense of reading the two things at the same time? (D. iii. 106)

Woolf's problem with the structure of her novel is echoed in Lily's with that of her painting: 'For whatever reason she could not achieve that razor edge of balance between two opposite forces; Mr Ramsay and the picture; which was necessary' (TL 209). The diary entry sheds light on the extensive use of parentheses throughout the novel, which becomes a way of finding an alternative narrative temporality, a modernist simultaneity which breaks with the conventions of linear form. It also provides a link between the 'double vision' (linked in turn to the structures of ambivalence) upheld by the novel: the doubleness of thought (Lily's 'feel[ing] violently two opposite things at the same time' or Cam's sense that 'they were doing two things at once'); the doubleness of the central image of the novel, the lighthouse, which for James is both 'a silvery, misty-looking tower with a yellow eye that opened suddenly and softly in the evening' and 'a stark tower on a bare rock' (*TL* 220); and the doubleness of the novel's closure, which mirrors the dualities (and the splitting) of sea and shore, art and life, past and present, repetition and newness, the ideal and the real, experience and representation (Mr Ramsay's arrival at the lighthouse rock, Lily's drawing of the line which is also the lighthouse). Standing on the lawn as she sets up her canvas, Lily 'felt curiously divided, as if one part of her were drawn out there – it was a still day, hazy; the Lighthouse looked this morning at an immense distance; the other had fixed itself doggedly, solidly, here on the lawn'. Between these two selves and these two locations her empty canvas rises up, 'white and uncompromising (*TL* 171).

In the final section of the novel, the multiple perspectives and eye lines of 'The Window' are reduced to a narrower range of vision, alternating between the view from the boat (to the island shore and then the lighthouse rock) and the view of the boat from the island shore. This distance marks, here as in *Jacob's Room*, the space of valediction and mourning. It is also, in *To the Lighthouse*, the distance across which 'secret messages' seem to be signalled, an unseen semaphor or ethereal communication which is one among a number of the novel's transmissions across space and time. As in *The Voyage Out*, Woolf uses alternating viewpoints, and the distance between sea and shore, as a measure of relativity and of the workings of memory and consciousness, whereby emotions that are at times remote – 'at the end of the corridor of years' (*TL* 190) – can at other moments flood the mind with their immediacy. In the final section of the novel, Woolf depicts James, Cam, and Lily 'remembering, repeating and working-through', to borrow Freud's terms, memory and loss.

As Lily begins to paint, a world is again hollowed out. The scoring of the canvas 'with brown running nervous lines' begins to surround a space, to create depth behind surface, to enclose Lily in the 'hollow' of a wave; the modelling of the white space 'with greens and blues' (the colours habitually invoked by Woolf in her descriptions of the painter's art) is also a spattering or 'spurting' of 'scenes, and names, and sayings, and memories and ideas' which 'her mind kept throwing up from its depths'. Words and images from the past (the first part of the novel) return: 'and she heard some voice saying she couldn't paint, saying she couldn't create, as if she were caught up in one of those habitual currents which after a certain time experience forms in the mind' (TL 173). The words are those of Charles Tansley, Mr Ramsay's protégé: 'Women can't paint, women can't write...'(TL 54); the 'current' is one which the woman artist or writer learns to circumnavigate, though with difficulty.

Where Lily explains her first, unfinished painting in formal, structural terms, by the time she comes to paint the second her loss – the death of Mrs Ramsay, the ruptures and breaks of the war – opens up a model of painting in which art is not separable from memory and desire. The shift between the two paintings could also be seen as a shift in Woolf's relationship to the question of art and psychoanalysis, a critique of Roger Fry's account of art as insulated from human need, as a self-contained artefact. Lily does not give up on the architecture or geometry, the structure of her painting, but her understanding of where to place the line that will bring the two halves together – left and right, past and present – comes out of the work of memory and an acknowledgement of emotional loss.[23]

As she paints, Lily recalls a scene from the past that is not narrated in 'The Window': 'And she began to lay on a red, a grey, and she began to model her way into the hollow there. At the same time, she seemed to be sitting beside Mrs. Ramsay on the beach' (TL 186). This is not a repetition, a scene 'remembered' by the narrative, and it is thus distinct from the images and memories which travel from 'The Window' to 'The Lighthouse'. 'Distance' (temporal, spatial, and aesthetic) is transmuted into proximity and simultaneity. The scene – of being on the beach with Charles Tansley and Mrs Ramsay – seems to be temporally and spatially coterminous or 'on a level' with the present: it 'survived, after all these years, complete, so that she dipped into it to re-fashion her memory of him [Charles], and it stayed in the mind almost like a work of art' (TL 175). The past has also been preserved for the present: 'She rammed a little hole in the sand and covered it up, by way of burying in it the perfection of the moment. It was like a drop of silver in which one dipped and illumined the darkness of the past' (TL 187). The 'she' is not clearly attached either to Mrs Ramsay or to Lily, so that 'the moment' could be said to belong to both; the 'crystal of intensity', the 'diamond in the sand' sought by the questers on the beach in 'Time Passes' exists here in molten and fluid form, capable of illuminating the text of the past.

As Lily paints, a door seems to open 'and one went in and stood gazing silently about in a high cathedral-like place, very dark, very solemn' (TL 186). The lines are echoed in 'A Sketch of the Past', when Woolf describes her first memories of her mother: 'Certainly there she was, in the very centre of that great Cathedral space which was childhood; there she was from the very first' (MB 94). In To the Lighthouse, solemnity exists alongside the fantastical; the scene recalls one of the most famous texts of Victorian childhood, Lewis Carroll's Alice Through the Looking Glass (also a 'journey' to a lost world of childhood through a pane of glass which is window and mirror), with its bespectacled, knitting Sheep:

> 'Can you row?' the Sheep asked, handing her a pair of knitting-needles as she spoke.
>
> 'Yes, a little – but not on land – and not with needles – ' Alice was beginning to say, when suddenly the needles turned into oars in her hands, and she found they were in a little boat, gliding along between banks: so there was nothing for it but to do her best.
>
> 'Feather!' cried the Sheep, as she took up another pair of needles.[24]

Dream-like disruptions of the conventional logics of time and space – 'At the same time, she seemed to be sitting beside Mrs Ramsay on the beach' – prepare us for Mrs Ramsay's apparitional 'return' for Lily: 'Mrs Ramsay – it was part of her perfect goodness to Lily – sat there quite simply, in the chair, flicked her needles to and fro, knitted her reddish-brown stocking, cast her shadow on the step. There she sat' (TL 219).

Mrs Ramsay 'returns' for Lily, not for Mr Ramsay. The intensity of Lily's need for her is that of both a lover and a child: 'To want and not to have, sent all up her body a hardness, a hollowness, a strain. And then to want and not to have – to want and want – how that wrung the heart, and wrung it again and again!' (TL 194). Yet Lily's response on 'seeing' Mrs Ramsay is to seek out Mr Ramsay: 'She wanted him.' Lily's negotiations in the final part of the novel, like those of Cam and James, are with the relationship between Mr and Mrs Ramsay, man and wife, father and mother, the marriage contract. For both James and Lily, this is captured in a memory of position or placing, that of Mr Ramsay standing over Mrs Ramsay as she sat in the window with James (we recall Helen and Terence 'standing over' Rachel in *The Voyage Out*), through which the novel explores the relationship between, at one level, stance and distance and, at another, the sexual and the familial. For Lily, the stance or 'standing-point' ('stopping there he stood over her, and looked down at her') is followed by a gesture ('He stretched out his hand and raised her from her chair') which, for the reader, recalls Mr Ramsay's stretching out his empty arms after Mrs Ramsay's death and, for Lily, 'repeats' a scene which is the keynote of the Ramsay's marriage:

> He stretched out his hand and raised her from her chair. It seemed somehow as if he had done it before; as if he had once bent in the same way and raised her from a boat which, lying a few inches off some island, had required that the ladies should thus be helped on shore by the gentlemen. An old-fashioned scene that was, which required, very nearly, crinolines and peg-top trousers. Letting herself be helped by him, Mrs Ramsay had thought (Lily supposed) the time has come now; Yes, she would say it now. Yes, she would marry him. And she stepped slowly, quietly on shore. <...> [Lily] was not inventing; she was only trying to smooth out something she had been given years ago folded up; something she had seen. For in the rough and tumble of daily life, with all those children about, all those visitors, one had constantly a sense of repetition – of one thing falling where another had fallen, and so setting up an echo which chimed in the air and made it full of vibrations. (*TL* 215)

The 'gestural' scene (stopping, looking down, stretching out his hand, raising her up) thus becomes not only part of a series but a repetition of a first, a 'primal', scene that may or may not have occurred, but which takes its shape and meaning from what succeeds it. Such complex temporalities are what found psychoanalytic understandings of the relationship of past to present and present to past.

The substance of Lily's memory has already been recalled by James, from his different perspective. We remember from 'The Window' James's anger at his father's 'interruption' and distortion of 'the perfect simplicity and good sense of his relations with his mother'. Ten years later the scene and its attendant emotion returns to James:

> They look down, he thought, at their knitting or something. Then suddenly they look up. There was a flash of blue, he remembered, and then somebody sitting with him laughed, surrendered, and he was very angry. It must have been his mother, he thought, sitting on a low chair, with his father standing over her. He began to search

among the infinite series of impressions which time had laid down, leaf upon leaf, fold upon fold, softly, incessantly upon his brain <...> how a man had marched up and down and stopped dead, upright, over them. *(TL* 184-5)

James's role in the novel has often been interpreted in classical Freudian terms as an enactment of the Oedipal crisis; the son, desiring the mother, feels a parricidal rage against the father who comes between them. In 'The Lighthouse', James is literally becalmed, like the Ancient Mariner, by this narrative, and metaphorically bound, as Oedipus was bound by the chains with which his father sought to secure his death: 'A rope seemed to bind him [James] there and his father had knotted it and he could only escape by taking a knife and plunging it...'*(TL* 203).

James's 'memories' recapture a prelapsarian garden, a world before the coming of loss, division, and conflict, the place of the mother. It is the shadow of the father which 'in this world <...>stayed and darkened over him <...>smiting through the leaves and flowers even of that happy world and making them shrivel and fall' *(TL* 201). 'Powerless to move', James can resolve the misery of loss and the tension of ambivalence only by reducing his awareness of the dual nature of the lighthouse as both a 'silvery, misty-looking tower with a yellow eye that opened suddenly and softly in the evening' (the lighthouse for the mother) and as a 'tower, stark and straight' on a rock (the lighthouse for the father) to a single, male-identified, perception: 'So it was like that, James thought, the Lighthouse one had seen across the bay all these years; it was a stark tower on a bare rock. It satisfied him' *(TL* 220). James and Mr Ramsay 'shared that knowledge': there 'were two pairs of footprints only; his own and his father's. They alone knew each other' *(TL* 200). This recognition is dependent upon the repression of the mother and her sphere.

For Cam, sitting in the boat, the island shore recedes into unreality, a place of ghosts, as remote and silent as the 'little town' pictured on Keats's Grecian Urn, that elegiac vessel, without 'a soul to tell | Why thou art desolate'. Turning away from the past towards the future, Cam is caught up in the adventure of the trip to the lighthouse, but her role is a passive one. In 'The Window' she is 'Cam the Wicked'; in the final part of the novel, she is elided by father and brother with Mrs Ramsay in the terms of an undifferentiated femininity. The father's place (the study, the world of books) is remembered by

Cam as a sanctuary distinct from the world of the garden. We could read this as an assertion of Woolf's own sense of herself as the inheritor of her father's literary heritage, although Cam remains excluded from the terms of his knowledge: 'what might be written in the book which had rounded its edges off in his pocket, she did not know' (TL 206). (And Woolf, if she is 'in' the novel, is dispersed between a number of its characters and voices, rather than simply embodied in one.) Unlike James, Cam preserves no direct memories of her mother, though her words return to her in reverie and she is linked to her at the level of metaphor: 'a fountain of joy', 'shapes of a world not realised but turning in their darkness'(TL 205). But, and as for James, the father's injunction to 'Come now' breaks into, takes over from, the first language, the mother's voice.

For both Cam and James the choices – of love, identification, futurity – would seem to be polarized between the way of the father and the way of the mother. Yet the novel, as Gillian Beer notes, also 'disperses parenthood and all its symbolic weight. Want and will give way, the want and the will of the fisherman's wife, of Lily Briscoe, of Mrs Ramsay, Mr Ramsay, of Cam and James'.[25] The ending of the novel acknowledges loss but eschews the weight of tragedy and the portentousness of 'symbol'. Lily's painting is an 'attempt at something': Woolf, as she wrote to Roger Fry, 'meant *nothing* by the Lighthouse'. Meaning is indeterminate. 'Gesture' is now muted. Mr Ramsay springs 'lightly' on to the lighthouse rock; Mrs Ramsay appears 'simply' for Lily, 'on a level with ordinary experience' (TL 219); Lily draws the line down the centre of her painting: 'It was done, it was finished. Yes, she thought, laying down her brush in extreme fatigue, I have had my vision' (TL 226).

6

Writing Lives:
Orlando, The Waves and *Flush*

I doubt that I shall ever write another novel after O. I shall
invent a new name for them.

(*D*. iii. 176)

Yesterday morning I was in despair: You know that bloody
book which Dadie and Leonard extort, drop by drop, from
my breast? Fiction, or some title to that effect [*Phases of
Fiction*]. I couldn't screw a word from me; and at last
dropped my head in my hands: dipped my pen in the ink,
and wrote these words, as if automatically, on a clean sheet:
Orlando: A Biography. No sooner had I done this than my
body was flooded with rapture and my brain with
ideas. <...> it sprung upon me how I could revolutionise
biography in a night <...>

Letter to Vita Sackville-West, 9 Oct. 1927. (*L*. iii. 428–9)

I'm glad to be quit this time of writing 'a novel'; & hope
never to be accused of it again.

(*D*. iii. 185)

As she was completing and revising *To the Lighthouse*, Woolf
began to record in her diaries her impulses towards two very
different kinds of writing. One would be a kind of 'play-poem'
(*D*. iii. 139); 'away from facts: free, yet concentrated; prose yet
poetry; a novel & a play' (*D*. iii. 128); 'an abstract mystical eyeless
book' (*D*. iii. 203). Many of the ideas and images circulating
around this 'play-poem' were to be realised in *The Waves*. The
second impulse was the desire for 'an escapade after these
serious poetic experimental books whose form is so closely
considered. I want to kick up my heels & be off' (*D*. iii. 13):

I sketched the possibilities which an unattractive woman, penniless, alone, might yet bring into being. <...>It struck me, vaguely, that I might write a Defoe narrative for fun. Suddenly between twelve & one I conceived a whole fantasy to be called 'The Jessamy Brides' – why, I wonder? I have rayed round it several scenes. Two women, poor, solitary at the top of a house. One can see anything (for this is all fantasy) the Tower Bridge, clouds, aeroplanes. Also old men listening in the room over the way. Everything is to be tumbled in pall mall. It is to be written as I write letters at the top of my speed: on the ladies of Llangollen; on Mrs Fladgate; on people passing. No attempt is to be made to realise the character. Sapphism is to be suggested. Satire is to be the main note – satire & wildness. The Ladies are to have Constantinople in view. Dreams of golden domes. My own lyric vein is to be satirised. Everything mocked. And it is to end with three dots ... so. (*D*. iii. 131)

This 'fantasy' was to be realised, although in a different guise, in *Orlando*. The 'two poor solitary women' appear remote from Orlando's patrician splendour, but the conception of a 'fantasy' revolving around women and sexuality remains.

Woolf's early plans for the novel-biography that was to become *Orlando* also suggest that it was in conception not wholly distinct from *The Waves*. A few months after the diary entry quoted above, she recorded her ideas for a book that would be 'a way of writing the memoirs of one's own times during peoples lifetimes. It might be a most amusing book. The question is how to do it. Vita should be Orlando, a young nobleman. There should be Lytton. & it should be truthful; but fantastic. Roger. Duncan. Clive. Adrian. Their lives should be related' (*D*. iii. 157) The chorus of six voices charting the passage from childhood to adulthood in *The Waves* was to be in part a way of exploring the interrelated lives of a group of friends; later Woolf was to write a more formal biography of Roger [Fry]. *Orlando* came to focus in its entirety on Vita as Orlando, 'a young nobleman', and to be less 'the memoirs of one's own times' than an historical pageant. The relationship between memoir and history, biographical and historical writing, becomes, however, one of the most important aspects of the text.

It is apparent from reading Woolf's diaries for the early months of 1927 that her growing erotic friendship with the writer Vita Sackville-West was becoming entwined with her ideas for her next piece of writing. Woolf's visit to Knole – Sackville-West's ancestral home – gave her some of the central historical and biographical images that animate *Orlando*:

Vita stalking in her Turkish dress, attended by small boys, down the gallery, wafting them on like some tall sailing ship – a sort of covey of noble English life: dogs walloping, children crowding, all very free & stately: & [a] cart bringing wood. How do you see that? I asked Vita. She said she saw it as something that had gone on for hundreds of years. They had brought wood in from the Park to replenish the great fires like this for centuries: & her ancestresses had walked so on the snow with their great dogs bounding by them. All the centuries seemed lit up, the past expressive, articulate; not dumb & forgotten; but a crowd of people stood behind, not dead at all; not remarkable; fair faced, long limbed; affable; & so we reach the days of Elizabeth quite easily. (*D.* iii. 125)

This passage contains a hint of the ways in which *Orlando* was to be a 'gift', although not an unambiguous one, from Woolf to Vita Sackville-West. In asking her 'How do you see that', Woolf is suggesting that she will weave her narrative around Vita's own conception of her family history, going back through the centuries. By October of that year, the plan for *Orlando* was complete: 'a biography beginning in the year 1500 & continuing to the present day, called Orlando: Vita; only with a change about from one sex to another' (*D.* iii. 161). One 'gift' that Woolf had earlier asked of Sackville-West had been a new name for the novel form: 'I want you to invent a name by the way which I can use instead of 'novel'. Thinking it over, I see I cannot, never could, never shall, write a novel. What, then, to call it?' (*L.* iii. 221). The relationship between the two women, and the writing that resulted from it and sustained it, becomes intertwined with the question of freedom from the restrictions of both genre and gender.

It is also striking that Woolf was referring to *Orlando* as a 'biography' from the outset; it was not only to be a way of escaping the restrictions of the novel but of 'revolutionis[ing] biography in a night'. The word 'night' is telling here; not only is this to be a biography imbued with the fantasy and eroticism of the nocturnal, as opposed to the sober realities of the day, but, rather like Shakespeare's *A Midsummer's Night's Dream* or *As You Like It*, with its own cross-dressing Orlando, it will transgress everyday realities.

Orlando ridicules the tenets laid down by the Victorian guardians of the biographical genre. Where they insist that the living individual is not a proper subject for biography, Woolf took as her 'subject' her friend and lover whose name, 'Vita', means 'life', and made of the word life a mocking-bird song: 'Then they come here, says the bird, and ask me what life is; Life, Life, Life!' (*O*. 189). She stretches the boundaries of the individual beyond breaking-point; Orlando is alive during the 400 years of text-time, first as a man and then as a woman. She satirizes Victorian biography and its narrative plod from the subject's birth to his death, 'without looking to right or left, in the indelible footprints of truth; unenticed by flowers; regardless of shade; on and on methodically till we fall plump into the grave and write finis on the tombstone above our head' (*O*. 47). She shows how transgressive the biography of a woman can be: 'the truth is that when we write of a woman, everything is out of place – culminations and perorations; the accent never falls where it does with a man' (*O*. 215). She mocks her narrator's pretensions to objectivity, and reveals the impossibility of reconstructing the past as it was; documents burn or develop holes in crucial places, the perspectives of the present make the past obscure or incomprehensible. And yet the drive of the text is towards a grand historical sweep and a denial of limit and closure.

Orlando is a biography that is also a mock-biography (a contemporary referred to it as a 'pseudobiography') or a 'metabiography', reflecting on the conventions of the genre even as it uses them. It also satirizes historiography, drawing attention to the ways in which history is periodized and categorized, and simplistic concepts of 'the age' – the Eliza- bethan age, the age of Enlightenment, the Victorian era and, more ambiguously, modernity – while revelling in the historical imaginings that such reconstructions make possible. It is a literary history in many senses. It scatters literary allusions and literary figures throughout its pages; it shows up the ways in which our concepts of an age are drawn from literary works, thus blurring the division between fiction and history; it is, crucially, the mock-biography of a writer, whose poem 'The Oak Tree', like the oak tree on the estate, is a constant throughout change and comes to embody identity itself; it turns history into a series of imaginative or fictional reconstructions. Winifred Holtby called it 'a dramatised history of literary fashion'.[1] *Orlando* also plays on the relationship between historical and biographical categories, punning on the ways in which 'age' can refer both to biographical and historical stages. It recounts historical change (Woolf refutes the Victorian myth of progress in representing the Victorian age as a definite falling-off from the eighteenth century) and the life course of an individual, albeit one whose life is composed of many lives and selves. The life course is in turn one in which gender can in no sense be taken for granted, but entails the production of complex narratives of identity, change, and development. Woolf both deploys and satirizes the psychological and sexological theories of her time, encoding and sending up current theories of sexuality, androgyny, and homosexuality.

Orlando was by no means Woolf's first experiment in biography. A number of her early short stories play with the biographical genre; 'The Journal of Mistress Joan Martyn' and 'Memoirs of a Novelist' explore the relationship between a woman biographer and her female subject, and between private and public histories. Woolf was fascinated by the idea of writing a history made up out of the evidence and experience of women's lives, drawing upon memoirs and autobiographies; in 'The Lives of the Obscure' 'obscurity' ceases to be a negation and becomes a medium 'thick with the star dust of innumerable lives':

> It is one of the attractions of the unknown, their multitude, their vastness; for, instead of keeping their identity separate, as remarkable people do, they seem to merge into one another, their very boards and title-pages and frontispieces dissolving, and their innumerable pages melting into continuous years so that we can lie back and look up into the fine mist-like substance of countless lives, and pass unhindered from century to century, from life to life. Scenes detach themselves. We watch groups. (*E.* iv. 120)

The histories Woolf creates from these lives are eccentric and obscure in their implications: questions remain unanswered and secret stories unresolved. Their oblique relationship to the mainstream is precisely their fascination, although they are not outside history. The 'obscure' – and women form a large part of this category – could also be seen as the repository of a kind of collective memory, in which history is the medium not the monument.

Jacob's Room, as we have seen, uses the biographical form as a way of satirizing biographical conventions, in particular those in which blindness to gender differences and inequalities allow for highly partial versions of the 'representative' life. The relationship between biographer and subject is central to *Jacob's Room*, the biographer as 'outsider', excluded from the men's room, and the elusive biographical subject conjoining, or failing to conjoin, to make biographical knowledge thoroughly uncertain. In *Orlando* Woolf plays up the comedy of the biographical search or pursuit of the subject, as Orlando slips in and out of view through the centuries, and the shifting roles of 'insider' and 'outsider'. In the eighteenth century, Orlando, become a woman, finds herself positioned on the outside looking in and hears not a word spoken by the 'Great Men' whose voices, literary history would have us believe, reverberate through the centuries. Lytton Strachey had suggested that Woolf write a 'Shandean' narrative, in the manner of Lawrence Sterne's *Tristram Shandy*, and elements of this emerge in Woolf's play with silences, pauses, digressions, and parentheses which radically disrupt the narrative. Orlando even starts living her life as if it were a book; we are told of one life event or 'episode' that 'she skipped it, to get on with the text'.

This playful textualization of lives also emerges in 'The Lives of the Obscure', in which Woolf exploits the metaphoric relationship between lives and books to the point where the terms collapse into one another: 'the obscure sleep on the walls, slouching against each other as if they were too drowsy to stand upright' (*E*. iv. 118). The relationship between 'life' and 'literature' is at the centre of Orlando, and the mocking and celebratory cry of 'Life, Life, Life' relates not only to the presence of a 'living' biographical subject but is directed at the realist novelist's simplistic demand for the inclusion of 'life' in fiction, as if it were a known and measurable quantity or, in Woolf's words, 'commodity' (*O*. 147). *Orlando* exposes the pitfalls and fallacies of biographical representation: in particular, that of the 'lives' of writers, who do not on the whole lead lives packed with incident and whose defining activity involves thought and not action. Where the conventional biographer writes over the *longueurs* which are a necessary part of the writer's life and an inescapable aspect of many women's lives before the twentieth century, Orlando's biographer makes them all the more obvious in inventing desperate strategies to fill in the time while she writes.

The translation of 'life' into 'literature' thus has a triple aspect in *Orlando*. There is the life of a writer which is the story of writing; the turning of life into text and text back into life which characterizes the biographical enterprise in general; the broader problem of literary representation itself, which seeks to turn world into word:

He was describing, as all young poets are for ever describing, nature, and in order to match the shade of green precisely he looked (and here he showed more audacity than most) at the thing itself, which happened to be a laurel bush growing beneath the window. After that, of course, he could write no more. Green in nature is one thing, green in literature is another. Nature and letters seem to have a natural antipathy; bring them together and they tear each other to pieces. (O. 13)

The passage mocks, as *To the Lighthouse* fractures, the belief that it is the role of art to hold a mirror up to nature. In using the image of 'match[ing] the shade of green precisely', which would seem more appropriate in the context of interior décor or dress than of writing or nature, Woolf also suggests how much of fashion and convention is entailed in 'realist' representation and how little 'nature' can be seen as an originary principle, when 'she' comes already mediated through rhetorical devices.

Woolf made a sharp distinction between the 'poetic experimental' nature of *To the Lighthouse* and the 'fun' and 'fantasy' of *Orlando*, and does indeed include a parody of the lyricism of 'Time Passes' in her novel-biography. They share, however, not only a focus on time, memory, historical rupture, and sexual identities, but a sense of the complex relationship between model and copy, biographical and fictional representations. As I noted earlier, Woolf plays with the metaphors and the media of portraiture in constructing and deconstructing the 'vision' of Mrs Ramsay. In *Orlando*, she incorporated photographs of Vita Sackville-West and photographs of paintings of her ancestors to 'represent' Orlando in the different stages of her historically and sexually differentiated career. Arnold Bennett, in his bemused review of *Orlando*, referred to 'ordinary realistic photographs' of Vita Sackville-West, labelled 'Orlando': 'This is the oddest of all the book's oddities....' (M&M 232), thus missing the ways in which the photographs enact the poses and performances of the self. Instead of anchoring identity in biographical and historical reality, they point to its theatricality. In ways rather similar to Julia Margaret Cameron's historical and dramatic constructions, her Floras and Julias 'as' Madonnas and Magdalenes, they portray 'Orlando as a boy', 'Orlando as Ambassador', and, of course, Vita as Orlando, Orlando as Vita.

The adverbs 'as' and, in particular, 'like', are reiterated throughout the text, most intensively in the 'Elizabethan' section, and make up *Orlando*'s central rhetorical device, simile;

'everything was partly something else' (*O.* 224). Orlando and the Russian princess with whom he falls in love express their passion, real on his part if not on hers, through a spume of simile: 'plunging and splashing among a thousand images' (*O.* 32). While the River Thames remains frozen solid and deep during the Great Frost of 1608, 'he told her that he could find no words to praise her; yet instantly bethought him how she was like the spring and green grass and rushing waters' (*O.* 39). The language of metaphor and simile is a language of approximation, a rhetoric which clothes or veils reality – Orlando's search for words to describe Sasha relates to the fact that there is in her 'something hidden <...>something concealed' (*O.* 32) – and a way of turning one thing into another, enacting 'the strangest transformation[s]' (*O.* 39). It is part of the text's exploration of appearance and reality and hints at the ways in which veiling and unveiling are to become the metaphors for its 'strangest transformation', Orlando's change from a man to a woman, and of clothes as the means through which identity is to be figured.

Transformations in *Orlando*, and indeed in Woolf's work in general, tend to be represented as oscillations and/or 'vacillations' from one state of being to another; the finality of change is thus re-figured in states of flux and in repetition. The most striking of Orlando's 'vacillations' is, of course, sexual – 'she seemed to vacillate; she was man; she was woman; she shared the secrets, shared the weaknesses of each' (*O.* 113) – but the text is also structured upon oscillations which relate to 'character' as well as 'sex'.

Through these Woolf makes the link between historical periods and forms and concepts of subjectivity, and explores the relationship between the enduring and the mutable self or selves. Like Jacob Flanders, Orlando veers between despair and ecstasy. During the Elizabethan and Jacobean periods, he is subject to a melancholia which is explained through the Renaissance view that '[he] was strangely compounded of many humours', his mind working 'in violent see-saws from life to death' (*O.* 32). 'Life' and 'death' become, as we shall see, the key terms of the biographical enterprise. In 'the age of Enlightenment', when Orlando has 'become' a woman, she finds herself travelling though London in a coach with Alexander Pope. Her 'state of mind' is created by the chiarascuro effects of eighteenth-century street lighting, which produces stretches of darkness between patches of light. Paradoxically, and at odds

with the Enlightenment's valorization of the light of rational-
ism, Orlando experiences enlightenment during the stretches of
darkness, praising Pope as 'the most august, most lucid of
beams' (*O*. 143), and profound gloom, as well as disenchantment
with the 'Great Man', during the brief moments of illumination.
The passage (which mockingly looks back at the play of light in
To the Lighthouse), also sends up the view that subjectivity is
simply determined by the historical moment (the idea that street
lighting determines consciousness) and further suggests that 'as
a' woman, Orlando's 'state of mind' no longer mirrors 'the age'
but enacts an exact reversal of its dominant tropes.

In the nineteenth century, the oscillation between light and
darkness is transferred to heat and cold and from consciousness
to mores and the now forbidden realms of the body. Veering
between modesty and shame, Orlando experiences 'the spirit of
the age' (a key term in nineteenth-century thought) as a blush:

> The blushes came and went with the most exquisite iteration of
> modesty and shame imaginable. One might see the spirit of the age
> blowing, now hot, now cold upon her cheeks. And if the spirit of the
> age blew a little unequally, the crinoline being blushed for before the
> husband, her ambiguous position must excuse her (even her sex was
> still in dispute) and the irregular life she had lived before. (*O*. 162)

Modernity shifts the terms of the oscillation to identity itself – in
the twentieth century Orlando veers between a singularity and a
multiplicity of selves and subjectivities – and to Orlando's
twanging and vibrating body, 'oscillating' between two points.

Such oscillations often occur during the journeys that
punctuate the text, primarily journeys between the country
and the city. For Woolf, as we have seen, forms of transport are
primary vehicles for the exploration of identity; in *Orlando*, they
are part of the text's exploration of transportations from one
state of being and time to another. Motoring and/as modernity
dominates the final section, as it dominated Woolf's diary
entries during the summer of 1927, when she was planning
Orlando: 'All images are now tinged with driving a motor. Here I
think of letting my engine work, with my clutch out' (*D*. iii. 149).
Motoring (also very much associated with Vita, whose driving
skills Woolf greatly admired) allowed her 'to see the heart of the
world uncovered for a moment'; she liked 'the sense it gives one
of lighting accidentally, like a voyager who touches another
planet with the tip of his toe, upon scenes which have gone on,

have always gone on, will go on, unrecorded, save for this chance glimpse' (*D*. iii. 153).

At this time, she also wrote her essay 'Evening over Sussex: Reflections in a Motor Car', in which she explored these spatial-temporal effects of speed and links them to the ways in which the multiple selves which make up 'the self' emerge during the dispersals of identity effected by modern travel. The interplay between 'I' and 'we' central to Woolf's work emerges strongly here, as it does in 'Street-Haunting'. The 'we' must be gathered up by the 'I' for the homeward journey: 'Now we have got to collect ourselves; we have got to be one self.' The gathering-up also entails a recapitulation of what 'we' have 'made' that day through vision: 'that beauty; death of the individual; and the future' (*CDML* 84). The injunction to the 'we' to be 'one self' is a recognition of the fact that the singular identity of 'the individual' is a matter of propriety and not truth, the need 'to collect ourselves' a question of a restraint or repression demanded by domestic and social life.

Such meditations also make up the last section of *Orlando*; the interchange between essays, letters, diaries, and fictional writing is particularly strong during this period, as the relationship between real and fictional lives, Orlando and Vita, was at its most playful and its most intense. In the 'present moment' Orlando drives to London and enters a department store. Her ascent in the lift of Marshall and Snelgrove is part of the re-enchantment of the world; it also reconstructs the passage through the ages Orlando has already undergone. As the lift doors open on to each floor and its seductive wares, past scenes are recalled, so that history is displayed in front of her, and Orlando's Proustian return of memory is triggered through the scents and stuffs of the thoroughly feminine world of commodities. The sights and sensations of the past – 'smells of wax candles, white flowers, and old ships' – which have composed the scenarios of the historical are now ironically juxtaposed with the 'napkins, towels, dusters' offered to Orlando by a sales assistant whose 'descent' – and the pun here is on the downward motion of the lift and of lineage – may well be as 'deep' and 'proud' as her own, though it is hidden by 'the impervious screen of the present', which turns depth into surface or, it could be argued, creates the illusion of depth and profundity behind or beneath the surface.

Orlando's drive back to the country entails a fragmentation of

125

selfhood which both echoes the proliferation of selves in 'Evening over Sussex' and is its more violent aspect:

> After twenty minutes the body and mind were like scraps of torn paper tumbling from a sack and, indeed, the process of motoring fast out of London so much resembles the chopping up small of identity which precedes unconsciousness and perhaps death itself that it is an open question in what sense Orlando can be said to have existed at the present moment. Indeed we should have given her over for a person entirely disassembled were it not that here, at last, one green screen was held out on the right, against which the little bits of paper fell more slowly; and then another was held out on the left so that one could see the separate scraps now turning over by themselves in the air; and then green screens were held continuously on either side, so that her mind regained the illusion of holding things within itself and she saw a cottage, a farmyard and four cows, all precisely life-size. (*O*. 212)

In this passage Woolf plays with the conventional wisdom that the authentic life of the countryside heals the wounds inflicted by the dissipations of the city, and makes of the rural a simulacrum of itself, a series of 'green screens' which are linked to 'the impervious screen of the present' she encountered in Marshall and Snelgrove. The 'reassembling' of Orlando's identity through her house, her land, and her poem becomes a life-preserving, and biography-preserving, fiction and the continuities that the house, the land, and the poem ostensibly represent are revealed, at one level, as the wishful thinkings that they indeed were for Sackville-West, who, unlike Orlando, could not, 'as a woman', inherit Knole and who longed to create in her verse something that would endure.

I suggested earlier that the subversiveness of *Orlando* as biography lies partly in its celebration of the 'life' in 'life-writing'. Woolf was also aware, however, that biography is a deadly practice: 'Of the multitude of lives written, how few survive', she wrote in her essay 'The Art of Biography' (*CDML* 144). The letters Woolf and Sackville-West wrote to each other during and immediately after *Orlando*'s writing and publication allude to this sense of biography as both life- and death-writing, and to the violence of biographical representation, which immobilizes and even negates its subject in turning 'life' into letters: 'Did you feel a sort of tug, as if your neck was being broken on Saturday last at 5 minutes to one?', Woolf wrote. 'That was when he [Orlando] died – or rather stopped talking, with three little dots ... <...> The question now is, will my feelings for you be changed? I've lived in you all these months – coming out, what are you really like? Do you exist? Have I made you up?...' (*L*. iii. 474).

Woolf 's image of a neck broken in the 'present moment' recalls the American writer and politician Henry Adams's autobiography, *The Education of Henry Adams*, in which he tries to come to terms with the 'real' forces governing the twentieth century. As a historian, he has rejected temporal sequences and narrativity, stories and histories, finding them not only overly relativist but unaware of their own motivating principles. The failure to find a sequence outside the limitations of the social, the chaos of thought, and the artificiality of temporality is resolved only by his discovery of the sequence of force: 'and thus it happened that, after ten years pursuit, he found himself lying in the Gallery of Machines at the Great Exposition of 1900, his historical neck broken by the sudden irruption of forces totally new'.[2] Dynamic forces – electricity, vibrations, and rays – erupt into and fragment time and narrative. This is sequence without the innocence of story-telling to blunt its effects. The autobiographer, biographer, and historian will no longer have recourse to the consolations of narrative: 'Between the dynamo in the gallery of machines and the engine-house outside, the break of continuity amounted to abysmal fracture for a historian's objects.... man had translated himself into a new universe which had no common scale of measurement with the old'.[3]

Adams's representations of modernity are echoed in *Orlando*'s repeated references to the electric charges of modernity, the shock of time, and the buffering effect of historical sequence: 'For what more terrifying revelation can there be than that it is the present moment? That we survive the shock at all is only possible because the past shelters us on one side and the future on another' (*O*. 206). The last and most difficult part of Orlando may suggest that modernity and now-time are incompatible with biography and that Orlando's biography can only be rendered from the perspectives of the present when that present entails an escape from itself into the consolations of the past and of 'descent'. In this sense, *Orlando* enacts the death of biography even as it revolutionizes and revivifies it.

Woolf also suggests, however, that the biography of a woman resists closure and narrative 'death':

<...>we must snatch space to remark how discomposing it is for her biographer that this culmination to which the whole book moved, this peroration with which the book was to end, should be dashed from us on a laugh casually like this; but the truth is that when we write of a woman, everything is out of place – culminations and perorations; the accent never falls where it does with a man. (*O*. 215)

Yet even this declaration is too final; the question of what it means to 'write of a woman', or indeed of a man, has been fundamentally troubled throughout the text. The last pages of *Orlando* do not consolidate the self or round off the life course, as conventional biography does, but chart both its complexity and its fragility, a waxing and waning of subjectivity and identity.

It has recently been argued that cultural images of sex and gender-crossing, such as we find in *Orlando*, are not just transgressions of sexual difference, male/female, but indicate a broader 'category crisis', crossing over borderlines of which the binarism male/female is only one.[4] Sex change, in this model, *is* the figure of fantasy, 'the transgression of boundaries as a play with the limit, as a play of difference', in Makiko Minow-Pinkney's words.[5] As I have suggested, 'vacillations' and 'oscillations' (the either/or, and/or of *Orlando*) are dispersed throughout the text and are not contained in the moment of Orlando's change of sex. Orlando is by no means the only sexually ambiguous figure When he first sees Sasha, her sex is initially indeterminate, disguised by 'the loose tunic and trousers of the Russian fashion'; for a moment she appears to be a boy and only finally does Orlando see that 'she was a woman' (*O*. 27). Nor is there a single shift from male to female: sexual identity is an uncertain question from the first line onwards, fixed only by linguistic necessity (he or she). Orlando continues to dress as a man, when the mood takes her and 'the age' allows, after she has 'become' a woman. The scene of transformation does not put an end to sexual oscillation any more than it confirms the symmetry of heterosexual pairings: Orlando finds that her love for women is in no way diminished when she becomes one herself.

As I suggested in my discussion of *A Room of One's Own*, 'androgyny' is the concept in Woolf's work that has most troubled feminist critics, sometimes seeming to imply that the sexual ideal is a combination of male and female attributes which are known and given from the start, rather than a matter of convention, and that this happy marriage allows for a transcendence of sexual difference. As we have seen, Winifred Holtby, whose study of Woolf was written soon after the publication of *Orlando* and *A Room of One's Own* and was thus close to the debates of the period, both endorsed the ideal of the 'manly-womanly' and 'womanly-manly' and suggested that:

> We cannot recognize infallibly what characteristics beyond those which are purely physical are 'male' and 'female'. Custom and prejudice, history and tradition have designed the fashion plates; we hardly know yet what remains beneath them of the human being.... We might as well call the conflicting strains within the human personality black and white, negative and positive, as male and female. The time has not yet come when we can say for certain which is the man and which the woman, after both have boarded the taxi of human personality.[6]

In this passage Holtby not only suggests that it is convention and not nature which determines gender identity; she seems to anticipate the view that the male/female distinction is but one of the arbitrary distinctions by which the world is ordered and controlled. She also invokes the clothes imagery which runs throughout *Orlando*. Woolf not only reworks Carlyle's satiric 'philosophy of clothes' in his *Sartor Resartus*; she appears to be ironizing the psychoanalytic studies of clothing and sexuality of her period, anticipating by two years the publication of J. C. Flugel's *The Psychology of Clothes* (published by the Hogarth Press), with its somewhat literal application of Freud's theories of the castration complex, exhibitionism, and narcissism to male and female dress.[7] In *Orlando* clothes are not only part of the furnishings by which historical ages are differentiated; they are used to suggest that sexual identity may well be a matter of costume, performance, and disguise. The biographer's pursuit of Orlando, which echoes that in *Jacob's Room*, is rendered almost impossible 'by the fact that she found it convenient at this time to change frequently from one set of clothes to another':

> She had, it seems, no difficulty in sustaining the different parts, for her sex changed far more frequently than whose who have worn

only one set of clothing can conceive; nor can there be any doubt that she reaped a twofold harvest by this device; the pleasures of life were increased and its experiences multiplied. For the probity of breeches she exchanged the seductiveness of petticoats and enjoyed the love of both sexes equally. (*O.* 153)

Orlando's 'sex-change' thus becomes a performance subject to repeated iteration. The 'performative' dimensions of gender identity are enacted most elaborately in the scene of transformation. Orlando 'becomes' a woman and sexuality is a matter of veiling and unveiling, literally and linguistically, as in Woolf's use of sexual innuendo in the following sentence's ambiguous use of 'which' to refer to the shortfall either of the towel or of the 'naked form'; 'Chastity, Purity, and Modesty, inspired, no doubt, by Curiosity, peeped in at the door and threw a garment like a towel at the naked form which, unfortunately, fell short by several inches' (*O.* 98).

Innuendo both veils and unveils; it points to the sexual while at the same time disguising it. Woolf's use of the figure of 'androgyny' serves something of the same function in relation to lesbianism or 'Sapphism' and bisexuality; it is the acceptable version of sexual ambiguity or sexual transgression. *Orlando's* playfulness, as well, perhaps, as the literary reputation of its author and the aristocratic status of its subject, allowed it to elude the censorship whose full weight fell on Radclyffe Hall's representations of the lesbian as a tragic misfit in *The Well of Loneliness*, published a year after *Orlando*. Woolf indeed fends off censorship by invoking it; her 'Victorian' critic reads a passage of 'The Oak Tree' (a more or less explicit evocation of women's desire for women taken from Sackville-West's *The Land*) and asks 'Are girls necessary?'. Orlando 'passes' only because she is by now married. Where Hall turned directly to the sexological theories of Krafft-Ebing and Havelock Ellis to explain her heroine's 'inversion', Woolf airily waves them away:

> The change seemed to have been accomplished painlessly and completely and in such a way that Orlando herself showed no surprise at it. Many people, taking this into account, and holding that such a change of sex is against nature, have been at great pains to prove (1) that Orlando had always been a woman, (2) that Orlando is at this moment a man. Let biologists and psychologists determine. It is enough for us to state the simple fact; Orlando was a man till the age of thirty, when he became a woman and has remained so ever since. (*O.* 98)

There is, of course, no reason to take Woolf's dismissal of current models of sexual difference entirely at face value. One of the 'gifts' Woolf seems to have been offering Vita Sackville-West was a dramatization of her belief that 'as centuries go on ... the sexes [will] become more nearly merged on account of their increasing resemblances'.[8] Superficially, at least, *Orlando* shares with Radclyffe Hall's lesbian fictions the narrative of an 'evolution' from male to female identity (Hall's Miss Ogilvy, in the short story 'Miss Ogilvy Finds Herself', dreams a return to her stone-age existence as a man and dies in the fulfilment this 'memory' provides) though not their assumption of fixed-gender identities and their 'trapped-soul' model of homosexuality. Orlando's first vision of Sasha reproduces in miniature Freud's model of the accession to psychical or 'mental' femininity; the first stage is a primary bisexuality, the second a psychic masculinity, and only finally does the (biologically) female child 'become' feminine. Orlando is first 'masculine', then 'feminine'; the continuity between these two stages is provided by his/her love of women, which, in turn, echoes Freud's account of both the male and female child's pre-Oedipal identifications with the mother. In the broader schema of a 'history of sexuality', Woolf seems to outline an increasing feminization of culture. Certainly Orlando becomes more 'feminine' as the advance of the Victorian age outlaws sexual and gender freedoms and imposes a 'compulsory heterosexuality' on its members; sexual behaviours are not prior to culture, Woolf suggests, but substantially determined by it.

The point of reading Freud's or Havelock Ellis's accounts of sexuality and gender in tandem with Woolf's writing is to show that her text shares the preoccupation with the narratives of sexual and gender identity of her culture and period. These storylines, often not only mutually exclusive but internally contradictory, weave their way through *Orlando*, and are used both seriously and satirically. Where Freud mapped the history of the race/species (phylogeny) onto the individual (ontogeny), Woolf simultaneously narrates historical and biographical development; she also hints, as does Freud's model of phylogeny, at an anti-narrative, a 'history' in which nothing changes. Fundamentally, we are told, Orlando remains the same. Like Freud, Woolf shows how circuitous the route to femininity is and how fragile are all sexual identities and identifications. For neither Freud nor Woolf was the antithesis between masculinity and femininity clear-cut. And for both the question of a movement between masculinity and femininity raised the issue of the 'repression' of whichever sexual identity was not in place or play. In Freud's words, 'both in male and female individuals masculine as well as feminine instinctual impulses are found, and... each can equally well undergo repression and so become unconscious'.[9] This either/or, and/or model of sexual identity is as vertiginous as anything to be found in *Orlando*, and is indeed echoed in Woolf's assertion that: 'Different though the sexes are, they intermix. In every human being a vacillation from one sex to the other takes place, and often it is only the clothes that keep the male or female likeness, while underneath the sex is the very opposite of what it is above' (*O*. 132–3).

Throughout *Orlando* Woolf alludes to unconscious realms, 'a pool where things dwell in darkness so deep that what they are we scarcely know' (*O*. 224). There is a model of repression at work in the text which renders history itself subject to psychic processes. Orlando does not simply retain the past he/she lives through; he forgets as much as he remembers, although images from the past still burden the present. The text and history move forward not only through violent transitions from one age to the next but during periods of amnesia, trances, and death-like states. Orlando lives through the centuries but never retains or contains the totality of time. Death does not close the text but it does punctuate it.

In describing the Great Frost, Woolf writes that the severity of the frost was such that 'a kind of petrification sometimes ensued'. Figures are frozen in the form of their last living gesture while, in the Thames, 'shoals of eels lay motionless in a trance, but whether their state was one of death or merely of suspended animation which the warmth would revive puzzled the philosophers' (*O*. 25). The either/or of death and suspended animation is later used in the context of Orlando's transitional, trance-like states: 'He lay as if in a trance, without perceptible breathing' (*O*. 47). These passages are then followed by discussions of the extent to which Orlando can recollect his/ her previous life. Little remains of his memory of the period of the Great Frost and his affair with Sasha – 'as if he were troubled by confused memories of some time long gone or were trying to recall stories told him by another'. More of the past is retained in the transition from man to woman, though 'some slight haziness there may have been, as if a few dark drops had fallen into the clear pool of memory' (O. 98).

Woolf's reference to 'petrification' may well be related to the question of biography as life-writing and/or death-writing, as Clare Hanson suggests.[10] Woolf certainly employed the metaphor of embalming in her critiques of Victorian biographical writing, to express the way in which weighty and ponderous biographies kill off the subject whose 'life' is ostensibly being recounted, fixing him or her like a fly in amber. It appears again in her description of the writing of Sir Thomas Browne in *Orlando*, which clearly pertains to Orlando's trances: Browne's 'words <...> lie entombed, not dead, embalmed rather, so fresh is their colour, so sound their breathing' (O. 57). Biographical representation, it would seem, creates a state which is between life and death; less an oscillation than a suspension.

Revolutionized, or revitalized, biography, on the other hand, like fiction, might be capable of animating the inert or dead organism, in a form of 'vitalism' which is condensed in Vita's name, or a 'Galvanism' echoed in the electrical energies of *Orlando*'s modernity (and here we might also recall the eels, electric or otherwise, of the Great Frost).

The account of 'petrification' also makes the effects of the Great Frost remarkably similar to those of the volcanic eruption which buried Pompeii and turned its inhabitants to stone. For Freud, the burial of Pompeii was the most vivid metaphor for the processes of psychic 'burial' he called repression: 'There is, in fact, no better analogy for repression, by which something in the mind is at once made inaccessible and preserved, than burial of the sort to which Pompeii fell a victim...'.[11] Orlando's 'petrification' is inseparable from the question of memory in the text, thus strongly suggesting a model of the repression of the past as a burial, and its recall through repetition: 'But descending in the lift again – so insidious is the repetition of any scene – she was again sunk far beneath the present moment; and thought when the lift bumped on the ground, that she heard a pot breaking against a river bank' (O. 210).

Mock-biography it may be, but *Orlando* makes a crucial point about biography written in the light of theories of the unconscious; the self is composed not only of multiple identities but of multiple temporalities. Yet the existence of the unconscious suggests a continuity of identity through time more profound than the quick-change artistry would suggest. Hence also the effects of deferral in the text: Orlando's 'castration' is painless, and the moment of sexual horror does not intrude into the narrative until near its end:

> She saw with disgusting vividness that the thumb on Joe's right hand was without a finger nail and there was a raised saucer of pink flesh where the nail should have been. The sight was so repulsive that she felt faint for a moment, but in that moment's darkness, when her eyelids flickered, she was relieved of the pressure of the present. (O. 223)

'Shock' in fact releases Orlando from now-time and allows her both to re-enter her past and to stand in liminal time on the edge of her future, hearing the chimes at midnight.

> I rather think the upshot will be books that relieve other books: a variety of styles & subjects: for after all, that is my temperament, I think: to be very little persuaded of the truth of anything – <...> now, if I write The Moths [The Waves] I must come to terms with these mystical feelings.
>
> (D. iii. 203)

Woolf, as her diary entries reveal, intended there to be a marked contrast between *Orlando* and the 'very serious poetical work which I want to come next' (D. iii. 131) that became *The Waves*. As I suggested at the beginning of this chapter, the two novels in fact share many of the same preoccupations: experiments with time and narrative; the representation of lives in biography; the unfixing of identities. Yet the contrast between *Orlando* and *The Waves* was of great importance to Woolf, as was the exploration at this time of what she saw as 'depth' rather than 'surface'. Her diaries are used to describe 'mystical' experiences and 'visions', and the writing of *The Waves*, became linked to her glimpse of 'a fin passing far out': 'I have netted that fin in the waste of waters which appeared to me over the marshes out of my window at Rodmell when I was coming to the end of To the Lighthouse', she wrote as she was completing *The Waves* (D. iv. 10) (She grants this perception to Bernard in the novel.)

The original working title of the novel, *The Moths*, was suggested by an incident recounted to Woolf in a letter from Vanessa Bell. Writing from her house in the South of France, Bell recorded that 'I sit with moths flying madly in circles round me and the lamp', and described the pains to which she had been to capture, kill (with ether and chloroform) and 'set' an enormous moth for the benefit of her children:

One night some creature tapped so loudly on the pane that Duncan [Grant] said 'Who is that?' 'Only a bat' said Roger 'or a bird', but it wasn't man or bird, but a huge moth – half a foot, literally across. We had a terrible time with it. My maternal instinct which you deplore so much, wouldn't let me leave it. Then I remembered – didn't Fabre try experiments with this same creature & attract all the males in the neighbourhood by shutting up one female in a room ? – just what we have now done. So probably soon the house will be full of them.

However, you'll only tell me its what comes of allowing instinct to play a part in personal relationships. What a lot I could say about the maternal instinct, but then also what a lot about Michael Angelo and Raphael. I wish you would write a book about the maternal instinct. (QB, 126).

Woolf replied: 'By the way, your story of the Moth so fascinates me that I am going to write a story about it. I could think of nothing else but you and the moths for hours after reading your letter. Isn't it odd? – perhaps you stimulate the literary sense in me as you say I do your painting sense.'

On completing *The Waves*, Woolf reminded Vanessa Bell that her story of the moth underlay the novel. While there are only faint traces of this origin in the final version, most visible, perhaps, in the representation of Susan, defined by her 'maternal instinct', Woolf's diaries and letters at this time return to the question of the shape of lives, her own and Vanessa's in particular, and of physical ageing and changing, as well as of the desire, or lack of it, to bear children, concerns which find their echoes in *The Waves*. 'Old age is withering us', she writes in her diary, but adds: 'Only in myself, I say, forever bubbles this impetuous torrent. So that even if I see ugliness in the glass, I think, very well inwardly I am more full of shape & colour than ever.' (*D*. iii. 219). She uses the imagery of pregnancy to define creativity: 'As for my next book, I am going to hold myself from writing till I have it impending in me: grown heavy in my mind like a ripe pear; pendant, gravid, asking to be cut or it will fall. The Moths still haunts me, coming, as they always do, unbidden, between tea & dinner, while L. plays the gramophone' (*D*. iii. 209). Later, creativity is felt as a quickening: 'this is I believe the moth shaking its wings in me' (*D*. iii. 287).

Early in her imaginings of the novel, Woolf had written in her diary that 'One must get the sense that this is the beginning: this is the middle; that the climax – when she opens the window & the moth comes in. I shall have the two different currents – the moths flying along; the flower upright in the centre; a perpetual crumbling and renewal of the plant. In its leaves she might see things happen. But who is she? I am very anxious that she should have no name.' (*D.* iii. 229). A few months later she decided that the Moths would work neither as the title nor, by implication, as the central motif of the novel: 'Moths, I suddenly remember, don't fly by day. And there cant be a lighted candle. Altogether, the shape of the book wants considering.' (*D.* iii. 254). In the shift from night to day, the movement of the waves comes to replace that of the moth or moths. Waves define, as the image of the moth could not, the passage from dawn to dusk which structures the novel; *The Waves*, like *Mrs Dalloway*, *To the Lighthouse*, and *Between the Acts*, uses the time-span of the day to explore the temporality of a life or lives. In Woolf's diary, days come to be perceived as waves: 'The thing to do is now to live with energy & mastery, desperately. To despatch each day high handedly. To make much shorter work of the day than one used. To feel each like a wave slapping up against one.' (*D.* iii. 303).

The Waves could be seen as a negotiation of the paradox which I previously noted: that Woolf's interest in 'autobiography' exists alongside her desire for 'impersonality'. In her essay 'Women and Fiction', written at this time, she discusses the 'turn towards the impersonal' being taken by a new generation of women writers, linking this not only with women's increasing involvement with political life but, less obviously, with a shift from the novel to poetry: 'The greater impersonality of women's lives will encourage the poetic spirit, and it is in poetry that women's fiction is still weakest'. (*WW* 51). *The Waves* was conceived as 'prose yet poetry' (she reread Wordsworth's epic verse autobiography *The Prelude* in the early stages of planning the novel) and as 'a novel & a play'. The six selves of the narrative, she wrote, are represented by 'dramatic soliloquies', interspersed with the 'poetic interludes' which describe the passage of the sun across the sky and the rhythms of the tide. Increasingly *The Waves* became bound up with musical imagery: Woolf wrote to Ethel Smyth, the composer, that she was writing 'to a rhythm and not to a plot' (*L.* iv. 204). The rhythm of the waves was intended to underlie the patterning of the whole work.

'Impersonality' also concerned Woolf at this time as a self that exists below the surface: 'Down there I can't write or read; I exist however. I am. Then I ask myself what I am?' (*D.* iii. 112). It is almost as if identity itself becomes 'the thing that exists when we aren't there' (D. iii. 114). *Jacob's Room* and *Orlando* represent the difficulties of the biographical pursuit of the subject: *The Waves* speaks to a desire for an 'autobiography' detached from ego. 'This shall be Childhood; but it must not be my childhood', she wrote of the novel's opening section (D. iii. 236; emphasis in original). Woolf's early imaginings of the novel included the concept of an 'autobiography' in which the central, female protagonist would have 'no name'; she wished to create what theorists of autobiography have claimed is impossible, an autobiography fuelled by a desire for anonymity.

The 'I am', Woolf suggests, exists in the place where she cannot read or write. In her diaries, she presents the creation of *The Waves* taking place outside writing; it becomes a mental act which is not so much about states of mind, but a state of mind itself. 'What I want is not to write it, but to think it for two or three weeks', she wrote; one of the problems in the construction of the novel she sought to solve was 'Who thinks it?' Some years later, she referred to the novel's creation as 'Writing's one mind'. The novel pushes the metaphor of the 'stream of consciousness' in new directions; it becomes an exploration of the relationship between psychic life and the 'impersonal' elements of waves and water rather than a narrative 'technique'.

Woolf also expressed in her diary a desire 'to go adventuring on the streams of other peoples lives – speculating, adrift' (D. iii. 187). The quest for (and the questioning of) an 'essential' selfhood is bound up with an equally strong sense that identity is not isolable. As she wrote to G. Lowes Dickinson after the novel's publication:

> I did mean that in some vague way we are the same person, and not separate people. The six characters were supposed to be one. I'm getting old myself – I shall be fifty next year; and I come to feel more and more how difficult it is to collect oneself into one Virginia; even though the special Virginia in whose body I live for the moment is violently susceptible to all sorts of separate feelings. Therefore I wanted to give the sense of continuity, instead of which most people say, no you've given the sense of flowing and passing away and that nothing matters'. (L. iv. 397)

'We are not single', Bernard reiterates in the novel. The six 'characters' – Bernard, Susan, Rhoda, Neville, Jinny, Louis – 'speak' their thoughts and experiences as separate entities, rarely in dialogue, yet the novel's construction brings them together by listening in to them at synchronous moments in their lives and by regrouping them at various stages. Percival, the voiceless figure in the novel, unites them as their object of desire and, in his early death, is, like Jacob, an absent centre around whom presence arranges itself. Bernard is the novel's dominant voice; the creator of stories, he is also the 'chronicler' of these intersecting lives, and the last part of the novel is given over to him, as he re-narrates their histories to a silent and unseen auditor. To an extent, however, each of the six creates the others' lives by incorporating elements of their stories into his or her own.

Woolf traces the six lives from childhood to middle age, but seeks to show continuities rather than developments. In so far as the six voices are differentially marked, they retain the same differences of style and imagery throughout. Susan's corporeal substance, her closeness to the natural world, is confirmed in her motherhood; Jinny expresses herself through her body; Rhoda's psychic fragility is throughout expressed as a 'facelessness'; Bernard expends himself in fictions and in other people's lives; Neville conserves himself for his scholarship and his love of Percival; Louis covers over insecurity by conforming to the rules and pursuing money and power.

In many ways, *The Waves* creates a far more 'solid' fictional world than accounts of its insubstantialized poetic mysticism would suggest. It is significant, for example, that Bernard tells their stories to an acquaintance over a restaurant table; the communication occurs in the public sphere of 'intersubjective' relations, not in the private, inner world of the mind. Yet Woolf was not, she stated, attempting to produce 'characters'. Her concern was rather with the *experience* of identity and with its articulation through a discourse that, for the most part, cannot be named either as speech or as thought. It is striking that, in a novel ostensibly seeking out the forms of 'impersonality', she should have turned to the 'I' of first-person narration. (The 'omniscient' narrator of *The Waves* speaks only, perhaps, in the 'interludes' and in the 'Bernard said', 'Neville said', that mark the divisions between the 'soliloquies'.) Equally striking is that these 'I's' cannot stabilize identities which are as much dispersed as created by language. (See Kate Flint, Introduction to *The Waves* (London: Penguin, 1992), xxxviii.) 'Life is not susceptible perhaps to the treatment we give it when we try to tell it', says Bernard in his 'summation'. The perception is not a new one in Woolf's writing, but *The Waves* was her most radical and uncompromising experiment in a different kind of telling.

As Woolf was writing *The Waves*, she commented acerbically in her letters and diaries on the conservatism of contemporary realist novels, a large number of which she read in manuscript for the Hogarth Press. She gave a great deal of thought at this time to the question of poetry in fiction, and explicitly linked her experiment in *The Waves* with *Jacob's Room*, particularly through their radical revision of 'character' in fiction: 'What I now think (about the Waves) is that I can give in a very few strokes the essentials of a person's character. It should be done boldly, almost as caricature. [...] I think it is possible that I have got my statues against the sky'. (*D*. iii. 300).

Daniel Ferrer notes the link between this declaration and a passage in 'A Sketch of the Past',[12] in which Woolf recalls the ways in which certain people in her childhood 'were very like characters in Dickens. They were caricatures; they were very simple; they were immensely alive. They could be made with three strokes of the pen, if I could do it'. (*MB* 73) The use of 'a very few strokes' may also have been suggested to her by the techniques of animated films: in the Spring of April 1931, Woolf records movie-going in France: 'Laughed violently at animals in hotel. A light risible method – the French – of telling the story of a cycle race – done by quick drawings on a sheet' (*D*. iv. 22). The image of 'statues against the sky' suggests both a monumental, epic form of narration and the child's-eye view of the world which Woolf ascribes to Dickens and which recalls the titanic figures of Mr and Mrs Ramsay in *To the Lighthouse*.

The image is also linked to the concepts of emergence, beginnings, and the dawn of the world and the self that run throughout *The Waves*. The 'beginnings' could be seen as ontogenetic – linked to the history of the individual, as in Woolf's representations of childhood as origin and emergence – and as phylogenetic – linked to the history of humanity. As a number of recent critics have argued, Woolf's 'vision' in the novel intersects with her growing interest in anthropological and scientific theories, including the work of the physicist James Jeans and of the evolutionary thinker Gerald Heard, author of *The Emergence of Man* (1931). Such 'influences' were, however, absorbed into her work in complex, multiple and often oblique, rather than systematic, ways. Woolf recorded in her diary for 18

December 1930, during the final rewriting of *The Waves*, a conversation with 'Lord David [Cecil], Lytton and Clive': 'Talk about the riddle of the universe (Jeans' book) whether it will be known; not by us; found out suddenly: about rhythm in prose' (*D.* iii. 1930). As Michael Whitworth notes, it is 'unclear whether the riddle of cosmology or composition has been "found out suddenly".... Woolf's fluid syntax indicates the ease with which borders could be crossed'.[13]

During the writing of the novel, Woolf had witnessed the solar eclipse of 29 June 1927, travelling to Yorkshire by train with Leonard and with the Nicolsons. The sight and symbolism of the eclipse clearly resonated in very powerful ways for Woolf, and, in the writing of the novel, it partially displaced the image of the moth. She gave very full and vivid accounts of the eclipse both in her diary and in an article, 'The Sun and the Fish', first published in the journal *Time and Tide* (3 Feb. 1928). In both diary and article she wrote of the ways in which the spectators watching as the sun was obscured and the light died were, to quote the diary entry, 'like very old people, in the birth of the world – druids on Stonehenge'. In 'The Sun and the Fish' she added: 'we had put off the little badges and signs of individuality. We were strung out against the sky in outline and had the look of statues standing prominent on the ridge of the world. We were very, very old; we were men and women of the primeval world come to salute the dawn'. (*E.* iv. 521)

In the final section of *The Waves*, Bernard uses the image of the eclipse to describe the starkness of the loss of identity; more specifically, the loss of the 'other' self, 'that self who has been with me in many tremendous adventures': 'Nothing came, nothing. [...] The scene behind me withered. It was like the eclipse when the sun went out and left the earth, flourishing in full summer foliage, withered, brittle, false'. The return of light to the world after the eclipse of the sun then becomes an image of absolute newness:

> So the landscape returned to me; so I saw fields rolling in waves of colour beneath me, but now with this difference; I saw but was not seen. [...] From me had dropped the old cloak, the old response; the hollowed hand that beats back sounds. Thin as a ghost, leaving no trace where I trod, perceiving merely, I walked alone in a new world, never trodden; brushing new flowers, unable to speak save in a child's words of one syllable. (*W.* 220)

In her diary, Woolf wrote of the eclipse: 'We had fallen. It was extinct. There was no colour. The earth was dead.... It was like recovery. We had been much worse than we had expected. We had seen the world dead. Then – it was over till 1999. What remained was a sense of the comfort which we get used to, of plenty of light and colour... Yet when it became established all over the country, one rather missed a sense of its being a relief & a respite, which one had had when it came back after the darkness.' (*D.* iii. 144) Woolf gives to Bernard, on the novel's final page, the perception that 'Dawn is some sort of whitening of the sky; some sort of renewal', a vision she echoed at the close of *The Years*.

In the second draft manuscript of the novel, Bernard articulates these words: 'I perceive that the art of biography is still in its infancy [...] or more properly speaking has yet to be born'. [*TW* 684] Bernard, as the 'chronicler' of lives, is also a biographer, though he questions the very notion of 'stories', and suggests that selfhood is far more complex and elusive than narrative and biographical conventions allow:

> What is my story? What is Rhoda's? What is Neville's? There are facts, as, for example: 'The handsome young man in the grey suit, whose reserve contrasted so strangely with the loquacity of the others, now brushed the crumbs from his waistcoat and, with a characteristic gesture, at once commanding and benign, made a sign to the waiter, who came instantly and returned a moment later with the bill discreetly folded up on a plate'. That is the fact, but beyond it all is darkness and conjecture (*W.* 108).

He has also been, he reveals towards the close of the novel, a biographical subject:

> Once I had a biographer, dead long since, but if he still followed my footsteps with his old flattering intensity he would here say, 'About this time Bernard married and bought a house... His friends observed in him a growing tendency to domesticity...The birth of children made it highly desirable that he should augment his income.' That is the biographic style, and it does to tack together torn bits of stuff, stuff with raw edges. (*W.* 199)

Woolf closely links the formulaic aspects of biography, its ways of organizing the narrative of a life, to the force of habit in the living of a life. As Bernard asserts, 'I became, I mean, a certain kind of man, scoring my path across life as one treads a path across the field (*W.* 200). He, like his creator, thus becomes absorbed, even beset, by the problems of biography.

The perception of the deadness and yet the necessity of biographical 'fact' observed by Bernard is also at the heart of Woolf's two major essays on biography, 'The New Biography' (1927) and 'The Art of Biography' (1939), the latter a discussion of Lytton Strachey's biographical works. In the first of these two essays, Woolf suggests that the 'problem of biography' lies in the difficulty of welding together 'truth' and 'personality', 'granite' and 'rainbow', and in both 'The New Biography' (a review-essay of Harold Nicolson's *Some People*) and 'The Art of Biography' (written more than a decade later), she focused on the tension between the use of fact and fiction in biographical writing. While she praised modern biography's creativity in combining fact and fiction, she also expressed doubts about combining historical fact and artistic invention: 'Let it be fact, one feels, or let it be fiction; the imagination will not serve under two masters simultaneously' (*E.* iv. 478) Yet she also suggested that the balance between fact and fiction has shifted in the modern age: 'it would seem that the life which is increasingly real to us is the fictitious life; it dwells in the personality rather than the act'. (*E.* iv. 478). In this account, biography becomes at one and the same time the representative modern genre and profoundly shaped by novelistic practice.

While Woolf was fully attentive to the new developments in biography, she retained some distance from the fictionalizing mode of new biographical texts, preferring to experiment with the biographical sketch or essay and the 'mock-biography'. Despite the fantastical aspects of both *Orlando* and *Flush*, Woolf upheld both the productivity of 'facts' in biographical writing and their appeal for her, with the understanding that 'facts' are not fixed entities but responsive to historical and cultural change and interpretation. She wrote in her diary on completing *The Waves* and beginning *Flush*, her 'biography' of Elizabeth Barrett Browning's dog: 'It is a good idea I think to write biographies; to make them use my powers of representation reality accuracy; & to use my novels simply to express the general, the poetic. Flush is serving this purpose' (*D.* iv. 40). She thus positions *Flush* on the side of biography rather than fiction.

Describing the inception of *Flush* in a letter to Lady Ottoline Morell (*L.* v. 162), she stated: 'I was so tired after the Waves, that I lay in the garden and read the Browning love letters, and the figure of their dog made me laugh so I couldn't resist making him a Life'. She expanded on this to another correspondent (the American businessman Frederick Adams, who had made an offer, not finally accepted, for the manuscript of *Flush*):

> I am very glad to think that you share my sympathy for Flush. The idea came to me that he deserved a biography last summer when I was reading the Browning letters. But in fact very little is known about him, and I have had to invent a good deal. I hope however that I have thrown some light upon his character. – the more I know him, the more affection I feel for him. The dog who acted his part here was black – but there can be no doubt that Flush was red. (*L.* v. 167)

'The Browning letters', the love letters of Elizabeth Barrett and Robert Browning, on which Woolf drew extensively in the writing of *Flush*, were also the basis for the extremely successful play *The Barretts of Wimpole Street*, written by Rudolf Besier and staged in London in the autumn of 1930, where Leonard and Virginia Woolf went to see it early in its run. The play was controversial, as Besier hinted at incestuous desires underlying Edward Barrett's tyrannical treatment of his invalid daughter. As Alison Light notes in her introduction to *Flush*, a number of critical responses to the play focused on 'the ethics of biography'. (*F.* xvii). Besier's drama became linked to the 'new biography' with which Lytton Strachey was so closely asso-ciated, from his 'debunking' of Victorian heroes in *Eminent Victorians* to his constructions of the interior worlds of monarchs in *Queen Victoria* and *Elizabeth and Essex*, with a strongly 'Freudian' cast to the latter which placed it in the new genre of 'psychobiography'.

Stracheyan biography was very much in Woolf's mind as she wrote *Flush*. In a draft version she parodied the virtuosic ending of Lytton Strachey's *Queen Victoria*, in which he undoes 'the life' by having the dying queen remember her experiences in reverse chronology, and something of this remains in the glimpses of past events and experiences that return to Flush at junctures throughout the text. She wrote to David Garnett: 'Yes, the last paragraph as originally written was simply Queen Victoria dying all over again – Flush remembered his entire past in Lyttons best manner; but I cut it out, when he was not there to see the joke'. (*L.* v. 232). The satire Woolf directs against Victorian heroes such as Thomas Carlyle, framed in a discussion of the motives for Carlyle's dog Nero's apparent suicide attempt in throwing himself from a top storey window – 'Some hold [...] that Nero was driven to desperate melancholy by associating with Mr Carlyle' (F. 97) – also has the ring of the coinage exchanged between Woolf and Strachey. Strachey's death in January 1932, Woolf suggested on a number of occasions, detracted from her pleasure in *Flush*; as she wrote to John Lehmann, 'I feel the point is rather gone, as I meant it for a joke with Lytton, and a skit on him' (*L.* v. 83). She disparaged the book to herself and to others, and framed its popular success in financial terms: 'We should net £2,000 from that dogged and dreary grind' (*D.* iv. 176). Yet *Flush* should not be seen as an aberration or 'freak' (as she termed it) in her *oeuvre*. There are strong connections between *Flush* and her other works: the vivid depictions of the London scene; representations of the Victorian home and its constraints on women's freedom (chiming strongly with *The Years*, *A Room of One's Own* and *Three Guineas*); the self-conscious and self-reflexive evocation of the biographical 'pursuit' so central to *Jacob's Room* and *Orlando*.

Vita Sackville-West, the 'subject' of *Orlando*, also played a part in the creation of *Flush*; she owned and bred spaniels, including Leonard and Virginia Woolf's dog Pinker (or Pinka), a 'model' for Flush. Vita's own 'breeding' and pedigree are ironically echoed in *Flush*, which opens with an account of spaniel genealogy – 'It is universally admitted that the family from which the subject of this memoir claims descent is one of the greatest antiquity' (F. 5) – and traces it back to Spain, the birthplace of Vita Sackville-West's grandmother Pepita. *Flush* is shot through with evocations of the canine caste system and the English obsession with breeding and the purity of types. On reaching Italy with the Brownings, Flush is amazed to discover that 'though dogs abounded, there were no ranks'. While Flush the 'snob' initially demands the deference owing to his pedigree, the text explores the value of hybridity, and Flush's 'education' in Italy comes to render him 'daily more and more democratic'. Woolf was of course writing of the Italy of the 1830s and 1840s, bound into the struggle for liberty and Italian unification, at a time – the early 1930s – when Italian Fascism under Mussolini had taken hold. As Anna Snaith has argued, *Flush*, with its attacks on tyranny at home, which *Three Guineas* will come to represent as the Hitlerism of the domestic sphere, and its celebration of 'racial' impurity, albeit translated into the canine world, should be seen in the context of Woolf's anti-

Fascist writings of the 1930s.[14]

Orlando, as we have seen, celebrates the complexities of sexual identity. In *Flush* this representation of the 'mixing' of the sexes is transmuted into the blurring of boundaries between animal and human. In selecting Flush the dog as the biographical viewpoint from which the Barrett-Browning romance is perceived (and thus sidestepping Elizabeth Barrett Browning's maid Lily Wilson as a possible centre of consciousness and perception, though a lengthy footnote to *Flush* suggests how her biography might have been written, and anticipates the representation of the servant Crosby in *The Years* (F. 94-6)), Woolf opened up some curious questions of species-being, of anthropomorphism and the projection of human qualities onto animals, and of likeness and difference.

If the dominant trope of *Orlando* is simile, that of *Flush* is chiasmus, the repetition of a phrase in inverted order, and it is most often used in the context of the relationship between Elizabeth Barrett and Flush. The 'pairing' between them first occurs in the represented thoughts of Flush's first owner Mary Russell Mitford (the writer friend of Elizabeth Barrett's on whom Woolf had written a number of essays in the 1920s) - 'Yes; Flush was worthy of Miss Barrett; Miss Barrett was worthy of Flush' (F. 13) – and the chiasmic structure of this sentence resonates with the text's repeated use of mirror images (also central to *Orlando*). It is, however, one of the few fully achieved chiasmus in the text; in most of the later uses of the trope, the inversion will not be an absolute mirroring, but will also incorporate repetition as difference.

On first entering Miss Barrett's room, Flush is surprised by his own reflection: 'Suddenly Flush saw staring back at him from a hole in the wall another dog with bright eyes flashing, and tongue lolling! He paused amazed. He advanced in awe'. (F. 17). His estrangement from self as well from the life he knows (Miss Mitford leaves him with Elizabeth Barrett in Wimpole Street) is resolved not through a recognition of his own image in the looking-glass, at this juncture at least, but through the mirroring of woman and dog:

'Oh, Flush!' said Miss Barrett. For the first time she looked him in the face. For the first time Flush looked at the lady lying on the sofa.

Each was surprised. Heavy curls hung down on either side of Miss Barrett's face; large bright eyes shone out; a large mouth smiled. Heavy ears hung down on either side of Flush's face; his eyes, too, were large and bright: his mouth was wide. There was a likeness between them. As they gazed at each other each felt: Here am I – and then each felt: But how different. [...] Between them lay the widest gulf that can separate one being from another. She spoke. He was dumb. She was woman; he was dog. Thus closely united, thus immensely divided, they gazed at each other. Then with one bound Flush sprang on to the sofa and laid himself where he was to lie for ever after – on the rug at Miss Barrett's feet. (*F.* 18-19).

'His flesh was veined with human passions', Woolf writes of Flush. Flush's training or formation, which includes a conversion scene with comic echoes of spiritual autobiography, is an education not only in constraint and 'suppression', but also in the complexity of emotions and feelings. The introduction of Robert Browning into Elizabeth Barrett's life is a major crisis in Flush's existence; he attacks Browning, is spurned by his mistress, and reciprocity fails: 'But though Flush might look, Miss Barrett refused even to meet his eyes. There she lay on the sofa; there Flush lay on the floor'. It is restored, in the perfection of the chiasmus, when Flush learns that 'love is hatred and hatred is love':

Things are not simple but complex. If he bit Mr Browning he bit her [Elizabeth Barrett] too. Hatred is not hatred; hatred is also love. Here Flush shook his ears in an agony of perplexity. He turned uneasily on the floor. Mr Browning was Miss Barrett – Miss Barrett was Mr Browning; love is hatred and hatred is love' (*F.* 44).

From this point on, Robert Browning and Flush are united in their hatred of Mr Barrett and of 'black and beetled tyranny'. But oppression and tyranny have their own complexities, and Robert Browning is revealed to be collusive with patriarchal law, which is upheld at the expense of both women and dogs. When Flush is stolen by the dog-thieves of Whitechapel, Elizabeth Barrett's father, brother, and lover are united in their refusal to rescue him by paying a ransom, even though Robert Browning pitches his protest against 'the execrable policy of the world's husbands, fathers, brothers and domineers in general' (*F.* 56). Miss Barrett finds that:

It was almost as difficult for her to go to Flush as for Flush to come to her. All Wimpole Street was against her. [...] Wimpole Street was determined to make a stand against Whitechapel. [...] Her father and her brother were in league against her and were capable of any treachery in the interests of their class. But worst of all – far worse –

Mr Browning himself threw all his weight, all his eloquence, all his learning, all his logic, on the side of Wimpole Street and against Flush. If Miss Barrett gave way to Taylor, he wrote, she was giving way to tyranny; she was giving way to blackmailers; she was increasing the power of evil over right, of wickedness over innocence. [...] So, if she went to Whitechapel she was siding against Robert Browning, and in favour of fathers, brothers and domineerers in general. Still, she went on dressing. (F. 55-6)

While the romance of Elizabeth Barrett and Robert Browning has Wimpole Street pitted against the lovers, *Flush* shows 'the forces of Wimpole Street...battling to keep Flush and Miss Barrett apart'. Their reunion is followed closely, in narrative terms, by the secret marriage of Miss Barrett and Mr Browning, and their departure, with Flush and Lily Simpson, for Italy. The kidnapping of Flush (which reveals the strength of Elizabeth Barrett's commitment to her dog) thus appears to be the catalyst for the rebellion against Wimpole Street, the rejection of London and the embrace of Italy.

The 'Whitechapel' episode of the text is the one for which Woolf had least evidence from the Barrett-Browning sources. She drew on Thomas Beames' *The Rookeries of London* of 1850 for her representation of the slums to which Flush was taken. Her description does fall back on a late nineteenth-century language of degeneration and human animality and brutality, which is at odds with the text's exploration, in its other sections, of the relative nature of the values conventionally attached to the human and the animal. In the 'Whitechapel' chapter Woolf also seems to incorporate some of the distaste for the working-class poor which Barrett Browning had articulated in her novel-poem *Aurora Leigh*, though a footnote in *Flush* does suggest some satire in Woolf's representation. 'The description of a London slum' in *Aurora Leigh*, she writes, although vividly realized, 'suffers from distortion natural to an artist who sees the object only once from a four-wheeler, with Wilson tugging at her skirts' (F. 94).

In keeping Flush's experiences to the fore, Woolf retains, as Light notes, a somewhat ironic distance from Elizabeth Barrett, who was always to play a central role in Woolf's lexicon, often as the focus for her ambivalence towards the Victorians and the Victorian woman writer in particular. Woolf's essay 'Aurora Leigh' (written in 1931, soon after she saw Besier's play and read Barrett Browning's poem 'with great interest for the first time' (L. iv. 301)) explored the disjuncture between the public fascination with Elizabeth Barrett Browning's life and the near-total neglect of her writing in the decades after her death:

> 'Lady Geraldine's Courtship' is glanced at perhaps by two professors in American universities once a year; but we all know how Miss Barrett lay on her sofa; how she escaped from the dark house in Wimpole Street on September morning; how she met health and happiness, freedom and Robert Browning in the church round the corner. (WW 133-4)

'What damage the art of photography has inflicted upon the art of literature has yet to be reckoned', Woolf writes, a point on which she touched in 'The Art of Biography' (1939), in which she linked biographical writing to the modern fascination with personalities: 'we live in an age in which a thousand cameras are pointed, by newspapers, letters and diaries, at every character from every angle'. (CDML 149-50). Woolf's essay on Barrett Browning is a clear-sighted evaluation of her novel-poem *Aurora Leigh*: she celebrates Barrett Browning's experimentalism in using poetic form to create a narrative of 'modern life', a play with generic expectations which resonates, though to very different ends, with Woolf's creation of the poetic novel in *The Waves*. *Flush*, however, repeats the biographical gesture of focusing on Barrett Browning's life rather than her work, but does so by deploying as a biographical filter a subject unable to read the poet's text. The effective word-blindness of biographers, their disregard for the writing of a writer, is thus taken to a parodic extreme in Woolf's representation of the Barrett-Browning romance through a consciousness – that of a dog - radically other to the written word.

Yet Woolf was also genuinely absorbed by the nature of the dog's consciousness. Her nephew Quentin Bell, in his biography of Woolf, sees *Flush* as a 'work of self-revelation'. Noting the ways in which Woolf, in all her relationships, pictured herself as an animal, creating an imaginary menagerie of those to whom she was closest, he suggests that '*Flush* is not so much a book by a dog lover as a book by someone who would love to be a dog'. (QB 175). The dog's world is realized most vividly in Woolf's representation of a sensorium governed by smell rather than sight: on first arriving in Wimpole Street:

> Flush [...] was more astonished by what he smelt than by what he saw. Up the funnel of the staircase came warm whiffs of joints roasting, of fowls basting, of soups simmering – ravishing almost as

food itself to nostrils used to the meagre savour of Kerenhappock's penurious fries and hashes. Mixing with the smell of food were further smells – smells of cedarwood and sandalwood and mahogany; scents of male bodies and female bodies; of men servants and maid servants; of coats and trousers; of crinolines and mantles; of curtains of tapestry, of curtains of plush; of coal dust and fog; of wine and cigars. Each room as he passed it – dining-room, drawing-room, library, bedroom – wafted out its own contribution to the general stew; while, as he set down first one paw and then another, each was caressed and retained by the sensuality of rich pile carpets closing amorously over it. (*F.* 16).

Flush's world is thus differently differentiated, while Woolf evokes a history in which bodies and bodily experience are central – and the passage above both genders bodies and sexualizes bodily experience - during a period, paradoxically, in which 'polite' bodies were kept most firmly under wraps. *Orlando*, too, places the body at the heart of biography; experience is, before all else, corporeal, and bodies are shaped by their historical circumstances. *Orlando* traces the living body through centuries of experience; *Flush* opens up the sensory particularities of the nineteenth century. Its close is where *The Years* will begin.

7

Fact and Fiction: *The Years* and *Three Guineas*

The Years, the writing of which Woolf was later to describe as 'like a long childbirth' (*D.* v. 31), was 'conceived' in 1931:

> I have this moment, while having my bath, conceived an entire new book – a sequel to a Room of One's Own – about the sexual life of women: to be called Professions for Women perhaps – Lord how exciting! This sprang out of my paper to be read on Wednesday to Pippa's society. Now for The Waves. Thank God – but I'm very much excited. (*D.* iv. 6)

The history of *The Years* is a complex one. In brief, Woolf's original plan was for a 'Novel-Essay', a 'novel of fact', in which essays would be interspersed with extracts from 'a [non-existent] novel that will run into many volumes': 'Its to be an Essay-Novel, called the Pargiters – & its to take in everything, sex, education, life &c; & come, with the most powerful and agile leaps, like a chamois across precipices from 1880 to here & now' (*D.* iv. 129). 'We must become the people that we were two or three generations ago. Let us be our great grandmothers,' she wrote in the first essay of *The Pargiters*, explaining that her use of the fictional extracts was to be an aid to this process for those unused to 'being somebody else'. The past provides 'that perspective which is so important for the understanding of the present' (*P.* 9).

In early 1933 Woolf decided not to have separate 'inter-chapters' (the essays), instead 'compacting them in the text' (*D.* iv. 146). Other elements were later used in *Three Guineas*, her polemical 'anti-fascist' essay on women's resistance to war. Woolf wrote the novel at speed and with relative ease, but its revising caused her years of difficulty and almost stopped her writing completely. *The Years* was finally published in 1937: *Three Guineas* appeared in 1938.

The earliest version of *The Years* was published as *The Pargiters* in 1977, revealing a great deal not only about its genesis but about Woolf's conceptions of the relationship between fiction, history, and politics in the 1930s. At times the essayistic discussions of the novel-extracts come close to being a commentary on the craft of fiction, as if the effort of 'giv[ing] ordinary waking Arnold Bennett life the form of art' (*D.* iv. 161) had brought back the fierceness of those early debates over 'art' and 'life'. Bennett had died in 1931, and Woolf clearly mourned him as a sparring-partner: 'a shop keeper's view of literature; yet with the rudiments, covered over with fat & prosperity & the desire for hideous Empire furniture, of sensibility.< . . .>he abused me; & yet I rather wished him to go on abusing me; & me abusing him' (*D.* iv. 16).

The terms of the debate between 'art' and 'life' have, however, shifted. Woolf appears to reoccupy the house of literary naturalism in the novel in all its versions. In *The Years* she shows how the Victorian home confined its occupants and how the course of history and the changes in ways of living could be charted through its dispersals and 'conversions' into flats, rooms, lodgings. She delineates the history of 'things', of 'solid objects'. Facts and details are embraced not eschewed. Woolf herself saw in *The Years* something of her second novel *Night and Day*, although one significant difference between the two is that the time-span of the later novel allowed for the exploration of patterns constructed over the years, repetitions and alterations, the laying-down of traces, of what survives.

The draft material of *The Pargiters* reveals what a radical and, in many ways, unworkable project Woolf had initially envisaged. *The Pargiters* directly addresses the crippling restrictions for women in the middle-class home, their exclusion from the seats of educational and professional prestige and power, and the structures of patriarchy in both private and public life. While men may appear to gain from these inequalities, their lives are also stunted by them.

Woolf's powerful analyses did not bend easily, however, to the exigencies of narrative and plot. Five novel chapters and six essays on, Woolf is still in 1880, whereas her original plan had been to move her readers into the projected future and to end in the year 2032. The writing and rewriting of the final sections also reveals some of Woolf's difficulties in negotiating the relation-ship between 'fact' and 'fiction'. Kitty Malone, a cousin of the Pargiters, visits the Oxford home of a fellow-pupil; the father is a self-educated working-class man, based on the dialect-scholar Dr Joseph Wright whom Woolf greatly admired and whose biography she had recently read. Woolf's writing falters as she tries to present the family from Kitty's point of view; in turning the biographical romance of Wright's life into 'fiction' she makes both 'fact' and 'fiction' unreal.

The dichotomy between 'fact' and 'fiction', upheld by Woolf throughout her writing career, became a particularly acute concern during the writing of *The Years*. 'Oh & I shall write a poets book next,' she wrote during its early stages. 'This one, however, releases such a torrent of fact as I did not know I had in me' (*D*. iv. 133). As the novel proceeded, Woolf speaks in her diaries of including 'facts, as well as the vision. And to combine them both' (*D*. iv. 151). When the book that was to become *Three Guineas* began to shape itself in her mind, the fact/fiction polarity is again reasserted, with the novel being placed firmly in the category of 'fiction' and the polemical work in that of 'fact': 'Now again I pay the penalty of mixing fact & fiction: cant concentrate on The Years. I have a sense that one cannot control this terrible fluctuation between the 2 worlds' (*D*. iv. 350). In short, the contrast was of central importance for Woolf, but the terms and the relationship between them are unstable and shifting.

'The relationship between fiction and history is more complex than anyone will ever say,' Paul Ricoeur writes.[1] In Woolf's work of the 1930s we find an intense questioning, as Patricia Laurence notes, of the distinctions between fact and fiction, history and literature, 'high' and 'low' art.[2] Woolf was becoming increas-ingly aware of the need to incorporate into her writing, and at times to resist, the linguistic and representational forms of the new media – journalism, radio, photography. *Three Guineas* names its origin as the imperious need to respond to a series of war photographs, to whose brute 'factuality' the text repeatedly and insistently returns. Thus to Woolf's experiments with genre, her 'new names for the novel' (with which this study has been particularly concerned), we must add her increasingly urgent and complex sense of the relationships between fiction and history and fiction and the emergent media, for which the fact/fiction dichotomy may well have acted not only as a convenient shorthand but as a strategy of containment.

In exploring the difficulties Woolf encountered in the writing of *The Pargiters/The Years* we need to begin, however, with another critical issue. 'Repression' played a key role in the novel in all its stages. *The Pargiters* thematized what *The Years* enacts – that which cannot be said. The starting-point for *The Pargiters* was a speech which Woolf gave to the National Society for Women's Service on 21 January 1931; it was published in shortened form as 'Professions for Women'. In the speech and the essay, Woolf discussed the struggles of the woman writer for freedom of expression. 'The Angel in the House', the spirit of Victorian womanhood, who demands of the woman writer that she flatter and cajole her male readers and, above all, that she 'be pure', has to be destroyed: 'If I had not killed her, she would have killed me – as a writer' (*P.* p. xxxi). The second obstacle cannot yet be removed: the woman writer's imagination 'has rushed away; it has taken to the depths; it has sunk – heaven knows where – into what dark pool of extraordinary experience. The reason has to cry "Stop!"' (*P.* p. xxxvii).

> Calm yourself, I say, as she [the imagination] sits panting on the bank – panting with rage and disappointment. We have only got to wait fifty years or so. In fifty years I shall be able to use all this very queer knowledge that you are trying to bring me. But not now. You see I go on, trying to calm her, I cannot make use of what you tell me – about womens bodies for instance – their passions – and so on, because the conventions are still very strong. If I were to overcome the conventions I should need the courage of a hero, and I am not a hero. (*P.* p. xxxviii–xxxix)

In the speech, Woolf makes a plea for a feminist gradualism; women must wait for a further fifty years (roughly the time-span of *The Years*) 'until men have become so civilised that they are not shocked when a woman speaks the truth about her body'. Upon the extent of men's tolerance of women's free speech depends not only 'the future of fiction' (*P.* p. xl) but of woman herself: 'I mean, what is a woman? I assure you, I dont know; I do not believe that you know; I do not believe that anybody can know until she has expressed herself in all the arts and professions open to human skill' (*P.* p. xxxiii). Woolf was attempting, it would seem, to write the novel that could not yet be written. It is striking that the question of women's relationship to art and writing is more or less written out of the final version of *The Years*.

The Pargiters makes explicit not only the effects of censorship and repression but its mechanisms. The Pargiter daughters, denied education and the freedom to move around the city in which they live – 'Eleanor and Milly and Delia could not possibly go for a walk alone – save in the streets around Abercorn Terrace' (*P*. 36-7) – exist in profound sexual and emotional bad faith, either unaware of their desires or forced to conceal them from themselves and each other. Their freedom is entirely circumscribed by the existence of a sexuality – 'street love, common love, love in general' – which they are forbidden to experience or even to recognize. Sex and sexuality are at one and the same time everywhere and nowhere in their lives. The Pargiter girls look out of the drawing-room window – the only vantage point available to them – at a young man and are told 'Don't be caught looking':

> They wanted to look at the young man; they knew it was wrong to look; they did look; they were caught looking; they disliked being caught; they were ashamed, indignant, confused – all in one – and the feeling, since it was never exposed, save by a blush, or a giggle, wriggled deep down into their minds, and sometimes woke them in the middle of the night with curious sensations, unpleasant dreams'. (*P*. 38)

Woolf illustrates this essay with a scene which survived into *The Years*. Rose, at 10 years the youngest of the Pargiters, makes a forbidden journey after dusk to a nearby shop:

> When she reached the pillar box there was the man again. He was leaning against it, as if he were ill, Rose thought, filled with the same terror again; [but] he was lit up by the lamp. There was nobody else anywhere in sight. As she ran past him, he gibbered some nonsense at her, sucking his lips in & out; & began to undo his clothes ... (*P*. 43)[3]

Woolf seems both to suggest that male sexuality does endanger women and that the damage is done through the concealment of such experiences. Where, she asks, does the shame and guilt derive from, a question she also posed in her autobiographical essay 'A Sketch of the Past' when describing her own experience of childhood sexual abuse at the hands of her half-brother. The whole realm of sexuality is shrouded in obscurity; the only clear message is that relationships between men and women were, and perhaps remain, dangerously distorted.

Just as Rose must conceal what she has seen, so the novelist cannot speak openly about such experiences: 'there is, as the three dots used after the sentence, "He unbuttoned his clothes ..." testify, a convention, supported by law, which forbids, whether rightly or wrongly, any plain description of the sight that Rose, in common with many other little girls, saw under the lamp post by the pillar box in the dusk of that March evening' (*P*. 51). The 'three dots', the ellipsis, are used throughout Woolf's writing as a way of marking the space of what cannot be said or, as at the close of *Orlando*, of refusing the narrative the finality of the full stop. In the passage above, Woolf 'exposes' the device of concealment, of covering over; a 'plain description' cannot yet be given, but she will not disguise the censorship, and indeed draws attention to it.

The Pargiters strains in the articulation of what, it is claimed, cannot yet be written. The extreme difficulties Woolf experienced in the later stages of the working of the novel, however, derived not from its writing but from its rewriting. In her diary entries she refers repeatedly to the need to compress and compact, to 'breaking up, the use of thought skipping, & parentheses' (*D*. iv. 203); she finally cut out, in Leonard Woolf's words, 'two enormous chunks'.[4] The original 'interchapters' take on a radically transmuted form as 'interludes', 'spaces of silence and poetry and contrast' (*D*. iv. 332), comparable to those in *The Waves*. The revisions entailed extensive cutting and ellipsis, a process which was in part a 'poetic' condensation but also formed a kind of censorship or repression of the naturalist detail of the earlier drafts, as if Woolf was playing out in her own novelistic practice the processes of 'full' articulation followed by erasure.

In *Three Guineas* Woolf seems to suggest that fiction itself is a form of repression or, at least, evasion. She is analysing the deep-seated, 'subliminal' motives underlying men's exclusion of women from public life and the suppressed, and sexually charged, male violence and anxiety that accompany this debate. Women, when confronted with such a rise in 'the emotional temperature', will find that:

> Intellectually, there is a strong desire either to be silent; or to change the conversation; to drag in, for example, some old family servant, called Crosby, perhaps, whose dog Rover has died ... and so evade the issue and lower the temperature.

But what analysis can we attempt of the emotions on the other side of the table – your side? often, to be candid, while we are talking about Crosby, we are asking questions – hence a certain flatness in the dialogue – about you. What are the powerful and subconscious motives that are raising the hackles on your side of the table? (*TG* 257)

Here, as elsewhere in *Three Guineas*, Woolf turns the tables so that it is men who are subject to irrational, 'primitive' urges and sensations while women analyse the other sex with their rational intellects.

The oddness of the passage stems, however, from the reference to *The Years*; Crosby is the Pargiters' long-serving maid, 'let go' in 1913, on the eve of the First World War, when the family house is vacated. Taking with her hoarded 'odds and ends' from the house, including the 'solid object', a 'walrus-brush', by which the relationship between time and entities is measured throughout the novel, she attempts to recreate Abercorn Terrace in her new room and thus to cover over the chasm created by change and loss. She also takes Rover, the family's old dog, with her; it dies a few days later. Crosby continues to do Martin Pargiter's laundry; he is embarrassed by her emotion at the dog's death, and made uncomfortable by the effort of 'talking to servants': 'Either one simpers, or one's hearty, he was thinking. In either case it's a lie' (*Y.* 179). The thought of this lie reminds him of all the other lies that are told; his father's concealment of his mistress, his own concealment of his private life: 'It was an abominable system, he thought; family life; Abercorn Terrace. No wonder the house would not let. It had one bathroom and a basement; and there all those different people had lived, boxed up together, telling lies' (*Y.* 180). Unlike his sister Eleanor, he does not think to consider the difference between the upper rooms in which the family lived and the dark basement in which Crosby spent her years.

Telling stories about servants and their dogs, *Three Guineas* seems to suggest, was a way of diffusing male anger and at the same time of asking 'undercover' questions about men's motives in denying to women the rights they themselves enjoy. Covering up – 'repression' of a sort – can be both an evasion and a political strategy. The underlying debate is the one most central to writers in the 1930s – that of the relationship between art and politics, and of the writer's responsibilities in the face of political exigencies. It is unsurprising that women writers have adopted a policy of indirection; at the same time, such a strategy could be a more effective way of obtaining answers than direct confrontation. From a different perspective, it may also be that Woolf wished to emphasize the absence of fictionality in *Three Guineas*, its hold on 'fact' and 'truth', by marking its difference from its twin-text *The Years*.

The Years is, of course, a thoroughly political novel in its analysis of the institutions of power – the universities, the Bar, the Army – and that masculine 'procession', described with such devastating satire in *Three Guineas*, in which the male members of the Pargiter family join while the women watch from the sidelines. Women's social and economic positions are far less secure than men's; Sara and Maggie Pargiter move from affluence to relative poverty, without narrative explanation, when their parents die suddenly. Kitty, now Lady Lasswade, is entirely at peace on the Yorkshire estate she has 'married into', but the enduring nature of the land and its ancient buildings is counterposed with her knowledge of the transient nature of her own relationship to it: 'Nothing of this belonged to her; her son would inherit; his wife would walk here after her' (*Y.* 224). In one sense, this gives her freedom, allowing her to see the land 'existing by itself, for itself', but Woolf reminds us that history and our sense of what endures is not separable from property relations and women's marginal place within them.

As in 'Professions for Women', change is also in part measured by the extent to which women have access to professional life; Peggy, a third-generation Pargiter, is a doctor, and it is her perspective that governs much of the lengthy final section of the novel. Yet Woolf is not pointing in any simple sense to 'progress'; the distinctions she draws between women tend to be based far more on their status as 'insiders' or 'outsiders' than on generation. Marriage and family are, with rare exceptions, seen as diminishing for women, taming or deadening their youthful aspirations and passions. Woolf is most interested in the perspectives of her 'odd women' – Eleanor Pargiter, her cousin Sara, whose quirky, poetic, angry view of the world is the counter-voice to the novel's surface realism, and her great-niece Peggy.

Despite the radical changes from first to final versions, Woolf did retain the use of 'a curious uneven time sequence – a series of great balloons, linked by straight narrow passages of narrative' (*D.* iv. 142). The novel 'leaps' across the years between

1880 and the present of the 1930s, in an irregular, stuttering movement that breaks up the smooth flow of passing time and generation: the sections are titled 1880, 1891, 1908, 1910, 1911, 1913, 1914, 1917, 1918, Present Day. There is thus a temporal clustering round the years of the First World War. *To the Lighthouse* jumps over the 'chasm' of the war years; *Orlando* glides effortlessly through them. *The Years* is the only one of Woolf's novels in which characters are shown living through the war, though its narrative representation is limited to one night in London in 1917. In 1914, a few months before the outbreak of war, Kitty Lasswade holds a dinner party in which her guests, searching for topics, discuss racing, the Russian ballet, and the Ireland of the 1880s. In 1917, the now middle-aged Eleanor Pargiter dines with her cousins Maggie and Sara, Maggie's husband Renny, and his friend Nicholas. As the Zeppelins drop bombs overhead, the group continue their dinner in the cellar. The light oddly illuminates them; two 'odd women' (the unmarried Eleanor and Sara), the Frenchman Renny, and the Polish homosexual Nicholas. War is represented here through the experience of 'outsiders', a theme at the centre of *Three Guineas*. Woolf elected not to 'bring in the Front', as she wrote to Stephen Spender soon after the novel's publication, not only because 'fighting isn't within my experience, as a woman', but because 'I think action generally unreal. Its the thing we do in the dark that is more real; the thing we do because peoples eyes are on us seems to me histrionic small boyish' (*L.* vi. 122). Increasingly Woolf came to despise 'publicity' and to espouse a 'philosophy of anonymity'.

The dinner in the cellar is one of many meals in the novel. The Pargiter girls' lives, like that of Katherine Hilbery, are circumscribed by the tea table; subsequent meals connote changed and differential social and gender relations. As in *A Room of One's Own*, women tend to be less well fed than men; the 'admirable mutton' eaten by Sara and her cousin Martin in a City chop-house in 1914 is an everyday occurrence for him but a rare or, rather, a well-done treat for her. Twenty or so years later, Sara serves her cousin North, Peggy's brother, with a tough and underdone leg of mutton, oozing 'red juice', in her shabby lodging house.

The Years also explores what Woolf elsewhere called the 'party consciousness', an eddying of individual and group conscious-nesses. Sara and North's dinner is the prelude to the family gathering which takes up most of the 'Present Day' section of the novel; at the other side of London Eleanor and Peggy are also dining together. We are shown North in the act of driving from Eleanor's to Sara's. When he arrives, Sara is talking on the telephone to Nicholas, whom North has just met, and their conversation is later interrupted by Eleanor's phone call. The omniscient narrator of the 'realist novel' tends to move across time and space without commenting on the transitions; Woolf, by contrast, points up the mechanisms of narrative connection by depicting her characters travelling across the spaces between 'scenes' and by using the telephone, one of the instruments of 'modernity', to make the links, and break down the distinctions, between one location or consciousness and another.

The phone transmits the voice; the visual image of the person must be constructed. This division of the individual into its verbal and visual aspects is a further aspect of the self-in-pieces represented in *Orlando*. For North, who has been away in Africa for some years, Sara 'came back in sections; first the voice; then the attitude; but something remained unknown':

'And you – ' she said, looking at him. It was as if she were trying to put two different versions of him together; the one on the telephone perhaps and the one on the chair. Or was there some other? This half knowing people, this half being known, this feeling of the eye on the flesh, like a fly crawling – how uncomfortable it was, he thought; but inevitable, after all these years.   (Y. 251)

Looking and being looked at, knowing and being known, subject and object, self and other, lose their distinctiveness; the fly's putative sensation in 'crawling over a face, and feeling, here's the nose, here's the brow' (a mapping through touch rather than vision) is not separable from that of the owner of the face crawled over. The passage quoted above echoes the 'making up' of Jacob in *Jacob's Room* out of hints and fragments, in a radical undermining of the concept of a fixed and unified identity which is also central to the final part of *The Years*. Guests at the party play Consequences, in which a figure is literally drawn in sections: 'Each of them had drawn a different part of a picture. On top there was a woman's head like Queen Alexandra with a fuzz of little curls; then a bird's neck; the body of a tiger; and stout elephant's legs dressed in child's drawers completed the picture' (Y. 313).

Throughout the 'Present Day' section of the novel Woolf

159

points up the strength of the desire to 'fix' character and its ultimate failure. Peggy seeks security in constructing an image of Eleanor and her past: 'It was so interesting; so safe; so unreal – that past of the 'eighties' (Y. 267). Eleanor, in fact, does not wish to return to the history that we have watched her live through 'in sections'; 'I want the present', she thinks (Y. 270). Peggy, attempting to construct the fixed image of Eleanor as a Victorian spinster which 'composed itself in [her] mind as she would tell it to the man in the hospital' (narration can be anticipatory as well as retrospective), finally admits defeat:

> She shook her head. I'm no use at describing people, she said to her friend at the hospital. They're too difficult ... She's not like that – not like that at all, she said, making a little dash with her hand as if to rub out an outline which she had drawn wrongly. As she did so, her friend at the hospital vanished.
> She was alone with Eleanor in the cab. And they were passing houses. Where does she begin, and where do I end? she thought ... On they drove. They were two living people, driving across London; two sparks of life enclosed in two separate bodies; and those sparks of life enclosed in two separate bodies are at this moment, she thought, driving past a picture palace. But what is this moment; and what are we? The puzzle was too difficult for her to solve it. She sighed. (Y. 269)

The relationship between 'I' and 'we' enacted here is a crucial one for Woolf, repeatedly played out in this final section of *The Years*. In the following passage, Eleanor, asked to think about 'her life', is visited by 'atoms' of the past, the phrase echoing 'the incessant shower of innumerable atoms' of 'Modern Fiction'. (The diagram she draws recalls not only the 'radial' structures of consciousness Woolf discussed with Jacques Raverat but the 'shape' which represents 'life' for both Katherine and Ralph in *Night and Day*, a 'little dot with the flames round it' (*ND* 7)).

> Millions of things came back to her. Atoms danced apart and massed themselves. But how did they compose what people called a life? She clenched her hands and felt the hard little coins she was holding. Perhaps there's 'I' at the middle of it, she thought; a knot; a centre; and again she saw herself sitting at her table drawing on the blotting-paper, digging little holes from which spokes radiated. Out and out they went; thing followed thing, scene obliterated scene. And then they say, she thought, 'We've been talking about you!' (Y. 295)

'My life's been other people's lives', Eleanor thinks.

One component of the scene recalled from 1891 is not present here: Eleanor's meditation on the continuing existence of the 'solid object' which 'might survive them all'. She is in fact remembering a moment in which a future was imagined; retrospect and prospect combine in a complex temporality which further militates against the surface linearity of the narrative and renders the past, like the present, open to the future. In the passage quoted above the juxtaposition of 'followed' and 'obliterated' radically disrupts linear progression. What comes after takes the place of what has preceded it, leaving us with serially passing moments, rather as the morning newspaper in *Between the Acts* 'obliterated the day before'. Time and consciousness also take on something of the structure of the palimpsest, a parchment on which one layer of writing is erased to clear the surface for another; it is both a writing-over and a writing-out, an accretion and an effacement. The accumulations of the past and of identity in *The Years* are also a cancelling-out, like Peggy's 'rub[bing] out' of the picture of Eleanor she has attempted to compose. Individuals, like histories, will not coalesce; this absence of fixity brings with it both fear and freedom.

At the same time, the mind is 'scored' with impressions which make repetition inevitable, and even make it impossible to think about such repetitions other than through familiar and repetitive images: 'Each person had a certain line laid down in their minds, [Peggy] thought, and along it came the same old sayings. One's mind must be criss-crossed like the palm of one's hand, she thought, looking at the palm of her hand' (*Y*. 288). Woolf suggests that there is a distinction between characters, like Eleanor, who glimpse something of a meaningful 'recurrence of some pattern' (*L*. vi. 116) and those of her generation who are caught in repetition, like 'a gramophone whose needle has stuck', as she wrote in *Three Guineas*.

The 'Present Day' section insistently plays out repetition, interruption, incompletion, fragmentation, failure. Maggie is twice interrupted in her attempts to make solid objects in a room cohere into a meaningful whole 'just as she was about to complete the pattern'. Eleanor's glimpse of 'a pattern' eludes her: 'Her mind slipped. She could not finish her thought' (*Y*. 297). Words and the rhymes they make obsessively return, cancelling out the content of sentences. Peggy feels compelled to continue with a speech she had not meant to make, while Nicholas begins to make a speech which he cannot complete: 'how can one speak when one is always interrupted?' (*Y.* 342). 'There is going to be no peroration<...>because there was no speech' (*Y.* 347). Where *Mrs Dalloway* and *To the Lighthouse* offered completion, of a scene or a moment, however transient, *The Years* breaks up patterns as or before they are formed: 'Directly something got together, it broke' (*Y.* 315). Kitty is denied 'the finish, the fillip' for which she seeks. The novel draws to a close with Eleanor's unanswered question: 'And now?'.

Peggy and North, the younger generation of Pargiters, are lonelier and wearier than their elders. They are aware of the demands that will be made of them; here Woolf alludes to the political situation in Europe and the advance of Fascism, increasingly exigent as the years of the novel's writing accumulated. Peggy and North's separate but shared response is a fantasy of total withdrawal, sleep, and seclusion. The image of the picture palace seen from the taxi returns to Peggy, but this time it is linked less, perhaps, to the creative dissolution of the self into the spectacle or of the boundaries between selves, than to a loss of centred selfhood and a fatal passivity: 'Again she saw the ruby-splashed pavement, and faces mobbed at the door of a picture palace; apathetic, passive faces; the faces of people drugged with cheap pleasures; who had not even the courage to be themselves, but must dress up, imitate, pretend' (*Y.* 312). This image of 'popular culture' is one Woolf rehearses without necessarily espousing; it had recently received an airing in Q. D. Leavis's *Fiction and the Reading Public* (1932) and had more political resonances in the work of the 'critical theorists' associated with the Frankfurt Institute for Social Research, notably in their critiques of the mass culture of Fascism.[5]

Peggy, while refusing the communal day dream of the cinema, yearns to dream alone in a private cinema of the mind: 'She wished that there were blinds like those in railway carriages that came down over the light and hooded the mind. The blue blind that one pulls down on a night journey, she thought. Thinking was torment; why not give up thinking, and drift and dream?' (*Y.* 312). This reverie, however, cannot be sustained; it is broken into by the laughter at the 'monster' created in the game of Consequences, which swells into her new vision of a way of 'living differently'.

North, another 'outsider', debates with himself over the

private versus the public life, the cultivation of the individual or the joining of societies and the signing of manifestos. His great-uncle Patrick mistakes the estate agent's details on the walls of the office in which the party is being held for 'manifestos' – 'North turned his back and pretended to read the particulars of a desirable property at Bexhill which Patrick had called for some reason "a manifesto". "Running water in all the bedrooms," he read. He overheard scraps of talk' (Y. 324). The talk stems from nice young public-school educated men who have espoused the cause of Justice and Liberty and who meet in hired halls: 'There was the pump-handle gesture; the wringing wet-clothes gesture; and then the voice, oddly detached from the little figure and tremendously magnified by the loudspeaker, went booming and bawling round the hall' (Y. 325). Here we have the more sinister aspect of the voice cut off, as on the telephone or the radio, from the person; it suggests a reason for both Eleanor's and Peggy's imaginings of a 'little telephone picture', a reintegration of the voice and the individual. The ironic link between estate agent's descriptions and political propaganda in the quotation above makes it clear that both are to be considered as salesmanship, purveyed through their own brands of rhetoric.

North imagines 'another life; a different life':

> Not halls and reverberating megaphones; not marching in steps after leaders, in herds, groups, societies, caparisoned. No; to begin inwardly, and let the devil take the outer form, he thought, looking up at a young man with a fine forehead and a weak chin. Not black shirts, green shirts, red shirts – always posing in the public eye; that's all poppycock. Why not down barriers and simplify? But a world, he thought, that was all one jelly, one mass, would be a rice pudding world, a white counterpane world. To keep the emblems and tokens of North Pargiter <...> but at the same time spread out, make a new ripple in human consciousness, be the bubble and the stream, the stream and the bubble – myself and the world together – he raised his glass. Anonymously, he said, looking at the clear yellow liquid.   (Y. 329–30)

North is and is not offering the reader a position in the debate between art and politics, individual and political life that clearly informs the end of *The Years*. While his thoughts are not free from the rhetorical structures he despises, as he raises his glass to his own peroration, he also espouses the interrelationship of 'I' and 'we' and the 'philosophy of anonymity' (D. iv. 186) that Woolf felt herself to be working towards at this period. Peggy does communicate to him her vision of a way of 'living differently'.

The novel closes with an image of the dawn: 'The sun had risen and the sky above the houses wore an air of extraordinary beauty, simplicity and peace' (Y. 349). The novel has, in fact, taught us to mistrust all 'finishes' and 'fillips', while such an ending may seem emptily optimistic in a novel acutely aware of the conflict and destruction to come and, as we have seen, insistently thematizing 'failure'. Yet Woolf did seem to hold to the idea of *The Years* as a 'creative, a constructive book' (*D*. v. 68), supporting, I think, a reading of the novel in which incompletion of all kinds testifies not only to repression and censorship but to a 'constructive', and profoundly political, refusal of the climactic moment and the charismatic individual, and a rebellion against historical necessity in the hope of free creation. As Woolf wrote to Stephen Spender:

> What I meant I think was to give a picture of society as a whole; give characters from every side; turn them towards society, not private life; exhibit the effect of ceremonies; Keep one toe on the ground by means of dates, facts: envelop the whole in a changing temporal atmosphere; Compose into one vast many-sided group at the end; and then shift the stress from present to future; and show the old fabric insensibly changing without death or violence into the future – suggesting that there is no break, but a continuous development, possibly a recurrence of some pattern; of which of course we actors are ignorant. And the future was gradually to dawn. (*L*. vi. 116)

Then a disclaimer which disrupts even this image of completion, opening it up again to the uncertainties of process: 'Of course I completely failed' (*L*. vi. 116)

Writing *The Years*, Woolf grappled with the terms and the interrelations of fiction, history, and politics, often through the dichotomies of 'fact' and 'fiction', 'fact' and 'vision', 'history' and 'truth'. 'If you object that fiction is not history,' she wrote in the first essay of *The Pargiters*, 'I reply that though it would be far easier to write history – "In the year 1842 Lord John Russell brought in the Second Reform Bill" and so on – that method of telling the truth seems to me so elementary, and so clumsy, that I prefer, where truth is important, to write fiction' (*P*. 9). As we have seen, she initially drew a distinction between the 'novel of fact' on which she was engaged and her earlier 'novel(s) of vision'. In the process of turning *The Pargiters* into *The Years*, however, she drew back from the 'didactic demonstrative' strain of the novel, her fear of 'the didactic' (*D*. iv. 145) increasing as she saw and heard the workings of Fascist propaganda, and, at times, protested about the 'politics, politics' increasingly governing her and Leonard's lives (*L*. v. 428). *The Years* became a more opaque and allusive text as she sought to reintegrate the elements of 'vision' and to incorporate a range of genres: satire, comedy, poetry, narrative (*D*. iv. 152). '[I] think it would be better acted,' she wrote to her niece in 1935 (*L*. v. 445). There had already been plans to produce a radio dramatization of her previous novel *The Waves*; Woolf's final novel, *Between the Acts*, takes up the increasingly choric dimensions of her work, the 'we' rather than the 'I'. These issues are explored in the next chapter.

In the 1930s, during and immediately after the writing of *The Years*, Woolf wrote a number of essays addressing the increasing politicization of art and redefining the question of art's 'use value'; 'use' often becomes synonymous with propaganda and didacticism. In 'Craftsmanship' (1937) she made the contentious claim that words 'never make anything that is useful, and words are the only things that tell the truth and nothing but the truth' (*CDML* 137). (The unequivocal nature of the truth demanded by the legal oath which she echoes here is somewhat undermined by her subsequent claim that truth is 'many-sided'.) In this essay, initially a radio broadcast, Woolf argued that there are two separate languages, 'one for fact, one for fiction'. The language of fact or 'useful statements', she asserts, could be condensed into a system of signs and codes, though the absoluteness of the distinction between use and aesthetic value breaks down when Woolf writes that 'Baedeker carries the sign language still further into the sublime realms of art' (*CDML* 138). (And, of course, the system of signs would not be viable on the radio, the medium through which Woolf was airing this argument.)

She also explored the idea of a sign language in her essay 'Reviewing'. Rejecting the idea that reviews are of value to authors, reviewers, or the public, Woolf suggested that the reviewer should be replaced by the Taster, who would affix a stamp to a short statement about the book in question – an asterisk to signal approval, a dagger disapproval. Meanwhile, the reviewer proper would become redesignated as a consultant, to whom the writer would submit his work 'in strict privacy and some formality' (*CDML* 160). The results for literature, Woolf speculates, would be that the writer would lose a spurious celebrity and withdraw into the darkness of the workshop, an obscure workman doing a job 'not unworthy of respect' (*CDML* 163). The scheme was fanciful, but testifies to Woolf's increasing rejection of the culture of publicity and her expressed desire for the quiet, darkened spaces of anonymity.

'The Leaning Tower' (1940) is addressed primarily to that group of young male writers that we now know as 'The Auden Generation'; Woolf knew many of them through their writings for the Hogarth Press and was close to John Lehmann and Stephen Spender. In this essay, first given as a speech to the Workers Educational Association, Woolf links 'the outsider' (increasingly her self-definition not only as a woman excluded from the institutions of power but as one who wishes to retain a critical distance from 'her' society) with 'the commoner'. She mounts an attack on the group of middle-class, public-school-educated poets (who have their fictional precursors in *The Years*) whose critiques of society are ultimately shaped by their unwillingness to bite the hand of the society that has so amply fed them. The distorting effects of two world wars, moreover, have resulted in 'the pedagogic, the didactic, the loud speaker strain that dominates their poetry. They must teach; they must preach' (*WE* 172). 'The Leaning Tower' gives a skewed account of 1930s writing, not least because it makes no mention of the women writers of the period, with whom Woolf was certainly familiar.

In 'Why Art Today Follows Politics' (1936) Woolf had defined the artist as a world-citizen (anticipating her claim in *Three Guineas* that 'as a woman I have no country'). The 'ancient voices prophesying war' that reverberate through Coleridge's *Kubla Khan* begin to echo in Woolf's essays, as they do in *Three Guineas*; she describes the artist as 'besieged by voices'. As she and Leonard listened to the wireless, they became all too familiar with the 'mad voice', the 'raging voices', of Hitler and the Nazis. In 'Thoughts on Peace in an Air Raid' (1940) she pits Blake's 'I will not cease from mental fight' ('Thinking is my fighting', she wrote in her diary in May 1940 (*D.* v. 285)) against the Coleridgean voices: 'The young airman up in the sky is driven not only by the voices of loudspeakers; he is driven by voices in himself – ancient instincts, instincts fostered and cherished by education and tradition. < . . . > We must help the young Englishmen to root out from themselves the love of medals and decorations' (*CDML* 170). The 'fighting instinct' she calls 'subconscious Hitlerism'.

In July 1937, a few weeks after his departure from England, Woolf's nephew Julian Bell was killed in Spain. He had wanted to fight for the Republic in the Civil War, but was persuaded by his family that if he had to go it should be as an ambulance driver. Two weeks after his death, Woolf wrote a memoir of Julian, in which she asked:

> What made him feel it necessary, knowing as he did how it must torture Nessa [Vanessa Bell], to go? He knew her feeling. <...> What made him do it? I suppose its a fever in the blood of the younger generation which we can't possibly understand. I have never known anyone of my generation have that feeling about a war. We were all C.O.'s [Conscientious Objectors] in the Great war. And though I understand that this is a 'cause', can be called the cause of liberty & so on, still my natural reaction is to fight intellectually: if I were any use, I should write against it: I should evolve some plan for fighting English tyranny. The moment force is used, it becomes meaningless & unreal to me.[6]

First conceived as a book about women and 'the Professions', *Three Guineas* began to take the form of an 'Anti fascist pamphlet' (*D*. iv. 282) and increasingly became an argument with Julian Bell, both before and after his death. As the passage from the memoir suggests, Woolf seems to have believed that her friends and associates would maintain the pacifist stance they had taken in the First World War; in fact, she became increasingly isolated in her view that the use of military force was never justified.

Woolf had been reading widely and collecting materials, primarily newspaper cuttings, throughout the 1930s for the book that became *Three Guineas*; she gathered 'ammunition' on the cultural and social history of women, male attitudes to women, the exclusion of women from public life, and on militarism, Fascism, and war. The photographs of 'ruined houses and dead bodies' from, presumably, the Madrid massacres, which became a central part of the argument of *Three Guineas* (though they are not shown in the text and have not survived into the Woolf archives), were probably sent by the Republican government in Spain (see *L*. vi. 85). Woolf also turned to biography, autobiography, and 'the daily paper, history in the raw', which provided her with an 'aid to the understanding of human motives'; specifically, the 'motives' of men who, like Julian, found 'some glory, some necessity, some satisfaction in fighting which we [women] have never felt or enjoyed' (*TG* 121).

Three Guineas takes the form of a letter, a reply to a male correspondent who has asked: 'How in your opinion are we to prevent war?' The question, Woolf (or her narrator) writes, is 'unique in the history of human correspondence, since when before has an educated man asked a woman how in her opinion war can be prevented?' The posing of the question marks a change in men's attitudes to women and in women's status; the answer to the question is a subtle and lengthy interrogation of sexual inequalities and differences, of the ways in which masculine power and privilege have been maintained at the expense of women's economic and intellectual autonomy, and of the relationship between 'patriarchy', militarism, and war. Woolf speaks in the name of 'the daughters of educated men'; a lengthy footnote suggests that she sees the needs of different classes of women as distinct, and, as in 'The Leaning Tower', she specifically rejects the 'pro-proletarian spectacles' of many of her contemporaries.

The rights of 'the daughters of educated men' to an education equal to that of their brothers and to entry into the professions are prerequisite to the question of their interests in preventing war and their abilities to do so. Without education, career, and income, women will be in no position to take up any form of autonomous political and ethical stance. The first of the eponymous guineas of the title is thus sent to the honorary treasurer of a women's college seeking new buildings, the second to 'the honorary treasurer of the society for helping the daughters of educated men to enter the professions'. The third guinea, and the text-letter of *Three Guineas*, goes to the original correspondent, treasurer of a society for the prevention of war. This guinea is not a subscription but an anti-subscription from a member (though the term is paradoxical) of the 'Outsiders Society', ' a free gift, given freely'.

'Free', 'freely', 'freedom' are amongst a number of loaded terms that circulate within this text. Both guineas and words are 'coinage', capable of use for good or ill. Words, like coins, become devalued by overuse or misuse: 'the word "free" is used so often, and has come, like used words, to mean so little, that it may be well to explain exactly, even pedantically, what the word "free" means in this context. It means here that no right or privilege is asked in return' (*TG* 226). The concept of words as coins has echoes in the writing of the Russian formalist critic

Victor Shklovsky, who argued that the role of the artist is to renew the worn currency of language.[7] Woolf gives this a number of new inflections. She argues that it is women who need to coin new words; she attacks the literary market place in which coins are exchanged for words and writers are unable to write 'freely'; and she extends the metaphor of words as coins into a complex interplay between 'facts' and 'values', and between fact, value, opinion, and truth.

She reminds us throughout *Three Guineas* that the question of 'value' is rarely 'free' from economic considerations; thus 'the enormous value that human beings place upon education' is to be deduced from the enormous sums they spend upon it – for their sons, that is. One of the arguments running through the text is that women need to 'free' 'value' from economic considerations as they gain more of the rights and privileges formerly denied them; if they do not, they will merely end up joining a system in which all activity is motivated by the greed and competitiveness which lead men to war. Hence the 'vows' she feels women must take, if they are to establish a new set of 'values' which will prevent war, to 'poverty, chastity, derision' and 'freedom from unreal loyalties' (*TG* 203).

The terms Woolf uses here – 'poverty', 'chastity' – are redefined for her purposes ('poverty' means sufficiency but not excess, 'chastity' refers not to sexual purity or abstention but to women's refusal to 'prostitute' themselves in marriage or the market place). 'Freedom from unreal loyalties' is a circuitous way of stating something for which there is no single word; it entails freedom from national pride, religious pride, college pride, and sex pride. While 'the English language is much in need of new words' (*TG* 205) and the question of preventing war is most completely answered 'by finding new words and creating new methods' (*TG* 272), 'we have no time to coin new words' (*TG* 203). Hence the difficulties of both the text and of the task, working both within and without the old terms and values, and of its 'economics'. Excess in the system corrupts, as she suggests in *A Room of One's Own*, but without it there is little opportunity for 'free' play with language, roles, and their redefinitions.

Woolf points up the status of *Three Guineas* as a transitional text and of the transitional status of women at the time she writes. Women's vantage points, and the vantage points of the text, move from the upper windows of the private house to its threshold, and then to the bridge between the private house and public life, figured as the bridges of London and of Ox(bridge): 'for both [of the great universities] have rivers, and both have bridges, too, for us to stand upon' (*TG* 142). Pausing at 'this moment of transition on the bridge', the narrator watches the members of the male procession in their extravagant vestments. But the Wordsworthian view of London from Westminster Bridge must be re-visioned; there is no time for dreaming, 'for there, trapesing along at the tail end of the procession, we go ourselves' (*TG* 184). One of the central questions Woolf poses is whether women should in fact agree to join the procession: 'how can we enter the professions and yet remain civilized human beings; human beings, that is, who wish to prevent war' (*TG* 200). The view from the upper window, the threshold, or the bridge is not only the perspective of the confined and the excluded but the 'bird's-eye view' of one who stands 'outside'. In this, Woolf anticipates recent feminist criticism in which women's 'sidelong' look at the world is refigured as anamorphic vision; a distorted image can be seen in its 'proper' proportions from a certain angle of perception. It is this view or vantage point, and any hope of opposing greed, militarism, and war, that would be lost, Woolf suggests, if women ceased to assert the difference of view, the difference of value.

Woolf is fully aware that this view of 'difference' is capable of exploitation by those who insist that it is women's role and duty to redeem a wicked world, while at the same time denying them equal rights and privileges on the grounds that these would be inappropriate or even corrupting. The figure of woman as redeemer or as man's conscience would seem to be a close relative of the Angel in the House. Woolf satirically notes her 'divine' manifestation in Goethe's 'The woman in woman | Lead forward for ever' (*TG* 199); for Woolf, women's 'transitional' status is primarily a social and political question and does not form part of the discourse of the 'new woman', with its biologistic definitions of woman as an 'evolving' creature who will renew a degenerate world. If women are to change society, Woolf suggests, they must be given not only the means but the motives to do so; their altruism should not be counted upon nor seen as part of their nature.

Language and vision, words and images, are the media through which the difference of view and the difference of value are made and manifested. One of the most contentious assertions of this feminist text is that the word 'feminist' is 'an old word, a vicious and corrupt word that has done much harm in its day and is now obsolete':

> That word, according to the dictionary, means 'one who champions the rights of women'. Since the only right, the right to earn a living, has been won, the word no longer has a meaning. And a word without a meaning is a dead word, a corrupt word. Let us therefore celebrate this occasion by cremating the corpse. Let us write that word in large black letters on a sheet of foolscap; then solemnly apply a match to the paper. Look, how it burns! What a light dances over the world! <...> The smoke has died down; the word is destroyed. Observe, Sir, what has happened as the result of our celebration. The word 'feminist' is destroyed; the air is cleared; and in that clearer air what do we see? Men and women working together for the same cause. The cloud has lifted from the past too. What were they working for in the nineteenth century – those queer dead women in their poke bonnets and shawls? The very same cause for which we are working now. <...> They were fighting the tyranny of the patriarchal state as you are fighting the tyranny of the Fascist state. Thus we are merely carrying on the same fight that our mothers and grandmothers fought; their words prove it; your words prove it.   (*TG* 227–8)

The first part of this passage must, I think, be understood ironically. Every argument Woolf makes in *Three Guineas* is a refutation of the belief that women's rights have been conclusively 'won'. The language of burning and blazing is part of a network of incendiary images running throughout the text, extending Woolf's claim in her diary that, in gathering together the materials for *Three Guineas*, 'I have collected enough powder to blow up St Pauls' (*D*. iv. 77). This statement has a true anarchist ring about it, but in *Three Guineas* she repeatedly transforms what is seen as a masculine enthusiasm for 'burning' into the more constructive and celebratory image of the 'blaze', echoing the scene in *The Years* in which mother and daughters (Eugenie, Magdalena, and Sara) make a celebratory bonfire of autumn leaves. The argumentative strategy of the passage quoted above serves to uphold the most important contention of *Three Guineas* as a whole; that patriarchy and Fascism are aspects of the same system, that a 'Dictator' can be defined as 'one who believes that he has the right <...> to dictate to other human beings' (*TG* 175), and that the dictator is 'here among us, raising his ugly head, spitting his poison, small still, curled up like a caterpillar on a leaf, but in the heart of England' (*TG* 175).

If men and women now find themselves on the same side in the struggle against the Dictator, it is because 'He is interfering now with your liberty; he is dictating how you shall live; he is making distinctions not merely between the sexes, but between the races. You are feeling in your own persons what your mothers felt when they were shut out, when they were shut up, because they were women' (*TG* 228). The fight, Woolf seems to concede, must be for a common cause; her guinea will go towards asserting 'the rights of all – all men and women <...> and may we live to see the day when in the blaze of our common freedom the words tyrant and dictator shall be burnt to ashes' (*TG* 229). In a characteristic move, however, Woolf follows this 'peroration' with an ellipsis: '... What possible doubts, what possible hesitations can those dots stand for?' (*TG* 229). They stand, it seems, for 'difference' and for a suspicion that the 'society' women are finally being invited to join is still a male club writ large, with its laws, rituals, and exclusions. Hence the need for the creation of 'the Outsiders Society', in which an ultimate refusal to become identical with the society or the group is figured in the oxymoron of the society's name.

The basis for 'the anonymous and secret society of Outsiders' is that, 'as a woman I have no country. As a woman I want no country. As a woman my country is the whole world' (*TG* 234). In marriage to a 'non-national', women lose their citizenship; their heritage is never unequivocally their own. 'Patriotism' stems from the same etymological root as 'patriarchy'; in *Three Guineas* Woolf attacks the rule of fathers, literal and figurative. Whereas in 'Professions for Women' Woolf writes of the need to perform a symbolic matricide – 'If I had not killed her', she writes of the mother-figure, 'The Angel in the House', 'she would have killed me' – in *Three Guineas* it is fathers who threaten to pluck the heart out of their daughters' aspirations and ambitions.

While Woolf did not seem to share her culture and milieu's interest in psychoanalysis when it spoke of individual sympto-motologies, she turned to psychological and psychoanalytic theories during times of historical conflict for an analysis of the workings of mass psychology. Towards the end of the First World War she records reading Wilfred Trotter's *Analysis of the Herd in Peace and War*; in 1939 she was reading Freud 'on groups' (*Group Psychology and the Analysis of the Ego* (1921) (*D. v.* 215)). In

Three Guineas she links the 'primitive' nature of a supposedly civilized society's most treasured rituals with the primitive 'infantile-fixation' of society's fathers. Woolf does not fully define the term 'infantile-fixation', though she quotes a lengthy, psychoanalytically informed, passage in which Freud's concepts of the 'castration complex', and of the representation of woman as castrated man, are used to explain 'the general acceptance of male dominance, and still more of feminine inferiority'. For Woolf, the home of 'infantile-fixation' is the Victorian family house and, in the father–daughter relationships of the Barretts, the Brontës, and the Jex-Blakes, she finds the desire of fathers to control and possess their daughters, and to deny other men emotional and sexual access to them. These 'ancient and obscure emotions' are fully ratified, Woolf argues, by our ostensibly 'civilized' and rational society.

For Freud, it is the 'Oedipus complex' through which 'ancient and obscure emotions' are replayed in perpetuity. Here the son's desire for the mother is played out, as well as the daughter's turning from mother to father as her object of desire. Woolf, too, looks to Greek tragedy, in Sophocles' renditions, for an understanding of those buried elements which are profoundly determining of our psychic and social beings, although her concern is not with Oedipus but with his daughter Antigone. In the classical legend, Antigone seeks to bury the corpse of her brother Polyneices, declared a traitor by the state; she is forbidden to do so by her uncle, Creon, king of Thebes. When she disobeys him, he orders that she be buried alive; she commits suicide first.

One interpretation of the play's message is that the state must be able to accommodate familial and ancestral obligations. Woolf has a rather different reading; Antigone is the forerunner of those nineteenth-century campaigners for women's rights who 'wanted, like Antigone, not to break the laws, but to find the law', and in so doing had to find 'the force which in the nineteenth century opposed itself to the force of the fathers'. The voice of Antigone echoes through the closing pages of *Three Guineas*, as it echoed through *The Years*. Anticipating Jean Anouilh's reading of the play, Woolf finds in Antigone the voice that opposes tyranny and Fascism. 'Let us shut off the wireless and listen to the past', Woolf writes:

That is the voice of Creon, the Dictator. To whom Antigone, who was to have been his daughter, answered, 'Not such are the laws set among men by the justice who dwells with the gods below.' But she had neither capital nor force behind her. And Creon said: 'I will take her where the path is loneliest, and hide her, living, in a rocky vault.' And he shut her not in Holloway or in a concentration camp, but in a tomb. And Creon we read brought ruin on his house, and scattered the land with the bodies of the dead. It seems, Sir, as we listen to the voices of the past, as if we were looking at the photograph again, at the picture of dead bodies and ruined houses that the Spanish Government sends us almost weekly. Things repeat themselves it seems. Pictures and voices are the same to-day as they were 2,000 years ago. (TG 269–70)

The photographs of 'dead bodies and ruined houses' that have punctuated the text (though we are not shown them) have been used to signify brute 'fact', the evidence beyond the vagaries of language and rhetoric, on which men and women must come to an accord; here they provide the link between past and present. But another photograph superimposes itself, 'the figure of a man <...> He is called in German and Italian Führer or Duce; in our own language Tyrant or Dictator. And behind him lie ruined houses and dead bodies – men, women and children' (TG 270). The task is, Woolf asserts at the close of *Three Guineas*, to recognize that 'we <...> are ourselves that figure' and thus to 'change that figure' from within (TG 271). In so doing, men and women must, for the time being at least, follow their related but separate paths. The key word here, and the one that will take us into Woolf's final novel, *Between the Acts*, is 'ourselves'.

8

Into the Heart of Darkness:
Between the Acts

Between the Acts, or *Pointz Hall* as it was initially called, was written as a counterpoint to Woolf's biography of *Roger Fry*. Fry had died in September 1934, and his family had asked Woolf if she would be his biographer. She took on the task, but found it a difficult and at times burdensome one, and her diary entries suggest that it became the focus for her feelings about the 'grind' of working with obdurate 'facts'. Woolf had felt anxious about beginning another novel after the tortures of *The Years*: 'I am doubtful if I shall ever write another novel,' she wrote in June 1937 (*D*. v. 91). In the event, however, she seems to have written *Between the Acts* with relative ease and considerable pleasure as an alternative to the biography. In May 1938 she described herself as 'living in the solid world of Roger, & then (again this morning) in the airy world of Poyntz Hall' (*D*. v. 141).

The question mark Woolf placed over her writing of further novels is also a questioning of the novel as a form. When the shape of a new novel did 'swim up', it was hybrid and many-faceted: 'The only hint I have towards it is that its to be dialogue: a poetry: & prose; all quite distinct' (*D*. v. 105). This was written in August 1937, as Woolf was completing *Three Guineas*. In the spring of 1938 she wrote in her diary: 'Last night I began making up again: Summers night: a complete whole: that's my idea' (*D*. v. 133). A few days later she wrote:

> here I am sketching out a new book; only dont please impose that huge burden on me again, I implore. Let it be random & tentative; something I can blow of a morning, to relieve myself of Roger: dont, I implore, lay down a scheme; call in all the cosmic immensities; & force my tired and diffident brain to embrace another whole – all parts

contributing – not yet awhile. But to amuse myself, let me note: why not Poyntzet Hall: a centre: all lit. discussed in connection with real little incongruous living humour; & anything that comes into my head; but "I" rejected: 'We' substituted: to whom at the end there shall be an invocation? "We" ... composed of many different things ... we all life, all art, all waifs and strays – a rambling capricious but somehow unified whole – the present state of my mind? And English country; & a scenic old house – & a terrace where nursemaids walk? & people passing – & a perpetual variety & change from intensity to prose. & facts – & notes; & – but eno'. (*D. v.* 135)

The final version of the novel remains remarkably close to this first conception. The 'scenic old house' is Pointz Hall, home of the Olivers; Bart and his sister Lucy Swithin, his son Giles and daughter-in-law Isa, and their two children. The novel is set on a June day in 1939 (a few months before the outbreak of the Second World War), when a village pageant is performed, directed by one of Woolf's artist as 'outsider' figures, Miss La Trobe. In the opening scene of the day (we enter the narrative on the previous evening) 'the nurses were trundling the perambulator up and down the terrace' (*BA* 9). The Olivers are visited on the day of the pageant by the flamboyant Mrs Manresa and her companion William Dodge, to whose homosexuality Woolf repeatedly alludes and who plays a crucial part in the novel's exploration of masculinity, aggression, and repression.

The shift from 'I' to 'We' is central to the novel, to Woolf's representations of subjectivity and consciousness, and to the critical period in history which marked the novel's inception and writing. Woolf's insistence that the novel be easy and airy is fulfilled in one sense in its comedy, but also belies the fact that this, her final novel, is perhaps her most unsettling. Its shifting, unstable narration and tone in some ways bring it closest to *Jacob's Room*, her First World War novel. *Between the Acts* depicts a world in which danger and destruction are barely held at bay. Its writing was marked by the coming of war; Woolf used the novel as a space in which to work through, or play out, the possible roles of art and the artist in the war which she had so dreaded. She did not live to see its publication; the unrevised draft was published in July 1941, four months after her death.

The first imaginings of the novel, quoted above, interestingly echo Woolf's plans for her diary as a whole, written some twenty years earlier:

What sort of diary should I like mine to be? Something loose knit, &
yet not slovenly, so elastic that it will embrace anything, solemn,
slight or beautiful that comes into my mind. I should like it to
resemble some deep old desk, or capacious hold all, in which one
flings a mass of odds & ends without looking them through. I should
like to come back, after a year or two, & find that the collection had
mysteriously sorted itself & refined itself & coalesced, as such
deposits mysteriously do, into a mould, transparent enough to
reflect the light of our life, & yet steady, tranquil, composed with the
aloofness of a work of art.   (*D*. i. 266)

The 'capacious' mind (as the 'hold all') has made the phonetically
slight but semantically significant transmutation into the 'capricious', and, though there is a shared sense in the two passages of
a way in which unity and diversity might come to co-exist, the
image of the 'steady, tranquil <...> work of art' cannot be
sustained. The novel is shot through with an understanding that
things can be held together neither through aesthetic containment nor through strenuous effort but will coalesce, if at all, as
Gillian Beer notes, through partial and fugitive methods of
association, recall, echo, rhyme, image, meaning.[1]

Woolf wrote *Between the Acts* at a time when she was much
concerned with 'personal' writings of various kinds – biographies, autobiographies, memoirs. She had noted the drive to
autobiography in the 1930s in her essay 'The Leaning Tower', a
drive she describes as 'auto-analysis' in her diary: 'I think
there's something in the psycho-analy[sis] idea: that the L.
Tower writer couldn't describe society; had therefore to describe
himself, as the product, or victim: a necessary step towards
freeing the next generation of repressions' (*D*. v. 267). *Between
the Acts* might seem to be far removed from any 'autobiographical impulse', yet, as the echoes between her plans for the
novel and her early aspirations for her diaries suggest, it had its
roots in a particular understanding of experience as collect –
both collection and collectivity. Hence the key image of the
novel – ' "I" rejected: 'We' substituted'.

The relationship between the novel and the contemporaneous
diary-writing are also close and significant. By the autumn of
1939 the Woolfs were based almost entirely in Rodmell (their
London home was destroyed in September 1940). At times Woolf
expressed irritation at the limitations and intrusions of the
village community, but more often she describes a sense of total
seclusion, of living on a 'desert island' or a 'little boat'. A flood in

the fields becomes an image from Genesis or pre-history: 'Oh may the flood last for ever – a virgin lip; no bungalows; as it was in the beginning < . . . > our island sea. [Mount] Caburn is become a cliff' (*D*. v. 336). Land has become sea. The intrusions of visitors are figured as 'invasions'; the broader, unspoken question is whether the channel will afford sufficient protection for England from invading landforces. (Throughout the writing of the novel, air attacks were taking place overhead.) In *Between the Acts* the occupants of Pointz Hall debate their distance from the sea (thirty-five, a hundred, a hundred and fifty miles?); Isa perceives the land going 'on for ever and ever' (*BA* 20), while Lucy Swithin reads of a time before recorded history when the land mass of 'England' was joined to the Continent, a time in which no dividing sea would have afforded protection, but in which such protection, in the absence of territorial or cultural barriers, would have been unnecessary.

'The war slowly enacts itself on a great scene: round our little scene', Woolf wrote in her diary as *Between the Acts* was completed; the 'private scene' (from which Woolf protected herself, she wrote, by 'drop[ping] a safety curtain' in the form of her reading of Michelet (*D*. v. 323)), the village scene and the theatre of war form concentric circles in the diaries and in the novel. At one point Woolf decided *Between the Acts* was to be a play in its entirety, though she then elected to make the play a part of the novel. Drama was the form of the times; both W. H. Auden and T. S. Eliot, for example, turned to theatre in the 1930s. Woolf was critical of Eliot's *Family Reunion*: 'He's a lyric not a dramatic. < . . . > A monologist' (*D*. v. 210). Dickens, she suggests, was the better dramatist, his fiction 'descend[ed] from the stage' (*D*. v. 215). In *Between the Acts*, Woolf rejects the voice of the 'monologist'. The novel is the intersecting point of a multiplicity of voices and discourses; for gossip and rumour, which emanate from and are addressed to no one and everyone; for language, past and present, at its most wayward and playful. It is overtly 'heteroglossic', in Mikhail Bakhtin's terms, intermingling the 'discourses' of the literary and the extraliterary, popular and high culture, the oral and the written.[2]

In this novel which, as I shall argue, thematizes 'ambivalence', the ' "I" rejected; 'We' substituted', cannot itself be enacted non-ambivalently. One of Woolf's key images of war time was of a whole people 'concentrated on a single point'. Two decades later she repeats the perception: 'the severance that war seems to bring: everything becomes meaningless: cant plan: then there comes too the community feeling: all England thinking the same thing – this horror of war – at the same moment. Never felt it so strong before. Then the lull & one lapses again into private separation –' (*D. v.* 215). A year later, when war had been declared, she wrote: 'I dont like any of the feelings war breeds: patriotism; communal &c, all sentimental & emotional parodies of our real feelings. But then, we're in for it' (*D. v.* 302). The last phrase capitulates to the inevitability of a 'we' who are 'in for it' together. As I argued in the previous chapter, Woolf's readings of Trotter and Freud chimed with her more negative sense of the 'group' as 'herd', an image of group identity satirically confirmed by the very active role played by a herd of cows in the village pageant: 'It was the primeval voice sounding loud in the ear of the present moment. Then the whole herd caught the infection. <...> Suddenly the cows stopped; lowered their heads, and began browsing. Simultaneously the audience lowered their heads and read their programmes' (*BA* 85). The term 'infection' is close to the 'contagion' Freud, paraphrasing Gustave le Bon's work on crowds, describes as the source of the group instinct.[3]

In the enforced communality of war, Woolf as a writer felt less the loss of the 'I' than of the audience which gave her back an 'identity'. Her diary entries for June and July 1940 describe the loss of 'the outer wall of security', of a public 'to echo back', of literary 'standards – which have for so many years given back an echo and so thickened my identity', of the sense of a future. 'The present moment', whose epiphanic fullness is celebrated in much of Woolf's earlier writings, now hangs on the 'precipice' of a future not only uncertain but inconceivable: 'We pour to the edge of a precipice ... & then?' (*D. v.* 299). Eleanor Pargiter's 'And now?' (*Y.* 349) becomes the '... & then?' dangling over the edge of the sentence and of the precipice. 'I can't conceive that there will be a 27th June 1941 <...> A clock ticks somewhere. Nothing said' (*D. v.* 299). 'All the walls, the protecting and reflecting walls, wear so terribly thin in this war.<...> Hence a certain energy and recklessness – part good – part bad I daresay. But its the only line to take. And perhaps the walls, if violently beaten against, will finally contain me' (*D. v.* 304), Woolf wrote in July. The violent beating against the walls (of literary tradition, of the 'standard') is not an attempted break-out but an attempt to establish limits, to create an echoing surround, and to mould the walls into a shape which could both hold and include ('contain') herself.

I have suggested that *Between the Acts* is closest to *Jacob's Room* in its use of unstable, shifting narration. Woolf also reworks the languages and images of her other novels: the fascination with the primeval and with evolutionary narratives of *The Voyage Out*, the historical pageantry of *Orlando*. Like *Mrs Dalloway*, *Between the Acts* is a one-day novel, although its time-span, running from night to night, takes it into darker places.

To the Lighthouse is perhaps its most significant precursor; *Between the Acts* returns to a family house but, as Sue Roe notes, evacuates the ghosts of the earlier, 'Victorian', novel.[4] When 'some wave of white went over the window pane' in *To the Lighthouse*, transparency becomes opacity and Mrs Ramsay 'returns' to and for Lily. In *Between the Acts* 'the flash of white in the garden' seen by old Bart Oliver through the dining-room window is the scullery maid, 'cooling her cheeks by the lily-pond' in whose 'dark heart' the servants insist, a lady had drowned herself: 'Ten years since the pool had been dredged and a thigh bone recovered. Alas, it was a sheep's, not a lady's. And sheep have no ghosts, for sheep have no souls. But, the servants insisted, they must have a ghost; the ghost must be a lady's, who had drowned herself for love' (*BA* 29). Ghosts are now overt fictions, made to fit. An empty room or house no longer contains busy matter or spirit, is no longer hollowed out to hold a world: 'Empty, empty, empty; silent, silent, silent. The room was a shell, singing of what was before time was; a vase stood in the heart of the house, alabaster, smooth, cold, holding the still, distilled essence of emptiness, silence' (*BA* 24). It is now 'the future [which] shadowed their present' (*BA* 70), not the past.

Or, at least, the past has become 'what was before time was'. Lucy, woken by birds 'attacking the dawn':

> had stretched for her favourite reading – an Outline of history – and had spent the hours between three and five thinking of rhododen-dron forests in Piccadilly; when the entire continent, not then, she understood, divided by a channel, was all one; populated, she understood, by elephant-bodied, seal-necked, heaving, surging, slowly writhing, and, she supposed, barking monsters; the iguana-don, the mammoth and the mastodon; from whom presumably, she thought, jerking the window open, we descend. (*BA* 8)

As Gillian Beer notes, 'the prehistoric is seen not simply as part of a remote past, but as contiguous, continuous, a part of ordinary present-day life'. Such an understanding cuts across any linear, progressivist narrative of the move from Nature to Culture, or from 'barbarism' to 'civilization'. It also throws into question models of a cultural regression to 'barbarism', though these are not absent from the novel nor from Woolf's responses to the coming of war. A notebook kept by Woolf during the writing of *Between the Acts* describes 'London in War' in these terms: 'Nature prevails. I suppose badgers & foxes wd. come back if this went on, & owls & nightingales. This is the prelude to barbarism.'[5]

Lucy Swithin finds pleasure in the reconstructions of 'prehistory'; the narratives of evolutionary descent seem not to conflict in any way with her equally sustaining religious beliefs. Yet Woolf also uses the imagery of prehistorical monstrosity to dramatize aggression and fear. Old Bart violently breaks up the completeness of his grandson's imaginary world with a 'game', masking his face with 'a beak of paper'. George, happily 'grouting in the grass', looked up 'and saw coming towards him a terrible peaked eyeless monster moving on legs, brandishing arms' (*BA* 10). Angry that his grandson is a 'cry-baby', Bart retreats into dreams of his youth in India. In representing the violence of the colonial encounter, inseparable from concepts of 'civilization' and 'barbarism', Woolf echoes the language of T. S. Eliot's *The Waste Land*: 'But no water; and the hills, like grey stuff pleated; and in the sand a hoop of ribs; a bullock maggot-eaten in the sun; and in the shadow of the rock; savages; and in his hand a gun' (*BA* 13). For Bart, however, this desolation is the material of nostalgic reverie and dream, not of nightmare.

The overwhelming emotion of his son Giles is an anger which is received as a sexual charge by Mrs Manresa, William, and, in more complex ways, by his wife Isa. Giles manifests a 'proper' anger at the war deaths occurring while the village plays, but the maturity of his stance is somewhat undercut by his childlike 'projection' of emotion onto his aunt Lucy: 'He hung his grievances on her, as one hangs a coat on a hook, instinctively' (*BA* 30). 'Instinctual life' and 'inner life' are inseparable in *Between the Acts*; the complex subjectivities which modernist consciousness explores have become starkly channelled into drives, instincts, and desires. At the novel's close Isa and Giles prepare for their next 'scene' (one that seems to be mirrored in

Miss La Trobe's vision of her next play): 'Alone, enmity was bared; also love. Before they slept they must fight; after they had fought, they would embrace. From that embrace another life might be born. But first they must fight, as the dog fox fights with the vixen, in the heart of darkness' (*BA* 29). Conrad's vision echoes through this last novel of Woolf's, as through her first.

In December 1939, Woolf recorded in her diary that she was 'gulping up Freud' (*D.* v. 249). The Freudian concept which particularly struck her was 'ambivalence', a new term in the language, defined by the psychoanalysts Laplanche and Pontalis as 'the simultaneous existence of contradictory tendencies, attitudes or feelings in the relationship to a single object – especially the coexistence of love or hate'.[6] 'Freud is upsetting', Woolf wrote:

> reducing one to whirlpool; & I daresay truly. If we're all instinct, the unconscious, whats all this about civilisation, the whole man, freedom &c? His savagery against God good. The falseness of loving one's neighbour. The conscience as censor. Hate ... But I'm too mixed. (*D.* v. 250)

The last phrase ostensibly refers to Woolf's 'thinking of a dozen things as usual', but is in fact a definition and an enactment of 'ambivalence': 'Hate ... But I'm too mixed' (*D.* v. 250). In *Between the Acts* it is Giles who feels pure hatred, while Isa is 'mixed': 'how much she felt <...> of love; and of hate' (*BA* 31). It is the women in the novel who, for the most part, can tolerate ambivalence (Isa's love and hate, Lucy's simultaneous, though undoubtedly simplistic, belief in evolution and Genesis), while the men are driven either by a single aggressive instinct or by the force of 'reason', which fears and forbids the incommensurable.

These preoccupations are both new and familiar in Woolf's writing. The concept of 'ambivalence' was being reframed in the 1930s in the context of war. The Hogarth Press published Joan Riviere's and Melanie Klein's *Love, Hate and Reparation* and Freud's *Civilization, War and Death*. Both Riviere and Freud argue that Love and Hate cannot be mapped in any simple way onto Good and Evil; it is not merely that they can coexist but that they contain each other. As Freud wrote in 'Why War?' (an open letter to Einstein answering the question posed by the League of Nations – 'Is there any way of delivering mankind from the menace of war?' – which may well have provided a model for *Three Guineas*):

Neither of these instincts [Love and Hate] is any less essential than
the other; the phenomena of life arise from the concurrent or
mutually opposing action of both ... The difficulty of isolating the
two classes of instinct in their actual manifestation is indeed what
has so long prevented us from recognizing them.[7]

Freud's is not an optimistic account; his arguments in fact
suggest that both Love and Hate are fuelled by aggressive and
self-preservative instincts. In *Between the Acts*, by contrast, Isa
imagines a step beyond 'ambivalence' which will 'contain'
'Love' and 'Hate': 'Love. Hate. Peace. Three emotions made the
ply of human life' (*BA* 57).

The coming of war made these questions crucial. Yet we can
also see in Woolf's turn to 'ambivalence' a reworking of the
structures of vacillation and of oscillation which run throughout
her work and which were highlighted in the discussion of
Orlando. In the either/or, and/or, and/and structures of Woolf's
writings we find the refusal of stark or simplistic choices and
resolutions and an insistence upon processes and open endings.

One of the most resonant images in *Between the Acts* is,
however, that of a fatal impasse, a neither/nor which is the no-
man's-land of ambivalence's 'betweenness', brought to an end
only by violence and destruction. During the interval of the
pageant, Giles indulges in a child's game, stone-kicking:

> He played it alone. The gate was a goal; to be reached in ten. The first
> kick was Manresa (lust). The second, Dodge (perversion). The third
> himself (coward). And the fourth and fifth and all the others were
> the same.
>
> He reached it in ten. There, couched in the grass, curled in an olive
> green ring, was a snake. Dead? No, choked with a toad in its mouth.
> The snake was unable to swallow; the toad was unable to die. A spasm
> made the ribs contract; blood oozed. It was birth the wrong way round
> – a monstrous inversion. So, raising his foot, he stamped on them. The
> mass crushed and slithered. The white canvas on his tennis shoes was
> bloodstained and sticky. But it was action. Action relieved him. He
> strode to the Barn, with blood on his shoes. (*BA* 61)

As Gillian Beer notes, Woolf, in *Between the Acts*, as in no other
novel, 'puts violence near the centre of meaning'.[8] The newspaper story to which Isa returns throughout the text is 'fact'; a
true story, which Woolf took from *The Times*, of a young girl,
lured into a barracks with a story of a 'a horse with a green tail',
hit about the face and raped by guardsmen.[9] Like the
photograph of 'ruined houses and dead bodies' which, though

it is not seen, punctuates *Three Guineas*, the newspaper report tells a story whose brute factuality (though Isa reads the 'tail/ tale' as 'fantastic') Woolf's 'fiction' must somehow negotiate. What role can 'art' play in the 'great scene' of war and violence? In her final, fragmentary works – 'Anon', 'The Reader', 'Reading at Random' – Woolf writes of an instinct to create, as powerful as the 'instinct for self-preservation'[10] and possessing the power of regeneration, and of a communal voice, 'sometimes man; sometimes woman'[11] (which we might contrast with the figure of the 'androgyne'). 'Only when we put two and two together', she wrote in her early drafts, 'two pencil strokes, two written words, two bricks do we overcome dissolution and set up some stake against oblivion'.[12] The 'Common History' book (of which these writings are fragments) planned in the months before her death, was to tell the story of English literature and society through, in Brenda Silver's words, 'the anonymous men and women who created them'.[13] As Silver notes, Woolf's struggles with the ordering and shaping of her book, her inability to see a transition from present to future, reflects the troubled question of historical continuity at the time she was writing – one that also radically disturbs *Between the Acts*.

The pageant in *Between the Acts* plays out (eccentrically, allusively) a history and a literature of Englishness, refusing the performances of conventional patriotism and Empire Day pageantry, having no 'Grand Ensemble. Army; Navy; Union Jack'. It is acted in the grounds of Pointz Hall, 'the very place', as Miss La Trobe exclaimed when she first saw it, 'for a play': 'There the stage; here the audience; and down there among the bushes a perfect dressing-room for the actors' (*BA* 36–7). The lines anticipate 'Anon', in which Woolf writes of the 'common life' of medieval theatre, staged in 'the uncovered theatre where the sun beats and the rain pours'.[14]

Walls, or their absence, ('All the walls, the protecting and reflecting walls, wear so terribly thin in this war.<...> perhaps the walls, if violently beaten against, will finally contain me' (*D*. v. 304)), are crucial to the staging of Miss La Trobe's pageant. As Daniel Ferrer has argued, *Between the Acts* displaces or effaces the limits on which representation is based, breaking down the boundaries between stage and audience, theatre and external world, stage and backstage.[15] Thus the natural world – cows, swallows, rain – intersects with or breaks into the pageant; the 'actors' are both themselves and their parts, both Eliza Clark of the village shop and Queen Elizabeth the First; the backstage promptings of the actors are fully audible to the audience.

Miss La Trobe's attempted *coup de théâtre* is the pageant's final scene, in which she moves from Victorian England to the representation of 'The present time. Ourselves' (*BA* 106):

> Miss La Trobe stood there with her eye on the script. 'After Vic.' she had written, 'try ten mins. of present time. Swallows, cows etc.' She wanted to expose them, as it were, to douche them, with present-time reality. But something was going wrong with the experiment. 'Reality too strong,' she muttered. 'Curse 'em!' She felt everything they felt. Audiences were the devil. O to write a play without an audience – *the* play. But here she was fronting her audience. Every second they were slipping the noose. Her little game had gone wrong. If only she'd a backcloth to hang between the trees – to shut out cows, swallows, present time! But she had nothing. She had forbidden music. Grating her fingers in the bark, she damned the audience. Panic seized her. Blood seemed to pour from her shoes. This is death, death, death, she noted in the margin of her mind; when illusion fails. Unable to lift her hand, she stood facing the audience.
>
> And then the shower fell, sudden, profuse. (*BA* 107)

The eruption of reality, the rain shower, the 'douche', provides, paradoxically, the necessary illusionism: 'Down it poured like all the people in the world weeping' (*BA* 107). The seamlessness of representation falters and fragments in *Between the Acts*, but there is no space beyond or outside it.

The pageant draws to its close with the display of 'a cloth roughly painted' to represent a wall and interpreted by Mr Page the reporter as an image of 'Civilization (the wall in ruins; rebuilt (witness man with hod) by human effort; witness also woman handing bricks' (*BA* 108). This 'flattering tribute to ourselves' is then replaced by another 'wall', this time a 'reflecting' wall (the image Woolf used in her diary), made up of fragments of mirror: 'Anything that's bright enough to reflect, presumably, ourselves?' (*BA* 109):

> Ourselves! Ourselves!
>
> Out they leapt, jerked, skipped. Flashing, dazzling, dancing, jumping. Now old Bart ... he was caught. Now Manresa. Here a nose ... There a skirt ... The trousers only ... Now perhaps a face ... Ourselves? But that's cruel. To snap us as we are, before we've had time to assume ... And only, too in parts ... That's what's so distorting and upsetting and utterly unfair.

Mopping, mowing, whisking, frisking, the looking glasses darted, flashed, exposed. (*BA* 109)

As the narrative breaks up into rhyming, chiming, cacophonous fragments, so this 'reflecting wall', composed not of a single mirroring surface but of shards and bits of mirror, breaks up what it reflects, 'shiver[ing] into splinters the old vision; Smash[ing] to atoms what was whole' (*BA* 109). It mirrors back 'ourselves' in parts and pieces, refusing to totalize the spectators as a unified group. The dissolution of identity, individual and collective, is accompanied by the breaking-down of the cultural barriers between the animal and the human world – 'The very cows joined in. Walloping, tail lashing, the reticence of nature was undone, and the barriers which should divide Man the Master from the Brute were dissolved' – and by the breaking-up of 'culture' itself, as the actors reappear to declaim 'some phrase or fragment from their parts' (*BA* 110). The distinction between audience and spectacle dissolves as the audience becomes the spectacle and the spectacle the audience; modernist 'estrangement' meets the 'communality' of medieval theatre.

The disintegration recorded or relayed in the final part of the pageant could well be read as a reflection of Woolf's broader sense of dissolution and destruction – of a culture, a history, a land. Certainly, Woolf satirizes the Reverend Streatfield's attempts to draw from the pageant a unifying message: 'To me at least it was indicated that we are members one of another. Each is part of the whole' (*BA* 114). Woolf, in fact, leaves us with fragments which sound out something other than annihilation – but ambiguously, ambivalently. The final syllabled sounds of the gramophone, which has ticked like a clock throughout the performance, try to spell this out: 'Dispersed are we', 'Harmony', 'Unity – Dispersity', 'Un ... dis ... And ceased' (*BA* 119). If we hear this as 'undeceased',[16] we are left with a negation that cancels out death, a 'Yes' and a 'No': '"Yes", Isa answered. "No," she added. It was Yes, No. Yes, yes, yes, the tide rushed out embracing. No, no, no, it contracted. The old boot appeared on the shingle' (*BA* 127). This is the rhythm of the waves, which does not cease.

Notes

PROLOGUE

1. Bernard Blackstone, *Virginia Woolf* (London: Longmans, Green & Co and the National Book League for the British Council, 1952, rev. edn. 1962), 37.
2. There has been a great deal written about Bloomsbury, and the Bloomsbury Group, and about Virginia Woolf's relationship to Bloomsbury culture. The Bloomsbury Group was not a formal association, but an influential intellectual and cultural grouping of friends, a number of whom were brought together during Thoby Stephen's time at Cambridge and who subsequently lived in London's Bloomsbury district: they included Lytton Strachey, Roger Fry, Clive Bell, Leonard Woolf, Maynard Keynes, Desmond MacCarthy, and Duncan Grant. Their culture encompassed the world of arts and letters, economics, history, politics, and psychoanalysis. For discussion of the Bloomsbury Group, see Quentin Bell, *Bloomsbury* (London: Weidenfeld & Nicolson, 1968), Leon Edel, *Bloomsbury: A House of Lions* (Harmondsworth: Penguin, 1979), S. P. Rosenbaum (ed.), *The Bloomsbury Group: A Collection of Memoirs, Commentary and Criticism* (London: Croom Helm, 1975), Leonard Woolf, *An Autobiography* (2 vols.); (Oxford: Oxford University Press, 1980), Jane Marcus (ed.), *Virginia Woolf and Bloomsbury: A Centenary Celebration* (Basingstoke: Macmillan, 1987), Raymond Williams, 'The Bloomsbury Fraction', in *Problems in Materialism and Culture* (London: Verso, 1980). For a discussion of Virginia Woolf's relationship to Bloomsbury aesthetics – particularly the art criticism of Roger Fry and Clive Bell – see Allen McLaurin, *Virginia Woolf: The Echoes Enslaved* (Cambridge: Cambridge University Press, 1973), and David Dowling, *Bloomsbury Aesthetics and the Novels of Forster and Woolf* (London: Macmillan, 1985).
3. The first book-length study of Woolf's representations of the city was Dorothy Brewster, *Virginia Woolf's London* (London: George Allen & Unwin, 1959). See the Select Bibliography for details of recent studies of this topic.
4. The category of 'now-time' is a translation of the German *Jetztzeit*, a term central to the philosophy of Walter Benjamin (1892–1940),

whose representations of temporality have important links with Woolf's – in particular with her emphases on time as threshold (*To the Lighthouse*), as interruption and freeze-frame (*Jacob's Room*), as the interrelationship of 'then' and 'now' (*The Years*), and as cessation and shock (*Orlando*). For an excellent discussion of time and modernity, see Peter Osborne, *The Politics of Time* (London: Verso, 1996).

5. Gillian Beer, 'Hume, Stephen, and Elegy in *To the Lighthouse*', in *Arguing with the Past: Essays in Narrative from Woolf to Sidney* (London: Routledge, 1989), 185.

6. In 'A Sketch of the Past' Woolf wrote of the childhood sexual abuse to which she was subjected by her half-brother Gerald Duckworth and of George Duckworth's fondlings when she was a young woman. Roger Poole (in *The Unknown Virginia Woolf* (Cambridge: Cambridge University Press, 1978; new edn., 1995), 27) writes:

   The chain of signifiers in Virginia's unconscious: Body:shame: mirror:Gerald–George:not touch:Greek:animal:no will weave its way all through the fiction and explain most of the apparent mysteries of the life.

   Louise DeSalvo (*Virginia Woolf: The Impact of Childhood Sexual Abuse on her Life and Work* (London: Women's Press, 1989)) defines Woolf as an 'incest survivor' and reads the novels, in particular their representations of childhood, as transformations of her early sexual trauma.

   These studies, although interesting, manifest the limitations of 'psychobiography' as a genre, in its attempts to analyse the writer as if he or she were a patient on the analytic couch. It might be useful to turn the tables and to ask why critics have been so preoccupied with the question of Woolf's sexuality and with her imputed frigidity, whether this is seen as an aspect of her neuraesthenic aestheticism or as a result of sexual trauma.

7. The concept of 'shock' as an aspect of modernity was extensively theorized by Walter Benjamin and by Freud in *Beyond the Pleasure Principle* (1920). Freud's model of the protective shield against stimuli and external excitations, which forms on the surface of the mental apparatus, is strikingly echoed in 'A Sketch of the Past'. Woolf represents art or vision as a shock which breaches the buffering (in Benjaminian terms, 'anaesthetic') effects of the psychic defences constructed in the face of (modern) experience. For a valuable discussion of this theme, see Charles Bernheimer, 'A Shattered Globe: Narcissism and Masochism in Virginia Woolf's Life-Writing', in Richard Feldstein and Henry Sussman (eds.), *Psychoanalysis and …* (New York: Routledge, 1990), 187–206.

CHAPTER 1. WOMEN'S FUTURE, WOMEN'S FICTION

1. John Mepham, *Virginia Woolf: A Literary Life* (Basingstoke: Macmillan, 1991), 17.

2. Woolf's short stories are collected in *The Complete Shorter Fiction of Virginia Woolf*, ed. Susan Dick (London: Grafton, 1991).
3. For early drafts and for the history of the novel's writing, see Virginia Woolf, *Melymbrosia: An Early Version of* The Voyage Out, ed. Louise DeSalvo (New York: Public Library), and Louise DeSalvo *Virginia Woolf's First Voyage: A Novel in the Making* (London: Macmillan, 1980).
4. For a discussion of the *Bildungsroman* as genre, see Georg Lukács *The Theory of the Novel* (London: Merlin Press, 1977), and Franco Moretti, *The Way of the World: The* Bildungsroman *in European Culture* (London: Verso, 1987).
5. For a fuller discussion of this theme, see Lyn Pykett, *Engendering Fictions* (London: Edward Arnold, 1995).
6. *Windows on Modernism: Selected Letters of Dorothy Richardson*, ed. Gloria Fromm (Athens, Ga.: University of Georgia Press, 1995), 281.
7. There has recently been an upsurge of interest in the 'New Woman' and in 'New Woman' literature. The term, said to have been coined by Sarah Grand in 1894, was used, both satirically and seriously, to refer to a new type of woman emerging at the end of the century who was no longer willing to be defined by the roles of wife and mother. Nora, the heroine of Ibsen's *The Doll's House*, is a central example: at the end of the play she walks out of the house, leaving her children and the husband who has patronized and infantilized her, declaring her intentions to cease to be a doll and to become a woman. For recent critical discussions of the 'New Woman' and the contexts which created her, see Elaine Showalter, *Sexual Anarchy: Gender and Culture at the Fin de Siècle* (London: Bloomsbury, 1991), Ann Ardis, *New Woman, New Novels: Feminism and Early Modernism* (New Brunswick, NJ: Rutgers University Press, 1990), Lyn Pykett, *The Improper Feminine: The Women's Sensation Novel and the New Woman Writing* (London: Routledge, 1992), and Sally Ledger, 'The New Woman and the Crisis of Victorianism', in Sally Ledger and Scott McCracken (eds.), *Cultural Politics at the Fin de Siècle* (Cambridge: Cambridge University Press, 1995), 22–4.
8. See Rachel Blau Duplessis, *Writing Beyond the Ending: Narrative Strategies of 20th Century Women Writers* (Bloomington, Ind.: Indiana University Press, 1985).

CHAPTER 2. A SHAPE THAT FITS

1. The Hogarth Press was essential to Woolf as a writer – she published all her novels and much of her non-fictional prose from *Jacob's House* onwards with the Press. It also made a central contribution to intellectual and cultural life, particularly in the fields of political pamphleteering, poetry, and psychoanalysis. (Leonard and Virginia Woolf became the sole publishers of Freud's work in English in 1924.) For an account of the Press and its significance for Virginia Woolf, see

Laura Marcus, 'Virginia Woolf and the Hogarth Press', in Ian Willison, Warwick Gould, and Warren Chernaik (eds.), *Modernist Writers and the Marketplace*, (Basingstoke: Macmillan, 1996), 124–50. The full history of the Press is given in J. H. Willis, *Leonard and Virginia Woolf as Publishers: The Hogarth Press 1917–41* (Charlottesville, Va.: University Press of Virginia, 1992).

2. For a helpful discussion of 'stream of consciousness' in Woolf, see James Naremore, *The World without a Self: Virginia Woolf and the Novel* (New Haven: Yale University Press, 1973), 60–76.

3. See Prologue, n. 6.

4. Gillian Beer, 'Virginia Woolf and Prehistory', in *Arguing with the Past: Essays in Narrative from Woolf to Sidney* (London: Routledge, 1989), 171.

5. Woolf was reading Freud's 'Group Psychology and the Analysis of the Ego' in 1939. The quotation is from her reading notebooks. See *Virginia Woolf's Reading Notebooks*, ed. Brenda Silver (Princeton: Princeton University Press, 1983), 116.

6. Winifred Holtby, *Virginia Woolf: A Critical Memoir* (London: Wishart, 1932; Chicago: Academy Press, 1978), 111.

7. Henry James, 'The New Novel', in Morris Shapira (ed.), *Selected Literary Criticism* (Harmondsworth: Penguin, 1968), 369.

8. Randall Stevenson, *Modernist Fiction: An Introduction* (Hemel Hempstead: Harvester Wheatsheaf, 1992), 59.

9. Despite the fact that the Hogarth Press was publishing Freud and other psychoanalytic theorists from 1924 onwards, that a number of Woolf's circle, including her younger brother Adrian Stephen and his wife Karin, were intensely involved in psychoanalytic culture, and that a number of Woolf's novels reveal considerable familiarity with psychoanalytic theories, Woolf claimed not to have read Freud until the late 1930s. In 1924 she wrote to Molly MacCarthy: 'I shall be plunged in publishing affairs at once; we are publishing all Dr Freud, and I glance at the proof and read how Mr. A. B. threw a bottle of red ink on to the sheets of his marriage bed to excuse his impotence to the housemaid, but threw it in the wrong place, which unhinged his wife's mind – and to this day she pours claret on the dinner table. We could all go on like that for hours; and yet these Germans think it proves something – besides their own gull-like imbecility' (*L*. iii. 134–5). For a full discussion of Woolf's complex and changing relationship to psychoanalysis, see Elizabeth Abel, *Virginia Woolf and the Fictions of Psychoanalysis* (Chicago: University of Chicago Press, 1989).

10. Lyn Pykett, *Engendering Fictions* (London: Edward Arnold, 1995), 94.

11. See *L*. iii. 136 n. 1. and Quentin Bell, *Virginia Woolf: A Biography* (2 vols.; London: Hogarth Press, 1972), ii. 106.

12. J. Hillis Miller, 'The Rhythms of Creativity in *To the Lighthouse*', in Robert Kiely (ed.), *Modernism Reconsidered* (London: Harvard University Press, 1983), 171.

13. Erich Auerbach, *Mimesis: The Representation of Reality in Western Literature* (Princeton: Princeton University Press, 1953), 536.

14. May Sinclair, 'The Novels of Dorothy Richardson', first published in

Egoist, 5 (Apr. 1918), 57–9; repr., in Bonnie Kime Scott (ed.), *The Gender of Modernism* (Bloomington, Ind.: Indiana University Press, 1990), 446.

15. Sue Roe, *Writing and Gender: Virginia Woolf's Writing Practice* (Hemel Hempstead: Harvester Wheatsheaf, 1990), 25.

16. Roger Fry's essays on art and aesthetics were published as *Vision and Design* in 1920. They were undoubtedly an important influence on Woolf, although she wrote on the book's publication: 'I think it reads rudimentary compared with Coleridge' (*D*. ii. 81).

17. For an excellent account of these thinkers and their theorizations of modernity, see David Frisby, *Fragments of Modernity; Theories of Modernity in the Work of Simmel, Kracauer and Benjamin* (Oxford: Polity Press, 1985).

18. Rachel Bowlby has an excellent discussion of this essay in her introduction to *The Crowded Dance of Modern Life*.

19. Charles Baudelaire, 'The Painter of Modern Life', in *The Painter of Modern Life and Other Essays*, trans. and ed. Jonathan Mayne (London: Phaidon, 1964), 13.

20. See Sylvia Plath, 'Lady Lazarus' (1962): 'I am only thirty. | And like the cat I have nine times to die. | This is Number Three. | What a trash | To annihilate each decade' (Sylvia Plath, *Collected Poems* (London: Faber, 1981), 244–5).

21. John Mepham, *Virginia Woolf: A Literary Life* (Basingstoke: Macmillan, 1991); 79.

22. Rachel Bowlby, *Virginia Woolf: Feminist Destinations* (Oxford: Basil Blackwell, 1988), 103.

23. Ibid. 106.

24. This assertion (surely in part an ironic version of the prevailing models of historical rupture) has generated a great deal of critical debate. Mark Goldman summarizes the accounts given of Woolf's choice of date: 'Aside from the obvious, official transition from the Edwardian to the Georgian period, there were other less obvious, though more significant, changes in the social structure which led to her conclusions about character in 1910. There was a subtle shift taking place at this time from a social, more stable view of man and his institutions to an individual, more subjective view of man in society. Mrs. Woolf saw the early reflection of such change in the work of Samuel Butler and Bernard Shaw. Walter Allen adds to this evidence the first Post-Impressionist exhibition in London (1910), so largely a Bloomsbury affair; the early translations of Dostoevsky, Chekhov, and other Russians; the dissemination abroad of Freud and psychoanalysis – all of which seemed to signal a new interest in the private soul and the expression of that interest in new and experimental forms of art' (Mark Goldman, *The Reader's Art: Virginia Woolf as Literary Critic* (The Hague: Mouton, 1976), 42). Randall Stevenson notes the importance of the 1910 Post-Impressionist exhibition, organized by Roger Fry, 'as the source of a new sort of vision strange and revolutionary enough to change humanity's apprehension of itself', but suggests that: 'A fuller explanation should

probably take account of December 1910 as the time when – following the General Election in that month – it became clear that the Liberal Government could, if necessary, abolish the powers of the House of Lords if forced to do so in order to carry out its programme of radical reform. Some of the hierarchies and stratifications of English life, deeply inscribed in its novelists' views of character and relationship, seemed as a result more shifting and precarious after December 1910 than they ever had before. For some authors this may have been an incentive to examine the depths of inner nature rather than look out upon society and the increasing uncertainties of the individual's place within it' (Randall Stevenson, *Modernist Fiction: An Introduction* (Hemel Hempstead: Harvester Wheatsheaf, 1992), 61).

25. Roger Fry, *Vision and Design*, (1920; Oxford: Oxford University Press, 1981), 15.

26. Perry Meisel has explored Woolf's concept of 'fitness' in relation to the aesthetic theories of Walter Pater. See Meisel, *The Absent Father: Virginia Woolf and Walter Pater* (New Haven: Yale University Press, 1980), esp. 59–61.

CHAPTER 3. WOMEN AND WRITING: *A ROOM OF ONE'S OWN*

1. Alex Zwerdling, *Virginia Woolf and the Real World* (Berkeley and Los Angeles: University of California Press, 1986), 211.

2. Viola Klein, *The Feminine Character: History of an Ideology* (1946) (3rd edn., London: Routledge, 1989), 59–60.

3. Zwerdling, *Virginia Woolf and the Real World*, 217.

4. Ibid. 227.

5. Kathleen Raine, *The Land Unknown* (London: Hamish Hamilton, 1975), 22.

6. René Descartes, *Discourse on Method and the Meditations*, trans. F. E. Sutcliffe (Harmondsworth: Penguin, 1968), 27.

7. John Sturrock, *The Language of Autobiography* (Cambridge: Cambridge University Press, 1993).

8. Woolf is referring to the passage in *Jane Eyre* in which Jane stands on the rooftop of Fairfield Hall: 'open<ing> my inward ear to a tale that was never ended – a tale my imagination created, and narrated continuously; quickened with all of incident, life, fire, feeling, that I desired and had not in my actual existence'. As Cora Kaplan has noted, this is the section of the passage from *Jane Eyre* that Woolf omits from her quotation in *A Room of One's Own*. Kaplan writes: 'In the sentences that Woolf omits in her own citation, Brontë insists that even the confined and restless state could produce "many and glowing" visions. Art, the passage maintains, can be produced through the endless narration of the self, through the mixed incoherence of subjectivity spoken from subordinate and rebellious positions within culture. It was this aesthetic that Woolf as critic explicitly rejected' (Cora Kaplan,

Sea Changes: Culture and Feminism (London: Verso, 1986), 172). The *Jane Eyre* passage links gender and class oppression, class rebellion and women's revolt, but also suggests that 'the association of feminism and class struggle leads to madness' (*Sea Changes*, 173). Woolf turns away from the difficult, incoherent links Brontë made between class, race, and gender subordination and rebellion, and offers instead a model of an achieved feminism which obviates the need for the feminist text: 'The woman writer is no longer < ...> angry. She is no longer pleading and protesting as she writes. < ...> She will be able to concentrate upon her vision without distraction from outside' (*WW* 48). 'This too', Kaplan writes, 'is a cry from the roof-tops of a desire still unmet by social and psychic experience' (*Sea Changes*, 175).

  9. Judith Walkowitz, *City of Dreadful Delight: Narratives of Sexual Danger in Late-Victorian London* (Chicago: University of Chicago Press, 1992), 48.

10. See Émile Zola, *Au Bonheur des Dames* (1883), and George Gissing, *The Odd Women* (1893). For an interesting discussion of the figure of the shopgirl, see Sally Ledger, 'Gissing, the Shopgirl and the New Woman', in *Women: A Cultural Review*, 6/3 (Winter 1995), 263–74.

11.   The chair she sat in, like a burnished throne,
           Glowed on the marble, where the glass
           Held up by standards wrought with fruited vines
           From which a golden Cupidon peeped out
           (Another hid his eyes behind his wing)
           Doubled the flames of seven branched candelabra
           Reflecting light upon the table as
           The glitter of her jewels rose to meet it,
           From satin cases poured in rich profusion.
           In vials of ivory and coloured glass
           Unstoppered, lurked her strange synthetic perfumes,
           Unguent, powdered, or liquid – troubled, confused
           And drowned the sense of odours; stirred by the air
           That freshened from the window, these ascended
           In fattening the prolonged candle-flames,
           Flung their smoke into the laquearia,
           Stirring the pattern on the coffered ceiling.'

           T. S. Eliot, *The Waste Land*, in *Collected Poems* (London: Faber, 1974), 66.

12. See, for example, 'Three Dreams in a Desert', in Olive Schreiner, *Dreams* (London: T. Fisher Unwin, 1905), 65–86.

13. Virginia Woolf, *Women and Fiction: The Manuscript Version of* A Room of One's Own, ed. S. P. Rosenbaum (Oxford: Blackwell, 1991), 114.

14. Winifred Holtby, *Virginia Woolf; A Critical Memoir* (London: Wishart, 1932; Chicago, Academy Press, 1978), 161.

15. Elaine Showalter, *A Literature of their Own* (London: Virago, 1982), 263–97.

16. Elizabeth Abel, *Virginia Woolf and the Fictions of Psychoanalysis* (Chicago: University Press of Chicago, 1989), 89.

17. Vita Sackville-West and Harold Nicolson, 'Marriage', *Listener*, 1 (26

June 1929), 899–900. In her diaries, Vita Sackville-West repeatedly referred to her 'dual' nature: 'I advance, therefore, the perfectly accepted theory that cases of dual personality do exist, in which the feminine and the masculine elements alternately preponderate' (Nigel Nicolson, *Portrait of a Marriage* (London: Weidenfeld & Nicolson, 1973), 118).

18. Otto Weininger, *Sex and Character* (London: Heinemann, 1906). Nicolson and Sackville-West refer to Weininger's model of an originary bisexuality (a combination of male and female characteristics) in 'Marriage'. Woolf, in using the letters 'M' and 'W' to refer to male and female in *A Room of One's Own*, may have been parodying Weininger's use of 'M' and 'W' to refer to ideal 'sexual types' (*Sex and Character*, 7). Woolf writes: 'And if I could not grasp the truth about W. (as for brevity's sake I had come to call her) in the past, why bother about W. in the future?' (*ROO* 28).

19. Rachel Bowlby, *Virginia Woolf: Feminist Destinations* (Oxford: Blackwell, 1988), 45.

20. Holtby, *Virginia Woolf*, 183.

CHAPTER 4. WRITING THE CITY: 'STREET HAUNTING' AND *MRS DALLOWAY*

1. *The Critical Writings of Katherine Mansfield*, ed. Clare Hanson (Basingstoke: Macmillan, 1987), letter to John Middleton Murry, 59.

2. See Rachel Bowlby, 'Walking, Women and Writing: Virginia Woolf as *Flâneuse*, in *Still Crazy After All These Years* (London: Routledge, 1992).

3. Jonathan Crary, *Techniques of the Observer: On Vision and Modernity in the Nineteenth Century* (Cambridge: Mass.: MIT Press, 1990), 96.

4. See Freud's essay *The 'Uncanny'* (1919), in *Art and Literature* (The Penguin Freud Library, vol. 14, Harmondsworth: Penguin, 1990).

5. Georg Simmel, 'The Metropolis and Mental Life' (1903), trans. repr. in Richard Sennett (ed.), *Classic Essays on the Culture of Cities*, (Englewood Cliffs, NJ: Prentice Hall, 1969), 47–60.

6. Maria DiBattista, 'Joyce, Woolf and the Modern Mind', in P. Clements and I. Grundy (eds.), *Virginia Woolf: New Critical Essays* (London: Vision Press, 1983), 105.

7. Bernard Blackstone, *Virginia Woolf: a Commentary* (London: the Hogarth Press, 1949), p. 98.

8. Hermione Lee, *Virginia Woolf* (London: Chatto and Windus, 1996), 461.

9. See David Bradshaw's introduction to the Oxford World's Classics edition of *Mrs Dalloway* (Oxford: Oxford University Press, 2000) and his article 'Vanished, Like Leaves': The Military, Elegy, and Italy in *Mrs Dalloway*', *Woolf Studies Annual*, vol. 8 (2002), 107–25.

10. Walter Benjamin, *Charles Baudelaire: A Lyric Poet in the Era of High Capitalism*, trans. Harry Zohn (London: Verso, 1983), 36.

11. Rachel Bowlby, *Virginia Woolf: Feminist Destinations* (Oxford: Blackwell, 1988), 80–98 *passim*.
12. Paul Ricoeur, *Time and Narrative*, trans. K. McLaughlin and D. Pellauer (Chicago: University of Chicago Press, 1984), ii.
13. Ibid. ii. 104.
14. Ibid. ii. 112.
15. Ibid. ii. 108.
16. Randall Stevenson, *Modernist Fiction: An Introduction* (London: Harvester Wheatsheaf, 1992), 86–7.

CHAPTER 5. THE NOVEL AS ELEGY: *JACOB'S ROOM* AND *TO THE LIGHTHOUSE*

1. Roger Fry, 'Vanessa Bell and Othon Friesz, *New Statesman*, 19 (3 June 1922), 237.
2. Gillian Beer, 'Hume, Stephen, and Elegy in *To the Lighthouse'*, in *Arguing with the Past: Essays in Narrative from Woolf to Sidney* (London: Routledge, 1989), 183.
3. Alan Bell, introduction to *Sir Leslie Stephen's Mausoleum Book* (Oxford: Clarendon Press, 1977), p. xv.
4. Freud, 'Mourning and Melancholia' (1917[1915]), in *On Metapsychology: The Theory of Psychoanalysis* (The Penguin Freud Library, vol. 11; Harmondsworth: Penguin, 1984), 253.
5. Winifred Holtby, *Virginia Woolf: A Critical Memoir* (London: Wishart, 1932; Chicago: Academy Press, 1975), 116.
6. John Mepham, 'Mourning and Modernism', in A. Clements and I. Grundy (eds.), *Virginia Woolf: New Critical Essays* (London: Vision Press, 1983).
7. Paul de Man, 'Autobiography as De-Facement', in *The Rhetoric of Romanticism* (New York: Columbia University Press, 1984), 75–6.
8. Alex Zwerdling, *Virginia Woolf and the Real World* (Berkeley and Los Angeles: University of California Press, 1986), 82, quoting Frances Marshall in *Recollections of Virginia Woolf*, ed. Joan Russell Noble (London: Peter Owen, 1972), 76.
9. Rachel Bowlby, Explanatory Notes to *Orlando* (Oxford: Oxford University Press, 1992), 318, n. 14.
10. Beer, 'Hume, Stephen, and Elegy in *To the Lighthouse'*, 185.
11. Ibid.
12. *Sir Leslie Stephen's Mausoleum Book*, 32–3.
13. For a discussion on 'in love' in Virginia Woolf, see Rachel Bowlby, *Feminist Destinations and Further Writings on Virginia Woolf* (Edinburgh: Edinburgh University Press, 1997).
14. Erich Auerbach, *Mimesis: The Representation of Reality in Western Literature*, trans. Willard Trask (Princeton: Princeton University Press, 1953).
15. Françoise Defromont, 'Mirrors and Fragments', trans. Rachel Bowlby,

in Rachel Bowlby (ed.), *Virginia Woolf* (Longman Critical Readers; Harlow: Longman, 1992), 63.

16. Suzanne Raitt, *Virginia Woolf's To the Lighthouse*, (Hemel Hempstead: Harvester Wheatsheaf, 1990).

17. Francis Cornford (ed.), *The Republic of Plato* (Oxford: Oxford University Press, 1941), 223 n. 1.

18. Walter Pater, *The Renaissance* (Oxford: Oxford University Press, 1986), 150.

19. Ibid. 150.

20. Ibid. 151.

21. Hermione Lee, 'Introduction' to *To the Lighthouse* (Harmondsworth: Penguin, 1992), p. xxv. See also Kate Flint, 'Virginia Woolf and the General Strike', *Essays in Criticism*, 36 (1986), 319–34, for an interesting discussion of Woolf's responses to the General Strike of 1926 and its impact on her writing of the 'Time Passes' section of *To the Lighthouse*.

22. Roger Fry, *Vision and Design* (1920; Oxford: Oxford University Press, 1981), 28.

23. See Elizabeth Abel, *Virginia Woolf and the Fictions of Psychoanalysis* (Chicago: University of Chicago Press, 1989), ch. 4 *passim*.

24. Lewis Carroll, *Alice Through the Looking-Glass* (Harmondsworth: Penguin, 1962), 261.

25. Beer, 'Hume, Stephen, and Elegy in *To the Lighthouse*', 201.

CHAPTER 6. WRITING LIVES: *ORLANDO, THE WAVES* AND *FLUSH*

1. Winifred Holtby, *Virginia Woolf: A Critical Memoir* (London: Wishart, 1932; Chicago: Academy Press, 1978), 167.

2. Henry Adams, *The Education of Henry Adams* (Boston: Houghton Mifflin, 1918), 382.

3. Ibid. 381.

4. See, for example, Marjorie Garber, *Vested Interests: Cross-Dressing and Cultural Anxiety* (New York: Routledge, 1992).

5. Makiko Minow-Pinkney, *Virginia Woolf and the Problem of the Subject* (Brighton: Harvester, 1987), 122.

6. Holtby, *Virginia Woolf*, 182–3.

7. J. C. Flugel, *The Psychology of Clothes* (London: Hogarth Press, 1930). Flugel's book is best known for its account of 'The Great Masculine Renunciation' which took place at the end of the eighteenth century, whereby 'men gave up their right to all the brighter, gayer, more elaborate, and more varied forms of ornamentation, leaving these entirely to the use of women, and thereby making their own tailoring the most austere and ascetic of the arts' (p. 111).

8. Nigel Nicolson, *Portrait of a Marriage* (London: Weidenfeld & Nicolson, 1973), 117.

9. Sigmund Freud, 'A Child is Being Beaten' (1919), in *On Psychopathology* (Penguin Freud Library, vol. 10; Harmondsworth: Penguin, 1979), 190–1.
10. Clare Hanson, *Virginia Woolf* (Basingstoke: Macmillan, 1994), 96.
11. Sigmund Freud, 'Delusions and Dreams in Jensen's *Gradiva*, (1907[1906]), in *Art and Literature* (Penguin Freud Library, vol. 14; Harmondsworth: Penguin, 1985), 65.
12. Daniel Ferrer, *Virginia Woolf and the Madness of Language* (London: Routledge, 1990), p. 67.
13. Michael Whitworth, 'Virginia Woolf and Modernism', in Sue Roe and Susan Sellers (eds.), *The Cambridge Companion to Virginia Woolf* (Cambridge: Cambridge University Press, 2000), 148.
14. Anna Snaith, 'Of fanciers, footnotes, and fascism: Virginia Woolf's *Flush*'. *Modern Fiction Studies*, 48/3 (Fall 2002), 614–36.

CHAPTER 7. FACT AND FICTION: *THE YEARS* AND *THREE GUINEAS*

1. Paul Ricoeur, *Time and Narrative*, trans. K. McLaughlin and D. Pellauer (Chicago: University of Chicago Press, 1984), ii. 229.
2. See Patricia Laurence's excellent essay 'The Facts and Fugues of War: From *Three Guineas* to *Between the Acts*', in Mark Hussey (ed.), *Virginia Woolf and War: Fiction, Reality and Myth* (Syracuse, NY: Syracuse University Press, 1991), 225–46.
3. In this edition of *The Pargiters*, square brackets and italics represent a deletion editorially restored.
4. Leonard Woolf, *An Autobiography*, ii. *1911–1969* (Oxford: Oxford University Press, 1980), 302.
5. See *The Essential Frankfurt School Reader*, eds. Andrew Arato and Eike Gebhardt (New York: Orizen Books, 1978), and Theodor W. Adorno, *The Culture Industry: Selected Essays on Mass Culture*, ed. J. M. Bernstein (London: Routledge, 1991).
6. Quentin Bell, *Virginia Woolf: A Biography* (2 vols.; London: Hogarth Press, 1972), 258–9. Bell includes an edited version of Woolf's memoir of Julian Bell (dated 30 July 1937) as an Appendix to the biography.
7. Victor Shklovsky, 'The Resurrection of the Word' (1914), trans. Richard Sherwood, in Stephen Bann and John E. Bowlt (eds.), *Russian Formalism* (Edinburgh: Scottish Academic Press, 1973), 41–7.

CHAPTER 8. INTO THE HEART OF DARKNESS: *BETWEEN THE ACTS*

1. Gillian Beer, Introduction to *Between the Acts* (Harmondsworth: Penguin, 1992), p. xii.
2. The Russian critic Mikhail Bakhtin's term 'heteroglossia' appears in

his 'Discourse in the Novel', trans. Caryl Emerson and Michael Holquist, in Michael Holquist (ed.), *The Dialogic Imagination* (Austin, Texas: University of Texas Press, 1981), 263.

3. Sigmund Freud, 'Group Psychology and the Analysis of the Ego', in *Civilization, Society and Religion* (Penguin Freud Library, vol. 12; Harmondsworth: Penguin, 1985), 101.

4. Sue Roe, *Writing and Gender: Virginia Woolf's Writing Practice* (Hemel Hempstead: Harvester Wheatsheaf, 1990), 156.

5. 'London in War' is a manuscript sketch written in late October 1939 (Monk's House Papers, List A, 20: quoted by Brenda Silver in ' "Anon" and "The Reader": Virginia Woolf's Last Essays', ed. Brenda Silver, Twentieth Century Literature, 25 (1979), 367).

6. J. Laplanche and J.-B. Pontalis, *The Language of Psychoanalysis*, trans. Donald Nicholson-Smith (London: Hogarth Press and the Institute of Psychoanalysis, 1983), 26.

7. Einstein and Freud, 'Why War?' (1933 [1932]), in Freud, *Civilization, Society and Religion*, 356.

8. Beer, Introduction to *Between the Acts*, p. xxi.

9. See Stuart N. Clarke, 'The Horse with a Green Tail, *Virginia Woolf Miscellany*, 34 (1990), 3–4.

10. ' "Anon" and "The Reader": Virginia Woolf's Last Essays', ed. Brenda Silver, *Twentieth Century Literature*, 25, (1979), 356–441.

11. Ibid. 382.

12. Ibid. 358.

13. Ibid. 357.

14. Ibid. 398.

15. Daniel Ferrer, *Virginia Woolf and the Madness of Language*, trans. Geoffrey Bennington and Rachel Bowlby (London: Routledge, 1990), 101.

16. Beer, Introduction to *Between the Acts*, p. xv.

Select Bibliography

WORKS BY VIRGINIA WOOLF

Published Works
The Voyage Out (London: Duckworth, 1915).
Night and Day (London: Duckworth, 1919).
Monday or Tuesday (London: Hogarth Press, 1921).
Jacob's Room (London: Hogarth Press, 1922).
Mrs Dalloway (London: Hogarth Press, 1925).
The Common Reader: First Series (London: Hogarth Press, 1925).
To the Lighthouse (London: Hogarth Press, 1927).
Orlando (London: Hogarth Press, 1928).
A Room of One's Own (London: Hogarth Press, 1929).
The Waves (London: Hogarth Press, 1931).
The Common Reader: Second Series (London: Hogarth Press, 1932).
Flush: A Biography ((London: Hogarth Press, 1933).
The Years (London: Hogarth Press, 1937).
Three Guineas (London: Hogarth Press, 1938).
Roger Fry (London: Hogarth Press, 1940).
Between the Acts (London: Hogarth Press, 1941).
A Haunted House and Other Stories (London: Hogarth Press, 1944).
A Writer's Diary, ed. Leonard Woolf (London: Hogarth Press, 1953).
Collected Essays, ed. Leonard Woolf (4 vols.; London: Hogarth Press, 1966).
Mrs Dalloway's Party: A Short Story Sequence, ed. Stella McNichol (London: Hogarth Press, 1973).
The Diary of Virginia Woolf, ed. Anne Olivier Bell with Andrew McNeillie (5 vols.; London: Hogarth Press, 1977–84).
'"Anon" and "The Reader": Virginia Woolf's Last Essays', ed. Brenda Silver, *Twentieth Century Literature*, 25 (1979), 356–435.
The Letters of Virginia Woolf, ed. Nigel Nicolson and Joanne Trautmann (6 vols.; London: Chatto & Windus, 1975–80).
The London Scene: Five Essays (London: Hogarth Press, 1982).
Virginia Woolf's Reading Notebooks, ed. Brenda Silver (Princeton: Princeton University Press, 1983).
The Complete Shorter Fiction of Virginia Woolf, ed. Susan Dick (London: Grafton, 1991).

Moments of Being: Unpublished Autobiographical Writings, ed. Jeanne Schulkind (rev. edn. London: Hogarth Press, 1985).

The Essays of Virginia Woolf, ed. Andrew McNeillie (6 vols.; Hogarth Press, 1986–91).

A Passionate Apprentice: The Early Journals, 1897–1909, ed. Mitchell A. Leaska (London: Hogarth Press, 1990).

Carlyle's House and Other Sketches, ed. David Bradshaw (London: Hesperus Press, 2003).

Editions of Manuscript Drafts

The Waves: The Two Holograph Drafts, ed. J. W. Graham (London: Hogarth Press, 1976).

The Pargiters: The Novel-Essay Portion of The Years, ed. and intro. Mitchell A. Leaska (London: Hogarth Press, 1978).

Melymbrosia: An Early Version of The Voyage Out, ed. Louise DeSalvo (New York: Public Library, 1982).

Pointz Hall: The Earlier and Later Typescripts of Between the Acts, ed. Mitchell A. Leaska (New York: New York University Press, 1983).

To the Lighthouse: The Original Holograph Draft, ed. Susan Dick (London: Hogarth Press, 1983).

Women and Fiction: The Manuscript Versions of A Room of One's Own, ed. S. P. Rosenbaum (Oxford: Blackwell, 1991).

BIBLIOGRAPHY

Bibliography of Woolf's Writings

Kirkpatrick, B. J., *A Bibliography of Virginia Woolf*, (3rd. edn., Oxford: Oxford University Press, 1980).

Bibliography of Criticism

Majumdar, R., *Virginia Woolf: An Annotated Bibliography of Criticism 1915–1974* (New York: Garland, 1976).

Mepham, John, *Virginia Woolf: Criticism in Focus* (Bristol: Bristol Classical Press, 1992.) Helpful survey and discussion of books and articles on Woolf.

Fudurer, Laura Sue, 'Criticism of Virginia Woolf from 1972 to December 1990: A Selected Checklist', in *Modern Fiction Studies: Virginia Woolf Special Edition*, 38, 1 (Spring 1992).

Biographical Studies

Bell, Quentin, *Virginia Woolf: A Biography* (2 vols.; London: Hogarth Press, 1972). A fascinating, beautifully composed study of Woolf's life by her nephew.

Caws, Mary Ann, *Virginia Woolf* (London: Penguin, 2001). A heavily illustrated short biography of Woolf.

Peter Dally, *Virginia Woolf: the Marriage of Heaven and Hell* (London: Robson Books). The author of this biography, a psychiatrist, explores Woolf's life 'from the perspective of her madness', defined as 'cyclothymic depression'.

DeSalvo, Louise, *Virginia Woolf: The Impact of Childhood Sexual Abuse on her Life and Work* (London: Women's Press, 1989). Influential psychobiographical study of Woolf's life and work.

Dunn, Jane, *A Very Close Conspiracy: Vanessa Bell and Virginia Woolf* (London: Cape, 1991). Biographical study of the relationship between the two sisters and their 'twin' arts, painting and writing.

——— *Virginia Woolf and Vanessa Bell* (London: Virago, 2001). A biographical study of the relationship between the two sisters and their creative lives.

Lee, Hermione, *The Novels of Virginia Woolf* (London: Chatto and Windus, 1996). Highly acclaimed biography.

Gordon, Lyndall, *Virginia Woolf: A Writer's Life* (Oxford: Oxford University Press, 1986). Lucid and insightful account of Woolf's 'writing life', focusing on *To the Lighthouse* and *The Waves* and their subjective and biographical significance for Woolf.

Mepham, John, *Virginia Woolf: A Literary Life* (Basingstoke: Macmillan, 1991). Excellent introduction to Woolf, particularly helpful on her publishing activities and on the 'material' aspects of her life as a writer.

Nicolson, Nigel, *Virginia Woolf* (London: Weidenfeld, 2001). An affectionate biography by the son of Vita Sackville-West, including Nicolson's own childhood recollections of Woolf.

Poole, Roger, *The Unknown Virginia Woolf* (Cambridge: Cambridge University Press, 1978; new edn., 1995). New edition contains a preface detailing and answering critical responses to Poole's 'psychobiographical' reading of Woolf and giving an account of the last two decades of Woolf criticism. The study criticizes Woolf's treatment by the medical profession and provides an interesting study of Woolf as an existentialist thinker.

Rose, Phyllis, *Woman of Letters: A Life of Virginia Woolf* (London: Routledge & Kegan Paul, 1978). Perceptive, lucid critical biography, putting feminism at the centre of Woolf's work.

Critical Studies

The following list is a selection from the enormous number of critical works published on Woolf, particularly since the 1970s. I have not included journal articles.

Abel, Elizabeth, *Virginia Woolf and the Fictions of Psychoanalysis* (Chicago: University of Chicago Press, 1989). Original and complex study of Woolf's knowledge of and relationship to psychoanalysis, giving a detailed account of British psychoanalytic culture in the 1920s and

1930s. Particularly interesting on the relationship betwen 'Kleinian' and 'Freudian' models in Woolf's work.

Auerbach, Erich, *Mimesis: The Representation of Reality in Western Literature*, trans. Willard Trask (Princeton: Princeton University Press, 1953). One of the most important works of literary criticism of the twentieth century, Auerbach's study of the representation of reality from Homer to the present ends with an account of narrative strategies and narrative time in *To the Lighthouse*. Auerbach's chapter on Woolf ('The Brown Stocking') is reprinted in Bowlby, *Virginia Woolf* (Longman Critical Readers; Harlow: Longman, 1992).

Banfield, Ann, *The Phantom Table: Woolf, Fry, Russell and the Epistemology of Modernism* (Cambridge: Cambridge University Press, 2000). Banfield's study, the first full treatment of the influence of the 'Cambridge Apostles' and their theory of knowledge on Woolf's thought, argues for a revision of the relationship between realism and formalism to account for Woolf's dual reality of sense impressions and logical forms.

Barrett, Eileen, and Cramer, Patricia (eds), *Virginia Woolf: Lesbian Readings* (New York, NY: New York University Press, 1997) A collection of essays focusing on the ways in which Woolf's private and public experience and knowledge of same-sex love influence her shorter fiction and novels.

Beer, Gillian, *Virginia Woolf: The Common Ground* (Edinburgh: Edinburgh University Press, 1996) A collection of essays on the writings demonstrating how Woolf's conceptualizations of history and narrative are intimately bound up with her ways of thinking about women, writing and social and sexual relations.

Barrett, Michèle, 'Introduction' to Virginia Woolf, *Women and Writing* (London: Women's Press, 1979). First edited collection of Woolf's essays on women's writing and feminine aesthetics, with a substantial introduction arguing for Woolf as a 'materialist' thinker concerned with the social and economic circumstances of women writers' lives and the conditions enabling female creativity. See also Barrett's essay on *A Room of One's Own and Three Guineas* in J. Briggs (ed.), *Virginia Woolf: Introductions to the Major Works* (London: Virago, 1984).

Beer, Gillian, *Arguing with the Past: Essays in Narrative from Woolf to Sidney* (London: Routledge, 1989). Contains four outstanding essays on Woolf, including 'Hume, Stephen, and Elegy in *To the Lighthouse*'.

Bowlby, Rachel, *Virginia Woolf: Feminist Destinations* (Oxford: Basil Blackwell, 1988). A brilliant study of Woolf's feminism and modernism, tracing the 'lines' of Woolf's models of women's changing lives and identities through her texts and intertwining them with Freud's fictions of femininity. Bowlby's extensive writings on Woolf (including introductions to *Orlando* (Oxford) and to two volumes of essays, *A Woman's Essays* and *The Crowded Dance of Modern Life* (Penguin)) are reprinted in *Feminist Destinations and Further Writings on Virginia Woolf* (Edinburgh: Edinburgh University Press, 1997).

——— (ed.), *Virginia Woolf* (Longman Critical Readers: Harlow: Longman, 1992). A valuable collection of essays covering the broad range of

Woolf's writing, with particular emphasis on feminist criticism of her work.

Briggs, J. (ed.), *Virginia Woolf: Introductions to the Major Works* (London: Virago, 1984). A collection of the excellent introductions to the new Penguin editions of Woolf's writings.

Brosnan, Leila, *Reading Virginia Woolf's Essays and Journalism* (Edinburgh: Edinburgh University Press, 1997). Dealing with Virginia Woolf's non-fiction writing from historical and theoretical perspectives, this work covers Woolf's essays and journalism, including the juvenilia, reviews, critical essays, autobiographical writings, 'A Room of One's Own' and 'Three Guineas'.

Caughie, Pamela L., *Virginia Woolf and Postmodernism: Literature in Quest and Question of Itself* (Urbana, Ill.: University of Illinois Press, 1991). Important study of Woolf as a postmodernist thinker. Explores some of Woolf's least critically discussed writings, including *Flush*.

—— (ed.), *Virginia Woolf in the Age of Mechanical Reproduction* (New York: Garland Publishing, 2000). Ten essays offering collectively a sustained reflection on the relationship between Walter Benjamin's analyses of mass culture and technology and Woolf's cultural productions of the 1920s and 1930s.

Caws, Mary Ann, and Luckhurst, Nicola, *The Reception of Virginia Woolf in Europe* (London: The Athlone Press, 2001). A collection of essays addressing European responses to Woolf over the course of the century.

Clements, P., and Grundy, L., *Virginia Woolf: New Critical Essays* (London: Vision Press, 1983). Valuable collection of essays.

Defromont, Françoise, *Virginia Woolf: Vers la maison de lumière* (Paris: Éditions des Femmes, 1985). A translated extract from this brilliant psychoanalytic study of Woolf's writing is included in Rachel Bowlby (ed.) *Virginia Woolf* (Longman Critical Readers; Harlow: Longman, 1992).

Dalgarno, Emily, *Virginia Woolf and the Visible World* (Cambridge: Cambridge University Press, 2001). An exploration of Woolf's engagement with visible and non-visible realms of experience, including textual analyses of individual novels and an elaboration of the theory of the subject emerging from Woolf's discourse of visibility in her autobiographical writing.

DiBattista, Maria, *Virginia Woolf's Major Novels: The Fables of Anon* (New Haven: Yale University Press, 1980). Focuses on genre in Woolf's writing, on her place in the tradition of English comic fiction, and on the importance of the figure of 'Anon' for her work and thought.

Dick, Susan, *Virginia Woolf* (London: Edward Arnold, 1989). A brief but useful study of Woolf's novels, at its best on narrative techniques. Recommended for students.

Dowling, David, *Bloomsbury Aesthetics and the Novels of Forster and Woolf* (London: Macmillan, 1985). Helpful discussion of Woolf's relationship to the aesthetic theories of the 'Bloomsbury' art critics Clive Bell and Roger Fry, worked through her novels.

Dusinberre, Juliet, *Virginia Woolf's Renaissance: Woman Reader or Common Reader?* (London: Palgrave, 1997). Explores Woolf's search, in *The Common Reader* and other non-fictional writings, for an alternative literary tradition for women, making connections between Woolf's work and the early modern period through addressing questions such as printing, the body, and the relation between amateurs and professionals.

Ferrer, Daniel, *Virginia Woolf and the Madness of Language* (trans. Geoffrey Bennington and Rachel Bowlby (London: Routledge, 1990). Detailed, complex readings of four Woolf novels (*Mrs Dalloway*, *To the Lighthouse*, *The Waves*, and *Between the Acts*), focusing on the 'crisis of representation' in modernist writing and reading the works through psycho-analytic and post-structuralist understandings of language, subjectivity, and meaning.

Gillespie, Diane, *The Sisters' Arts: The Writing and Painting of Virginia Woolf and Vanessa Bell* (Syracuse, NY: Syracuse University Press, 1988). A detailed and analytical account of Bell's paintings and of the representation of the visual arts in Woolf's novels.

Ginsberg, E. K., and Gottlieb, L. M., *Virginia Woolf: Centennial Essays* (Troy, NY: Whitston, 1983). Useful collection of critical essays.

Glenny, Allie, *Ravenous Identity: Eating and Eating Distress in the Life and Work of Virginia Woolf* (London: Palgrave, 2000). An exploration of Woolf's complex relationship with food and eating, and how this relationship is expressed in her work.

Goldman, Jane, *The Feminist Aesthetics of Virginia Woolf* (Cambridge: Cambridge University Press, 2001). Goldman develops the concept of a 'feminist prismatics' through which Woolf expresses her challenging and often seemingly contradictory feminism. Focuses in particular on contemporary aesthetics.

Goldman, Mark, *The Readers Art: Virginia Woolf as Literary Critic* (The Hague: Mouton, 1976). A helpful discussion of Woolf as essayist and critic.

Greene, Sally, (ed.), *Virginia Woolf: Reading the Renaissance* (Athens: Ohio University Press, 1999). A collection of essays from specialists in Renaissance as well as twentieth-century studies, exploring Woolf's engagement with Renaissance literature.

Gualtieri, Elena, *Virginia Woolf's Essays: Sketching the Past* (London: Palgrave, 2000). The sketch and the essay represented for Virginia Woolf the two forms of writing through which she articulated her understanding of the workings of literary history. This study analyses the intersection between essays and sketches in Woolf's non-fiction as part of an argument about the scopes and models of feminist criticism.

Guiget, Jean, *Virginia Woolf and her Works* (London: Hogarth Press, 1965). To some extent overtaken by more recent Woolf criticism, this remains a valuable study of the novels, reading Woolf through a Sartrean, existentialist filter.

Hanson, Clare, *Virginia Woolf* (Basingstoke: Macmillan, 1994). Lucid, theoretically informed study of Woolf's work.

Holtby, Winifred, *Virginia Woolf: A Critical Memoir* (London: Wishart, 1932; Chicago: Academy Press, 1978). First English book-length study of Woolf's writing, which closes with *The Waves*. Remains an original and highly perceptive account of Woolf's work.

Homans, Margaret, *Virginia Woolf: A Collection of Critical Essays* (Englewood Cliffs, NJ: Prentice-Hall, 1993). Collection of reprinted essays from some of the most interesting of Woolf's critics. Recommended.

Hussey, Mark, *The Singing of the Real World: The Philosophy of Virginia Woolf's Fiction* (Columbus, Oh.: Ohio State University Press, 1986). Argues for Woolf as a 'religious' novelist, concerned with the manifestations of the soul or 'essence' of the self and with pre-verbal experience.

—— (ed.), *Virginia Woolf and War: Fiction, Reality and Myth* (Syracuse, NY: Syracuse University Press, 1991). A valuable collection of essays, focusing on Woolf's pacificism and her responses to Fascism and war.

Laurence, Patricia Ondek, *The Reading of Silence: Virginia Woolf in the English Tradition* (Stanford: Stanford University Press, 1991). Subtle, detailed reading of the role of silence, interiority, and rhythm in Woolf's fiction.

Lee, Hermione, *The Novels of Virginia Woolf* (London: Methuen, 1977). A detailed and perceptive 'close reading' of Woolf's novels.

Levenback, Karen L., *Virginia Woolf and the Great War* (Syracuse: Syracuse University Press, 1999) This study focuses on how Woolf's sensitivity to representations of the Great War in the popular press and authorized histories affected both the development of characters in her fiction and her non-fictional and personal writings.

McLaurin, Allen, *Virginia Woolf: The Echoes Enslaved* (Cambridge: Cambridge University Press, 1973). Important study of the relationship between Woolf's modernism and the aesthetic theories of Roger Fry.

McNichol, Stella, *Virginia Woolf and the Poetry of Fiction* (London: Routledge, 1990). Exploration of the 'poetic' techniques of Woolf's prose.

Marcus, Jane, *Art and Anger: Reading Like a Woman* (Columbus, Oh.: Ohio State University Press, 1988). Feminist approach to Woolf, focusing on *A Room of One's Own* and *Three Guineas*, and strongly critical of much Woolf biography.

—— (ed.), *New Feminist Essays on Virginia Woolf* (Lincoln, Nebr.: University of Nebraska Press, 1981). Influential collection of feminist essays.

—— (ed.), *Virginia Woolf: A Feminist Slant* (Lincoln, Nebr.: University of Nebraska Press, 1983).

—— (ed.), *Virginia Woolf and Bloomsbury: A Centenary Celebration* (Basingstoke: Macmillan, 1987).

—— *Virginia Woolf and the Languages of Patriarchy* (Bloomington, Ind.: Indiana University Press, 1988). Original essays on some of Woolf's less discussed works, including *Night and Day* and *The Pargiters*.

Marder, Herbert, *Feminism and Art: A Study of Virginia Woolf* (Chicago: University of Chicago Press, 1968). Early study of Woolf's feminism, focusing on her concept of 'androgyny'.

—— *The Measure of Life: Virginia Woolf's Last Years* (Ithaca, NY: Cornell University Press, 2000). Uses Woolf's diaries to develop a picture of her life during the years 1930 to 1941.

Marsh, Nicholas, *Virginia Woolf: The Novels* (London: Palgrave, 1998). A study guide focusing on close reading of extracts from Woolf's novels.

Maze, John R., *Virginia Woolf: Feminism, Creativity, and the Unconscious* (Westport, CT: Greenwood Publishing Group, 1997). A psychoanalytic reading of the life-historical and psychopathological themes underlying the intellectual and emotional force of Virginia Woolf's novels.

Meisel, Perry, *The Absent Father: Virginia Woolf and Walter Pater* (New Haven: Yale University Press, 1980). Underrated study of Woolf. A complex and fascinating account of Woolf's unacknowledged intellectual debt to Walter Pater, which opens up many aspects of her aesthetics.

Miller, J. Hillis, *Fiction and Repetition: Seven English Novels* (Oxford: Blackwell, 1982). Contains two important essays on *Mrs Dalloway* and *Between the Acts*.

Minow-Pinkney, Makiko, *Virginia Woolf and the Problem of the Subject* (Brighton: Harvester, 1987). Rich, detailed readings of Woolf's novels through post-structuralist filters, linking her feminism and modernism.

Moore, Madeline, *The Short Season between Two Silences: The Mystical and the Political in the Novels of Virginia Woolf* (Boston: George Allen & Unwin, 1984). Links Woolf's feminism with her 'mysticism', focusing on Woolf's representations of women's spiritual relationships and creativity.

Naremore, James, *The World without a Self: Virginia Woolf and the Novel* (New Haven: Yale University Press, 1973). Remains one of the most important and insightful studies of Woolf. Particularly good on her narrative techniques.

Pawlowski, Merry, (ed.), *Virginia Woolf and Fascism: Resisting the Dictators' Seduction* (London: Palgrave, 2001). Essays dealing primarily with Woolf's fiction and non-fiction from *Mrs Dalloway* to *Between the Acts* in terms of their engagement with the rise of fascism.

Peach, Linden, *Virginia Woolf* (London: Palgrave, 2000). Reads Woolf's novels using theorists such as Foucault and Bakhtin to reveal the extent of her engagement with historical and political issues.

Raitt, Suzanne, *Virginia Woolf's To the Lighthouse* (Hemel Hempstead: Harvester Wheatsheaf, 1990). Perceptive and lucid account of the novel, using recent film theory to explore its gendered and visual dimensions.

—— *Vita and Virginia: The Work and Friendship of Vita Sackville-West and Virginia Woolf* (Oxford: Oxford University Press, 1993). First detailed study of the relationship between the two women and its impact on Woolf's work, and of Vita Sackville-West's novels. Good discussion of biography and narrative.

Richter, Harvena, *Virginia Woolf: The Inward Voyage* (Princeton: Princeton

University Press, 1970). An important philosophical exploration of Woolf's novels, focusing on patterns and themes in her work, including 'androgyny', 'impersonality' and 'the moment'.

Roe, Sue, *Writing and Gender: Virginia Woolf's Writing Practice* (Hemel Hempstead: Harvester Wheatsheaf, 1990). Perceptive, original study of the influence of gender on Woolf's writing practice. Excellent discussions of the later novels.

—— and Sellers, Susan (eds), *The Cambridge Companion to Virginia Woolf* (Cambridge: Cambridge University Press, 2000). A collection of essays providing readings of all nine novels, as well as the letters, diaries and essays. Reflects the constant evolution of Woolf scholarship especially in the light of feminist theories.

Rosenberg, Beth Carole, and Dubino, Jeanne, (eds), *Virginia Woolf and the Essay* (London: Palgrave, 1997). One of the first critical studies to focus exclusively on Woolf's essays. The collection begins with an introduction that surveys the historical reception of Virginia Woolf's essays, and then sketches out a methodological study of Woolf's essays by placing them within historical, literary-historical, reader-orientated, generic, and feminist contexts.

Rosenfeld, Natalia, *Outsiders Together: Virginia and Leonard Woolf* (Princeton, NJ: Princeton University Press, 2000). Analyses the work of both husband and wife to illuminate the complex dialogue between the two, and in particular the interrelationship between contemporary social and political theory and models of subjectivity revealed in their writing.

Ruotola, Lucio, *The Interrupted Moment: A View of Virginia Woolf's Novels* (Stanford, Calif.: Stanford University Press, 1986). Explores the complex role of 'interruption' in Woolf's novels and the movement between the 'aesthetics' of fragmentation/open-endedness and of closure/coherence in her work and thought.

Schlack, Beverly Ann, *Continuing Presences: Virginia Woolf's Use of Literary Allusion* (University Park, Pa.: Pennsylvania University Press, 1979). Identifies the extensive use of literary allusion in five of Woolf's novels.

Silver, Brenda R., *Virginia Woolf Icon* (Chicago: University of Chicago Press, 2000). Analyses the use to which Woolf's name and image has been put in both high and popular cultures, and the ways in which she has become an important site of conflict in debates about art, politics, anger, sexuality, gender, class, the canon, feminism, race and fashion.

Smith, Angela, *Katherine Mansfield and Virginia Woolf: A Public of Two* (Oxford: Clarendon Press, 1999). Through detailed comparative readings of their fiction, letters and diaries, Smith explores the intense affinity between the two writers, particularly in terms of their experience and expression of the liminal.

Snaith, Anna, *Virginia Woolf: Public and Private Negotiations* (London: Palgrave, 2000). Argues that Woolf's sense of the relationship between public and private is central to an understanding of her feminism, narrative techniques, attitudes to publication and her own role in public debate.

Spilka, Mark, *Virginia Woolf's Quarrel with Grieving* (Lincoln, Nebr.: University of Nebraska Press, 1980). Argues that Woolf's incomplete 'mourning' especially for her mother's death, had a central impact on her writing.

Squier, Susan, *Virginia Woolf and London: The Sexual Politics of the City* (Chapel Hill, NC: University of North Carolina Press, 1985). Detailed and lively study of Woolf's writings on the city and its gendered spaces.

Stape, J. H. and Haule, James M. (eds), *Editing Virginia Woolf* (London: Palgrave, 2002). A collection of essays dealing with the issues and problems surrounding the critical editing of Woolf's work, including her fiction, letters, diaries and biographical writing.

Stevenson, Randall, *Modernist Fiction: An Introduction* (Hemel Hempstead: Harvester Wheatsheaf, 1992). Very useful guide to modernist fiction and to the contexts of modernist writing, including Woolf's. Recommended for students.

Waugh, Patricia, *Feminine Fictions: Revisiting the Postmodern* (London: Routledge, 1989). Contains an interesting reading of *To the Lighthouse*.

Wheare, Jane, *Virginia Woolf: Dramatic Novelist* (Basingstoke: Macmillan, 1989). Useful study of narrative techniques in Woolf's 'realist' novels – *The Voyage Out*, *Night and Day*, and *The Years*.

Williams, Lisa, *The Artist as Outsider in the Novels of Toni Morrison and Virginia Woolf* (Westport, CT: Greenwood Press, 2000). Examines the literary relationship between Woolf and Morrison and how differing structures of domination define their art, analysing race and gender and the construction of whiteness.

Willis, J. H., *Leonard and Virginia Woolf as Publishers: The Hogarth Press 1917–41* (Charlottesville Va.: University Press of Virginia, 1992). Fascinating and comprehensive study of the Hogarth Press.

Zwerdling, Alex, *Virginia Woolf and the Real World* (Berkeley and Los Angeles: University of California Press, 1986). One of the most important recent studies of Woolf. Zwerdling focuses on Woolf as a 'political' writer and explores her engagement with the events and issues of her times.

Index

Dickens, Charles, 178
Dostoevsky, Fyodor, 191
Dowling, David, 187
Duckworth, George, 188
    Gerald, 18, 188
    Herbert, 3
    Stella, 3
Duplessis, Rachel Blau, 189

Edel, Leon, 187
Einstein, Albert, 94, 182, 198
Eliot, George, 11,
Eliot, T. S., 35, 39, 54, 178, 181,
    193
Ellis, Havelock, 130-1

Ferrer, Daniel, 139, 184, 196, 198
Flaubert, Gustave, 38
Flint, Kate, 138, 195
Flugel, J. C., 129, 196
Forster, E. M., 32, 74
Freud, Sigmund, 19, 25, 67, 86,
    90, 103, 110, 114, 129, 131, 172-
    3, 179, 182-3, 188, 190, 191, 194,
    195, 196, 197, 198
Frisby, David, 191
Fromm. Gloria, 189
Fry, Roger, 29, 34, 38, 85, 95, 111,
    115, 117, 175, 187, 191-2, 194,
    196

Galsworthy, John, 23, 27, 37, 39
Garber, Marjorie, 196
Garnett, David, 17, 143
Gebhardt, Eike, 197
Gissing, George, 53, 193
Goethe, J. W. 170
Goldman, Mark, 192
Grand, Sarah, 189
Grant, Duncan, 115, 187

Hall, Radclyffe, 55, 130-1
Hanson, Clare, 133, 196
Heard, Gerald, 139

Hogarth Press, 17-18, 48, 96,
    129, 166, 182, 189-90
Holtby, Winifred, 20, 55, 58-9,
    87, 119, 129, 190, 193, 195-6

Ibsen, Henrik, 13, 188

James, Henry, 24, 38, 190
Joyce, James, 23, 25, 27-8, 32, 35,
    39, 68-9

Kaplan, Cora, 192
Keats, John, 114
Keynes, John Maynard, 187
Klein, Melanie, 182
    Viola, 42, 191
Kracauer, Siegfried, 29
Krafft-Ebing, R. 130

Laplanche, J. 182, 198
Laurence, Patricia, 152, 197
Lawrence, D. H., 32, 83
Leavis, Q. D., 162
Le Bon, Gustave, 179
Ledger, Sally, 189, 193
Lee, Hermione, 72, 194
Lehmann, John, 166
Light, Alison, 143, 147
London, 61-3, 68-9
Lowes Dickinson, Geoffrey, 137
Lukács, Georg, 189
Lutyens, Edwin, 72

McLaurin, Allen, 187
MacCarthy, Desmond, 35, 187
    Molly, 190
Mansfield, Katherine, 62, 194
Marcus, Jane, 187
Marcus, Laura, 190
Marsh, Edward, 87
Marshall, Frances, 195
Meisel, Perry, 192
Mepham, John, 7, 32, 87, 177,
    189, 191, 195